Interactive
Museum Tours

Interactive Museum Tours

A Guide to In-Person and Virtual Experiences

Sharon Vatsky

ROWMAN & LITTLEFIELD
Lanham • Boulder • New York • London

Published by Rowman & Littlefield
An imprint of The Rowman & Littlefield Publishing Group, Inc.
4501 Forbes Boulevard, Suite 200, Lanham, Maryland 20706
www.rowman.com

86-90 Paul Street, London EC2A 4NE

British Library Cataloguing in Publication Information Available

Library of Congress Cataloging-in-Publication Data

Names: Vatsky, Sharon, author.
Title: Interactive museum tours : a guide to in-person and virtual
   experiences / Sharon Vatsky.
Description: Lanham, Maryland : Rowman & Littlefield, 2023. | Includes
   bibliographical references and index. | Summary: "This easy-to-follow
   yet comprehensive book provides everything an educator working in a
   museum or school, in person or online, needs to develop experiences that
   encourage close looking, spark the imagination, and support the
   development of critical thinking skills"-- Provided by publisher.
Identifiers: LCCN 2022052715 (print) | LCCN 2022052716 (ebook) |
   ISBN 9781538167403 (cloth)| ISBN 9781538167410 (paperback) |
   ISBN 9781538167427 (ebook)
Subjects: LCSH: Museum exhibits. | Virtual museum exhibits. | Interactive
   multimedia. | Museums--Educational aspects.
Classification: LCC AM151 .V37 2023 (print) | LCC AM151 (ebook) | DDC
   069/.5--dc23/eng/20230112
LC record available at https://lccn.loc.gov/2022052715
LC ebook record available at https://lccn.loc.gov/2022052716

for museum educators past, present, and future

and

Sierra

Contents

List of Illustrations   xi

Preface   xv

Acknowledgments   xxv

Part I: The Big Picture

Chapter 1:   Why Museum Tours Still Matter   3

Chapter 2:   An Introduction to Thematic Tours   11

Part II: Planning

Chapter 3:   The Tour Planning Template   17

Chapter 4:   Choosing a Theme   23

Chapter 5:   Object Selection and Sequencing   33

Chapter 6:   Writing and Sequencing Open-Ended Questions   41

Chapter 7:   The Role of Information   49

Chapter 8:   Multimodal Activities   59

Chapter 9:   Advance Organizers, Transitions, Reflections   69

Chapter 10: Getting Ready   75

Part III: Facilitation

Chapter 11: Greeting and Orientation   81

Chapter 12: Supporting Participation   91

Chapter 13: Reflection and Evaluation   101

Part IV: Adapting the Tour Planning Template for Diverse Audiences

Chapter 14: Audience at the Center: Adapting the Tour
Planning Template for Varied Audiences   115

Chapter 15: Adapting the Tour Planning Template for School Tours   121
Queena Ko

Chapter 16: Adapting the Tour Planning Template for
Students on the Autism Spectrum   129
Melanie Adsit and Jackie Delamatre

Chapter 17: Adapting the Tour Planning Template for Social-
Emotional Learning   139
Lisa Mazzola

Chapter 18: Adapting the Tour Planning Template for Family Tours   149
Emily Rivlin-Nadler

Chapter 19: Adapting the Tour Planning Template for Virtual Tours
for Adults   155
Sharon Vatsky

Chapter 20: Adapting the Tour Planning Template for Adults Who
Are Blind or Have Low Vision   165
Karen Bergman

Chapter 21: Adapting the Tour Planning Template for Adults with
Alzheimer's Disease and Other Dementias   175
Francesca Rosenberg

Appendix 1: Questionnaire on Gallery and Virtual Museum Teaching   185
Appendix 2: Tour Planning Checklist   189
Appendix 3: Tour Planning Template   191
Bibliography   193
Index   201
About the Author   213
About the Contributors   215

List of Illustrations

Preface 1 Camille Pissarro (1830–1903), *The Hermitage at Pontoise*, ca. 1867*   xviii

Preface 2 Camille Pissarro, (1830–1903), *The Hermitage at Pontoise*, ca. 1867, detail   xx

Figure 1.1 Educator Missy Lipsett facilitates a *One Work, One Hour* tour at the Guggenheim   7

Figure 4.1 Connecting Collections, Shoe icebreaker   23

Figure 4.2 Connecting Collections, Shoe icebreaker, detail   24

Figure 4.3 Teachers discuss reproductions of artworks and brainstorm possible themes   25

Figure 4.4 Detail from a brainstorming session on possible tour themes   26

Figure 5.1 A group of students discuss *Untitled (Ghardaïa)*, 2009, by Kader Attia*   35

Figure 6.1 Tayeba Begum Lipi, b. 1969, *Love Bed*, 2012*   43

Figure 6.2 Tayeba Begum Lipi, b. 1969, *Love Bed*, 2012, detail   44

Figure 7.1 An example of an *information strip* that provides a bit of contextual information   53

Figure 7. 2 Emily Rivlin-Nadler facilitates an *information auction*   54

Figure 8.1 Many activities can be adapted for in-person or
virtual experiences   59

Figure 8.2 Many activities can be adapted for in-person or
virtual experiences   60

Figure 8.3 Marc Chagall (1887–1985), *Paris Through the
Window*, 1913*   64

Figure 8.4 An example of an annotated drawing based on
Chagall's painting   64

Figure 13.1 Retrospective evaluation tool   108

Figure 13.2 Retrospective evaluation tool   108

Figure 13.3 Evaluation form from Luca   110

Figure 14.1 The 2:00 p.m. daily tour gathers in the rotunda of
the Guggenheim Museum   115

Figure 15.1 Njideka Akunyili Crosby (b. 1983) *Portals*, 2016   125

Figure 16.1 Students take turns placing circles to create a
collaborative collage in front of *Several Circles*, 1926,
by Vasily Kandinsky   135

Figure 17.1 Rineke Dijkstra, *Almerisa, Asylum Center Leiden, Leiden,
the Netherlands, March 14, 1994*   140

Figure 17.2 Rineke Dijkstra *Almerisa, Zoetermeer, the Netherlands,
January 4, 2008*   145

Figure 20.1 A Mind's Eye participant touches a raffia grass skirt
similar to the material in a nearby sculpture in the exhibition
Simone Leigh: Loophole of Retreat   166

Figure 20.2 A Mind's Eye participant creates a tactile drawing using
a stylus on foam   169

Figure 21.1 At the Museum of Modern Art, a group of older adults
stand close to a large painting of water lilies by the
artist Claude Monet   177

*More information and a color image of this work of art can be found at https://www.guggenheim.org/collection-online.

Preface

In 2018, my first book, *Museum Gallery Activities: A Handbook*, was published. The idea for it had been percolating in my mind for years and I was happy to have the opportunity to share the multimodal activities that I had devised, facilitated, observed, and participated in over the years. As I wrote, my mind frequently went to other aspects of creating interactive thematic tours that fell outside the confines of gallery activities. This book is an opportunity to talk about that larger process.

The premise of this book is based on a simple format, the Tour Planning Template, that emerged from discussions with museum educators from The Metropolitan Museum of Art, The Whitney Museum of American Art, The Museum of Modern Art, and the Solomon R. Guggenheim Museum as we planned a summer institute for teachers in the early 2000s. It provides a structure that is both clear and flexible. Although these four museums all focus on visual art, the same template can be equally useful when planning experiences in history and science museums.

The Tour Planning Template is the scaffold for this book, but so much goes into planning and facilitating a museum experience: research, thought, organization, empathy, reflection, and revision are only some of the elements. I wanted this book to unpack that process, and to reflect more than only my voice. To that end I created an email survey (see appendix 1) and sent it out to a broad network of museum educators. Of course, only a percentage were returned—each one is thanked in the acknowledgments—but that feedback was invaluable to this process. Many of the surveys were in alignment with my experiences but added nuance and additional perspectives to those understandings. Other respondents raised new issues to consider and include. At the heart of this book are those aggregated experiences of planning, facilitating, and reflecting on guided museum experiences. No two tours are alike. Even if you use the same theme, artworks, sequence, questions, and activities, the participants and their responses make each experience unique.

A LOOK BACK AND AHEAD

As I write this book, the whole museum and cultural landscape is shifting. COVID-19 has significantly impacted museums and in many places restricted the ability to continue in-person group experiences. The educators who conduct(ed) these tours have been disproportionally impacted, many of them losing their jobs, and dismissed after years of dedicated service.

Some museums successfully "pivoted," finding ways to continue to connect with audiences virtually. Nearly overnight, museum educators became the only front-facing staff (albeit virtual) in direct communication with the multiple audiences of their shuttered institutions.This required a sharp learning curve and many of the lessons learned about virtual teaching are shared in this book. In the process, museums discovered and developed new audiences, but sustaining these online audiences requires skill and attention. What do they want and how can we continue to keep them connected and engaged? Will museums have the interest and bandwidth to continue to serve both in-person and virtual audiences?

As museums have reopened, museum educators, having worked remotely for more than a year, returned to "the office" and found that they now had two or more jobs, sustaining the responsibilities that had been developed during the pandemic, the pre-COVID-19 demands of onsite work, while also assuming responsibilities for staff who had left the field or been dismissed.

For audiences, if visiting a museum pre-COVID-19 meant dealing with some hurdles like transportation and paying the admission price, the barriers to visiting a museum have certainly increased. Even for seasoned museum-goers new protocols have added additional layers of complication. Although required as health and safety measures, and to reassure visitors that health precautions are being followed, these measures also impact the ease of visitation. Many museums require visitors to buy their tickets online, in advance, for a specific timed entry. Proof of vaccination may be requested at the door. Masks may be required. Some of these restrictions are easing, but visitation has not reached prepandemic levels. After months of being cautioned that all public spaces can be dangerous, we have been conditioned to think differently about convening and connecting.

The Black Lives Matter movement has also resulted in institutional change. When I first entered the museum field more than thirty years ago, New York City's Department of Cultural Affairs was calling for the city's museums to diversify their exhibition schedules, audiences, staff, and board members. Although this was seen as a worthy goal, it is only recently, due to the unprecedented events of 2020 that museums have responded in significant and hopefully sustained ways. Some still question whether these changes are genuine and long ranging or just a reaction to pressure, but change it is. There is no doubt that—for whatever reason—museums have felt the need to respond and are collecting and exhibiting more works by artists of color, revamping their hiring practices, requiring staff to participate in DEAI (diversity, equity, accessibility, inclusion) trainings, and putting a new emphasis on the workplace environment.

The issues that face museums are daunting. Even before the pandemic, I could see that the type of museum experience that I am advocating for was in danger. Budget constraints and the availability of multimedia guides provided a rationale for the elimination of the long-standing 2:00 p.m. daily tour for museum visitors. This is truly troubling. One assignment I give my graduate students is to sign up for an educator-led and curator-led tour at any museum. Curator-led tours can be excellent and informative, but I have never joined one that was truly participatory except for the leader asking, "Are there any questions before we move on?" The curatorial tour and the education tour are just different *animals*. The primary goal of the curatorial tour is to inform the visitor about an exhibition, but an education tour will also focus on supporting participants in making personal connections with works of art and modeling a process that can be used to make these connections with other works once the tour has concluded.

It is hard to tell how museums will emerge from this time. Will these intimate and varied experiences in front of artworks that have been so important to me continue to be available to visitors or considered antiquated relics of an earlier time? At some points I have wondered if I am writing about an endangered species—whether the in-person inquiry-based museum tour will go the same way as the dodo bird and the slide rule, replaced by downloaded multimedia guides. I have nothing against multimedia guides, but they are not a substitute for a facilitated group experience.

I am sincere when I say that some of the most satisfying learning experiences of my life have come when sitting in front of a work of art with a group of people. I have had the opportunity and privilege to do this—perhaps hundreds of times over my career. I have been guided by some of the luminary museum educators in our field, but also by novices trying out their first tour. Sometimes the groups are large, where thirty or more individuals are gathered in front of a single work. At other times the groups have been intimate, where an educator is rehearsing a tour for just three or four colleagues, looking for feedback and tweaks. The assembled group may be composed of all art and museum-savvy professionals. Other times I sit with those completely new to visiting a museum, a group of teens, a class of adult English language learners.

For me, this process of looking together and sharing our perceptions is deeply gratifying. As an activity, there are few that I prefer. I like to be the facilitator/educator, but I am at least equally happy to be a participant. What is it that, to me, is so compelling about these experiences? Yes, they are about learning, but it's more than that. They are collaborative, thoughtful, creative, unique, supportive, experimental, and yes . . . fun—akin to delving into a complicated puzzle and discovering that you are capable of solving it.

Working in a museum you literally live with original works of art. One of my touchstones in the Guggenheim's collection is Camille Pissarro's *The Hermitage at Pointoise* (see figure preface.1). It was on nearly continual display during my two decades of work there. This is not cool. I shouldn't continue to be drawn to a work by a dead, white, male artist more than a century and a half after it was completed, but it has been part of thousands of museum tours and continues to offer up new and compelling insights.

When you first look at it most visitors see a depiction of a quaint European village. We have debated whether the season is spring, summer, or fall, but all

Preface 0.1. Camille Pissarro, (1830 -1903)The Hermitage at Pontoise, ca. 1867 Oil on canvas 59 3/16 x 78 3/4 inches (150.3 x 200 cm) *Solomon R. Guggenheim Museum, New York, Thannhauser Collection, Gift, Justin K. Thannhauser, 1978*

agree the weather is perfect. Lush mountains and greenery surrounding the rustic buildings that seem to be made from the materials that surround them—stone, clay, wood—a village in sync with its environment. Even the colors are keyed to reflect unity. When I ask participants to share a word that describes their initial response to this painting, they frequently offer up *bucolic, rustic, communal, idyllic.* Many visitors also comment on the interaction between the two women in the foreground (see figure preface.2). You can't miss them. Pissarro has structured the painting over a thinly disguised "map" of how to travel through it. The road that begins on the lower right corner almost screams, "Enter here!" These women are the first villagers you meet on your visual walk, but the encounter is ambiguous. As we focus on these figures, a participant notices that one of the women is holding a parasol to protect herself from the sun, while the exposed arm of the woman with her back to us is many skin tones darker. Pissarro seems to have wanted to make this disparity explicit. Then we pair up, taking the poses of the two women and imagine what they might be talking about. Taking the poses is revelatory. The woman whose back is to us leans in with her arms clasped behind her back, a pose that the group suggests might indicate subservience or deference. The way they are dressed seems to confirm our deduction. We posit that these are not peers, but women from different classes of society, one able to protect herself from the sun, the other deeply tanned from working in the elements. Pissarro believed in an idealized society of equals, where the disparity between rich and poor, bourgeois and peasant, was not as great, but in 1867, even in an idealized scenario, class divisions are still evident.[1] These are not understandings that come quickly or easily. I have not read about this from art historical accounts. These insights come from looking, thinking, and talking together. Whereas most visitors will glance at this work, think "nice landscape," and move on, prolonged looking and probing has yielded a much more nuanced interpretation.

This format doesn't work without willing participants. If no one talks, we all sit there in silence. Participatory tours depend on participation ... duh. I tell this to groups as we begin. "I am counting on you to share your thoughts and perceptions." Fortunately, I have never sat there in silence. I attribute this not to my great teaching, but rather to the works of art that are truly interesting to discuss when given some time and space. Sometimes they *compel* participants to talk. Some of my favorite contributions come from participants who begin their comments by saying, "I promised myself I wouldn't talk, my English isn't good, but I have been looking at this work and I have to tell you that . . ." Another favorite is the participant who changes their statement midway through their sentence because they notice something that suggests a new meaning. "I see that. . . . Oh, I just noticed . . . and now I see . . ."

There is something in the format itself, whether expertly or even less-proficiently facilitated, with a large or small group of seasoned museum goers or newbies that encourages you to look deeply, listen carefully, respect the thoughts of others, and notice your own responses. In my estimation even the best multimedia guide cannot supplant these experiences. Although wonderful to have a gifted educator leading the experience, it is the format—a group of curious people coming together to talk, to share, to make meaning that is most important. In this process we demonstrate that we truly see things from different perspectives. In looking at an artwork, someone mentions a detail, others declare, "I hadn't noticed that." Someone else inserts a comment, and another person adds, "I never thought of it that way." At a time when we are so polarized in our positions, this forum provides a place to marvel, accept and truly enjoy disparate points of view. Yes, these group experiences are about learning, but they are about so much more.

WHAT VISITORS WANT

In his most recent book, John H. Falk, a leading expert on free-choice learning, focuses on the benefits of museum visitation:[2]

> For nearly half a century, I have been thinking and theorizing about museum experiences—why people use museums, what they do during those experi-

Preface 0.2. Camille Pissarro (1830 -1903) The Hermitage at Pontoise, ca. 1867 (detail) Oil on canvas 59 3/16 x 78 3/4 inches (150.3 x 200 cm) *59 3/16 X 78 3/4 inches (150.3 X 200 CM) Solomon R. Guggenheim Museum, New York, Thannhauser Collection, Gift, Justin K. Thannhauser, 1978 78.2514.67*

ences, and what they take away, including the value they perceive they derive. Today, though, my explanation of the museum experience is starkly different than it was forty years ago, or even fifteen years ago.

For much of my career I focused on learning, and more recently identity, but these days I have come to believe that there is an even more basic value that sits at the heart of the museum experience—enhanced well-being. . . . I argue that well-being is a basic biological process, a mechanism for achieving balance with one's world. In fact, the pursuit of well-being is at the core of what it means to be alive, and the pursuit of human-specific dimensions of well-being are at the heart of what it means to be human.[3]

During the first meeting of each graduate class in museum education I pose this question to the students: "Think back to a positive learning experience that you have had. It can be at any time during your life and need not be school-based. Write down when and what that experience was." I give the group a bit of time to write. Then I ask, "What were the *qualities* that made the experience positive? Write down a few words that describe that experience." We then make a cumulative list. As each student describes the learning experience that came to mind, I add their adjectives to our growing list. One student says, "I took a new course and was feeling overwhelmed. The teacher encouraged me and gave me extra attention and time." What words do you want to add to the list? *Encouragement* and *attention*. Another student recounts, "I took a guided wilderness hike. It was *challenging* and *communal*." The list continues to build. Here are some of the adjectives that have been offered:

- Empowering
- Welcoming
- Trust
- Learning something new
- Modeling
- Empathetic
- Creative
- Shared experience
- Hands-on
- Team building
- Validating
- Can make mistakes
- Informed instructor
- No judgment
- Safe
- Social
- Comfortable
- Collaborative
- Supportive

- Interactive
- Skill sharing
- Confidence building
- Individualized
- Intimate
- Validating
- Fun

That word, *fun*, pops up again in another recent study.

According to Culture Track, a national research organization that studies the changing behaviors of cultural audiences, the are many reasons why people attend cultural activities, but the single greatest motivator is having *fun*. Cultural organizations may scoff at the word "fun" because it seems to distract from their missions, but audiences believe they are not mutually exclusive. "Fun," in fact, is a somewhat all-encompassing term that has to be better defined and understood in respect to cultural experiences; but it is an essential—and widely desired—element of them."[4]

It is interesting that my very small sample of fifteen graduate students so closely correlates with the Culture Track's 2017 study that polled 4,035 cultural consumers across the United States.[5] According to the study, when asked to list the *characteristics of an ideal cultural activity*, respondents voiced the following qualities: social, interactive, lively, hands-on, active, calm, immersive, reflective. "For culture to matter, it must enable people to find or make meaning. At this particular socio-political moment, reducing stress, providing fun, and offering perspective are pre-conditions for this to happen."[6] And that is *exactly* what interactive guided museum experiences can provide!

I am a lifelong arts educator. At age twenty I began teaching art to Head Start through eighth grade students in Hartford, Connecticut.[7] I was assigned to three schools. Wednesday mornings I had four twenty-five-minute art-on-a-cart classes followed by an eighth grade class. Five classes in one morning! I would prep materials, do the motivation, get the class started on an art project, then run down the hall to the next class. Some teachers would allow their classes to continue the artmaking process, for others when I headed out the door it was cleanup time. I saw some students only every other week. At one point I added up the number of students I taught. The total was more than one thousand. After years of teaching public school youth, I moved to adult education and then college teaching. When I made the transition to museum education administration, I made sure that that although much of my work was administrative, some teaching would stay in the mix. Even as a director, I continued to factor in time to work directly with visitors. Those were the days I felt the most impactful, the most productive.

My hope is that this book serves as reassurance for those who are doing this work and sometimes feel that they are only small cogs in the larger wheels of the museum. You are doing important, valuable work that makes a difference. There are many hopeful signs, including committing to welcoming new audiences and diversifying collections to include more women artists and artists of color, but there are also opposing forces, tight budgets, and more competition for time and attention. A report released in March 2022 by the U.S. Bureau of Economic Analysis concludes that as COVID-19 raged, the nation's arts and culture economy shrank by 6.4 percent—with fine arts education declining 37.4 percent and museums decreasing 22 percent.[8]

This book is about planning and facilitating a specific kind of tour—the interactive thematic tour. It is both a *how-to* and *tell-all* account. The opening chapters outline the rationale and structure of the Tour Planning Template and elaborate on the planning process. I spend a lot of time on planning. It is the gestation period when you have time to think through, learn, and question possible teaching strategies, but it is not until you facilitate the tour plan—actually do it—that you know if your planning has connected with your audience. These chapters offer ideas for supporting participation and reflecting on and learning from the tour so that you can continue to improve your practice. For the final chapters I invited seven gifted educators to share how they adapt the Tour Planning Template to best serve the audiences they work with. This last portion of the book demonstrates how sensitive museum educators, who take the time and effort to get to know their audiences, can use this basic template and adjust it to support specific audiences. Each of these chapters begins with the same basic Tour Planning Template but shapes it to accommodate a particular audience.

I believe that this format encompasses most of the attributes that cultural consumers are seeking. This book is an insider's guide to creating interactive tours offering not only my insights, but also those of many other skillful educators. Museum educators have the desire and capacity to offer these programs, both in person and virtually. It is my hope that museums realize the special experience these programs can provide and support the talented educators that facilitate them. This is a "how-to" book, but also a plea to continue these kinds of offerings. I think they encapsulate the best of what museums can provide.

NOTES

1. Richard R. Brettell, *Pissarro and Pointoise.* New Haven, CT: Yale University Press, 1990, 41.
2. John H. Falk, The Value of Museums: Enhancing Societal Well-Being. Lanham, MD: Rowman & Littlefield, 2021.
3. John H. Falk, *Why Well-Being Is at the Heart of Museum Experiences.* American Alliance of Museums blog, January 10, 2022. https://www.aam-us.org/2022/01/10/why-well-being-is-at-the-heart-of-museum-experiences/.
4. La Placa Cohen. Culture Track 2017. Top-Line Report. p. 11. https://s28475.pcdn.co/wp-content/uploads/2019/06/CT2017-Top-Line-Report.pdf.
5. Ibid, 5.

6. Ibid, 41.
7. Head Start is a federal program that promotes the school readiness of children from birth to age five from low-income families by enhancing their cognitive, social, and emotional development.
8. Databank USA: The Ailing Arts, July/August 2022, AARP Bulletin, 46.

Acknowledgments

This book is focused on a simple planning tool, the Tour Planning Template, which was created in conjunction for an annual summer teacher institute program, *Connecting Collections: Integrating Modern and Contemporary Art into the Classroom.* Since its inception in the early 2000s, dozens of museum educators from the Solomon R. Guggenheim Museum, The Metropolitan Museum of Art, Museum of Modern Art, and the Whitney Museum of American Art, have worked toward making this program a success. Hundreds of teachers have attended, from all over the world, and brought inquiry-based teaching strategies back to their local classrooms. I am truly gratified that a program I helped to create continues, more than twenty years after its inception. My thanks to the current Connecting Collections team and to those who have worked on the program through the years.

Unlike my first book that was largely a solo effort, as I envisioned this book, I wanted to include the knowledge and experience of many museum educators. To that end, a questionnaire (see appendix 1) about gallery teaching was sent to my network of colleagues. Of course, only a percentage were completed and returned, but those responses were extremely important to this project. Their wisdom and comments are woven into each chapter. My deep gratitude to Jen Brown, Ryan Hill, Olga Hubard, Carolyn Keogh, Missy Lipsett, Sarah Mostow, Shannon Murphy, Gabriela O'Leary, Vas Prabhu, Joyce Raimondo, Laurel Schmidt, Rebecca Shulman, Jamie Song, and Linda Sweet for sharing their process and insights.

Most of this book explores how to use the template to customize both in-person and virtual tour experiences, but each audience comes with its own characteristics. To expand on and demonstrate how museum experiences need to be crafted to accommodate varied audiences, I invited seven museum educators to contribute chapters. These chapters add crucial dimensions to this book and provide in-depth investigations into customizing museum experiences. My deep appreciation to Melanie Adsit, Karen Bergman, Jackie Delamatre, Queena Ko, Lisa Mazzola, Emily Rivlin-Nadler, and Francesca Rosenberg for their important contributions. My thanks also extends to Cyra Levenson, deputy director, Education and Public Engagement at the Solomon R. Guggenheim Museum and Nisa Mackie, Edward John Noble Foundation deputy director of Learning and Audience Engagement at the Museum of Modern Art for providing these staff members the flexibility to write for and contribute to this book.

I am grateful to Kara Largenton, associate manager, Rights & Reproduction and Susan Wamsley, digital asset manager at the Guggenheim Museum for their assistance in securing permissions to reproduce the images. You made the process as painless as possible. My thanks to Erinn Slanina, associate acquisitions editor, and Taylor Breeding, assistant production editor at Rowman & Littlefield Publishers. Throughout this project you have deftly guided me and generously offered your knowledge and expertise.

And finally, in December 2020 as I departed the Guggenheim Museum, I received an email from Charles Harmon, senior executive editor at Rowman & Littlefield Publishers asking if I had a concept (and the wherewithal) to embark on writing another book. I had worked with Charles previously but was surprised (and flattered) when he contacted me again. Thanks for wondering if there was another book in me. I didn't know there was. Your encouragement and support have been important motivators during this writing process.

Part I

The Big Picture

1

Why Museum Tours Still Matter

Early in my museum education career I was leading a group of third graders on their first museum visit. As I guided the class to the next tour stop the first child in line asked me, "What's the name of what you do?" I looked at her a bit puzzled, not quite understanding the question. She repeated, this time with a bit more emphasis and growing frustration, "What's the name of what you do?!" I finally understood the question and said, "I'm a museum educator." To which she replied, "That's what I want to be!"

This interaction happened decades ago, but it has stuck in my mind. In retrospect, I have gained a bit of insight into that moment. I thought I was teaching about the museum and the objects we were looking at, but this student was focusing on something else. She knew about the teachers who work in school classrooms, but this was different. You could be a teacher, but one that worked in a different kind of environment. She had glimpsed an interesting new possibility, but to learn more, she'd need to know what to call it.

She was way ahead of me. I didn't learn that there were educators in museums until I was in my twenties and was invited to participate in a teacher advisory committee at the Wadsworth Atheneum in Hartford, Connecticut. My undergraduate courses in art education mentioned nothing about museum education.

If you grew up in New York City, going on field trips to some of its many museums was probably an integral part of your learning. My mom, a teacher in the New York City's public schools, would take her thirty-five fifth grade students on the subway to visit some of the city's best known cultural institutions. She would allow me to skip school to join these trips. My favorite was the Hayden Planetarium, at the American Museum of Natural History. For a few years I aspired to be an astronomer.

Today, field trips to museums are in decline. Even before the COVID-19 pandemic, museums across the country were reporting steep drops in school tours, and other recent events have curtailed them even further. The decision to reduce field trips to museums reflects a variety of factors. Financial pressures force schools to make difficult decisions about how to allocate resources. With greater focus on raising student performance in math and reading, many testing days have been added to the school calendar, which may have the consequence of limiting the days available for field trips.[1] When schools do organize field trips, they are increasingly used as rewards, opportunities for socialization, or entertainment rather than for cultural experiences. As a member of my town's board of education, I review and approve all district-wide field trips, so I see this trend in real time. The destinations for the majority of field trips are to visit parks and amusement areas.

As school trips to museums decrease, several ambitious studies have been published that document the positive learning and attitudinal impact that guided museum visits can exert on K–12 students. In 2013, Crystal Bridges Museum of American Art and the University of Arkansas College of Education and Health Professions shared the results of a study analyzing the impact of school field trips on students in grades K–12. This major study included 10,912 students, surveyed at 123 schools. The research team found that even a single field trip to a museum can have significant benefits for students. "We found that students who attended a school tour at Crystal Bridges demonstrated stronger critical thinking skills, displayed higher levels of tolerance, had more historical empathy and developed a taste for being a cultural consumer in the future. . . . We also found that these benefits were much larger, in general, for students from rural areas or high-poverty schools, as well as minority students."[2] Interestingly, the school tour format described in the Crystal Bridges study strongly aligns with the Tour Planning Template described in this book. Each one-hour long visit includes discussions and activities at several thematically connected tour stops.

Another study published in 2018 from the National Art Education Association (NAEA) and the Association of Art Museum Directors (AAMD) showed that "facilitated classroom visits to an art museum had a measurable impact on key aspects of student learning." The four-year research project studied more than 2,600 students in grades four through six and included facilitated experiences at six art museums across the United States. The results demonstrated that there are a variety of educational benefits to class visits to art museums, across four areas:

- Questioning: Students ask more complex questions about works of art
- Multiple Interpretations: Students are more accepting of multiple interpretations of a work of art
- Physicality of Art: Students are more likely to think about art in terms of its material properties
- Emotive Recall: Students experience greater emotive recall of the program.[3]

Evidence from these studies demonstrate that art museum visits should be an increasing, rather than decreasing experience for students. Museums immerse children in a world outside of their own lives, expanding their horizons.

Something special that happens when students leave their school building for another place where a different kind of learning can be experienced.[4]

Class trips are important, but an even more significant factor in determining future visitation is whether you grew up visiting museums with family members. Several studies have shown that those who visited cultural organizations as children are significantly more likely to visit as adults.[5]

An initial assignment I give to graduate students in my museum education class is to write a museumcentric autobiography. I have read hundreds of these over the years. Many recall memories (mostly, but not all positive) of being taken to a museum in their early years. For most, their experience with a family member, a dad who shared his love of aviation with his daughter at the Smithsonian's National Air and Space Museum, an aunt who introduced her niece to wonders of The Metropolitan Museum of Art planted seeds that years later would yield adult museumgoers. A major factor in determining whether you will be a visitor to museums as an adult is whether you experienced them in childhood.

The New York City-based organization Cool Culture was one of the first to acknowledge the disparity in museum visitation according to family income and formulate an approach that supports building a habit of museum-going for lower income families. Its mission is "to amplify the voices of families and strengthen the power of historically marginalized communities through engagement with art and culture, both with cultural institutions and beyond."[6] Toward this goal Cool Culture provides fifty thousand families a year with unlimited free admission to ninety New York City cultural institution partners.[7] To encourage visitation, it supports families with activities, workshops, and events facilitated in multiple languages. Its work is paying off with more parents reporting increased comfort in museums and enhanced understanding of how to support their children's learning through the arts.

Hopefully, you are now convinced that guided museum experiences are important for youth, but what are the benefits for adults? It has been widely reported that adults visiting a museum typically spend less than thirty seconds looking a painting.[8] If you work at a museum and get to observe visitors on a regular basis, you might think that is an overestimation. James O. Pawelski, director of education for the Positive Psychology Center at the University of Pennsylvania makes this analogy, "When you go to the library, you don't walk along the shelves looking at the spines of the books and on your way out tweet to your friends, 'I read 100 books today! You can't really see a painting as you're walking by it."[9]

There is no single way to visit a museum. When visiting an exhibition on my own, I am as guilty as the next person of rushing through and only perusing the works on view. As an alternative, some have advocated for slowing down, but paradoxically most museums aren't designed for an individual visitor to stop in front of a single artwork for an extended period. There is usually no seating, other visitors are jockeying to see the same work, and just the sense that you are conspicuously standing there feels awkward and out-of-step with the active surroundings. It is distressing to acknowledge that the configuration of today's art museum is not conducive to looking at art. For most visitors, the only way they will ever spend extended time looking at an important artwork is by joining a guided tour.

According to art historian James Elkins,

> Looking for a long time is not the usual way people see artworks. The usual interaction with an artwork is a glance or a glimpse or a cursory look. What I have in mind is a different kind of experience: not just glancing, but looking, staring, gazing, sitting, or standing transfixed: forgetting, temporarily, the errands you have to run, or the meeting you're late for, and thinking, living, only inside the work. Falling in love with an artwork, finding that you somehow need it, wanting to return to it, wanting to keep it in your life.[10]

As an undergraduate at New York University, my gifted professor Robert Kaupelis gave this assignment to his introductory drawing class. He suggested that we each select a reproduction of a drawing that we were drawn to:

> "It's like you literally *live* with this drawing. You are to have an intimate affair with it. Carry it with you at all times. Let it be the first thing you look at in the morning and the last thing you look at before going to bed. Really get into and study this work. Just as you would with a new lover, try to find out all you can about the drawing and allow yourself to experience it to the utmost of your ability. As you would a new friend or lover, introduce the drawing to your friends and acquaintances; let them look it over and ask for their responses to it. As in true life, your friends will often see both strengths and weaknesses that you have failed to notice. As you agree or disagree with their reactions, you may find yourself and your feelings about the work begin to change, either for better or worse. . . . Living with a drawing in this fashion can be a most profound experience."[11]

Working in a museum you *can* literally live with original works of art. Their layers and meanings emerge after multiple viewings, but few visitors ever have that opportunity.

Looking closely at works of art while comfortably seated on a gallery stool is enough reason to join a guided tour, but what truly makes the experience special is the chance to look closely in dialogue with other people. The interactive aspect of the experience is as important and encourages multiple perspectives that support sharing ideas.

> It doesn't really work to try to look at paintings by yourself. I've come to the museum and stood there and asked myself the how do you feel thing and I look at it and I come up with a thought or two. But when I'm by myself, it doesn't seem as great as it does when there are people around you raising their hands and having thoughts. By yourself, once you have exhausted those

Figure 1.1. Educator Missy Lipsett facilitates a *One Work, One Hour* tour at the Guggenheim. *Filip Wolak © Solomon R. Guggenheim Foundation, New York. All Rights Reserved. 78.2514.67*

two thoughts, you're standing there looking at this painting and this painting is standing there looking at you, and there's nothing interactive about it. You're not with other people who can bring out things you didn't see, or explain things you couldn't figure out, or describe feelings you couldn't put into words.[12]

I want every museum visitor to have that experience. During a group tour it is not unusual to spend extended time in front of a work. Twenty minutes is typical, but some programs can devote an hour or more to focusing on a single work. Museum educator Missy Lipsett has conducted an ongoing series titled *One Work, One Hour.* What do they do during this tour? They consider and discuss a single work of art for sixty minutes. Not every artwork is prime for this kind of investigation, but many are. I am reluctant to use the word "transformative." I am not one for hyperbole, but these conversations are important, collaborative, and frequently memorable. We are all working together to solve a layered puzzle, deeply engaged in noticing, describing, and bringing the breadth of what we each know to the task of interpretation. We will "solve" each work of art in our own unique way, but sharing those perceptions, insights, and personal connection brings us closer to the work and each other.

According to their mission statement, Culture Track is a "cultural innovation platform, dedicated to addressing the most pressing challenges facing the worlds of culture and creativity through research, education, dialogue, and action. We believe that studying and tracking the shifting patterns of audience behavior is critical to shaping the future of culture."[13] Culture Track conducts extensive audience research that helps cultural organizations understand what visitors want. During the COVID-19 pandemic they focused on cultural institutions and their audiences. One of the most interesting findings to emerge from their research was the considerable increase in the perceived importance of arts and culture organizations. More than half (56%) of Americans view art and culture organizations as important to them.[14] Eighty-three percent wanted to see art and culture organizations help their community by providing emotional outlets including opportunities for people to laugh, relax, experience moments of beauty, rekindle hope, express themselves creatively, experience distraction or escape, and have help with healing, grieving, and processing emotions. Respondents who reported that they had become more worried, afraid, sad, or depressed during 2020/21 wanted cultural organizations to serve as emotional outlets for their communities. Nearly as many Americans (77%) wanted art and cultural organizations to serve their community by providing opportunities for connection and learning. This category includes providing opportunities to stay connected with other people, bringing people of different backgrounds together, connecting the past to the present, addressing societal inequity and racial injustice, and helping educate children.[15]

If you are thinking that it's a tall order to ask museums to fill all those needs, new research is demonstrating that museum visits may indeed have the ability to support many of these requests. University of Pennsylvania researchers Katherine N. Cotter and James O. Pawelski reported that adults visiting a museum had the potential to reduce stress levels, anxiety, lower chronic pain, increase their life span, and lessen the likelihood of being diagnosed with dementia! Beyond these individual gains, museum visits also positively boosted empathy and the way people interacted with each other.[16] In-person guided museum experiences have the potential—in small, incremental ways—to meet many of the expectations that audiences are needing and requesting, opportunities to slow down, focus, learn, and most of all, connect with others.

NOTES

1. Jay P. Greene, Brian Kisida, Daniel H. Bowen (2014), "The Educational Value of Field Trips: The Educational Value of Field Trips: Taking Students to an Art Museum Improves Critical Thinking Skills, and More," *Education Next* 14(1), 79, https://www.educationnext.org/the-educational-value-of-field-trips/.
2. Jay P. Greene, 21st Century Chair in Education Reform and head of the Department of Education Reform at the University of Arkansas College of Education and Health Professions, Brian Kisida, senior research associate and Daniel H. Bowen, doctoral fellow.
3. *Impact Study: The Effects of Facilitated Single-Visit Art Museum Programs on Students Grades 4-6*, National Art Education Association & Association of Art Museum Directors by RK&A, Inc. September 2018, https://www.arteducators.org/research

/articles/377-naea-aamd-research-study-impact-of-art-museum-programs-on-k
-12-students.

4. Amanda Krantz and Stephanie Downey (2021), "Thinking About Art: The Role of
Single-Visit Art Museum Field Trip Programs in Visual Arts Education," *Art Education*, 74:3, 41, https://www-tandfonline-com.tc.idm.oclc.org/doi/full/10.1080/00
043125.2021.1876466.

5. LaPlaca Cohen, Culture Track '17, https://culturetrack.com/wp-content
/uploads/2017/02/CT2017-Topline-Deck.pdf Slide 44.

6. Cool Culture, https://www.coolculture.org/.

7. Cool Culture, https://www.coolculture.org/programs-impact/.

8. Issac Kaplan, *How Long Do People Really Spend Looking at Art in Museums?*
Artsy, November 7, 2017, https://www.artsy.net/article/artsy-editorial-long
-people-spend-art-museums.

9. Stephanie Rosenbloom, *The Art of Slowing Down in a Museum*, New York Times,
October 9, 2014.

10. James Elkins, "How Long Does It Take to Look at a Painting?" Huffington Post, The
Blog, November, 8, 2010, updated December 6, 2017, https://www.huffpost.com
/entry/how-long-does-it-take-to-_b_779946.

11. Robert Kaupelis, Experimental Drawing, 1980, New York:, Watson-Guptill Publication, 15.

12. Rika Burnham, "If You Don't Stop, You Don't See Anything," *Teachers College Record*
Volume 95, Number 4, 1994, 520–25, https://www.tcrecord.org/content.asp?con-
tentid=88.

13. Culture Track, https://culturetrack.com/about-culture-track/what-is-culture
-track/.

14. Culture + Community in a Time of Transformation: A Special Edition of Culture
Track, 5–6, https://sloverlinett.com/wp-content/uploads/2022/01/Rethink-
ing-Relevance-Rebuilding-Engagement-CCTT-Wave-2-Survey-Full-Report.pdf.

15. Ibid, 27–28.

16. Elaine Velie, "Suffering from Anxiety? Try Visiting a Museum" (2022), *Hyperallergic*, https://hyperallergic.com/741124/suffering-from-anxiety-try-visiting-a
-museum/.

2

An Introduction to Interactive Thematic Tours

Each July since 2005, the education departments of The Metropolitan Museum of Art, the Museum of Modern Art (MoMA), the Solomon R. Guggenheim Museum, and until 2015 the Whitney Museum of American Art, have collaborated on a weeklong professional development institute for teachers, known as *Connecting Collections: Integrating Modern and Contemporary Art into the Classroom*. This collaboration has developed an intensive program focused on sharing object-based interpretive practices in art museums.

Each institute includes forty teachers who are diverse in the subjects they teach, the ages of their students, and where they live. Some call New York City their home, others have traveled halfway around the world to be part of the program. During the course of the week, teachers experience interactive tours that model various object-based teaching techniques that focus on exploring works of art. They are also provided with the tools and strategies that enable them to build their own interactive thematic tours.

Participants report in written evaluations that they leave the weeklong program with a greater understanding of how to effectively incorporate modern and contemporary art into their curricula. One participant likened it to an intellectual spa: "We were surrounded by amazing works, thought-provoking instructors, and enthusiastic colleagues. I felt pampered aesthetically, intellectually, and spiritually. This was a great summer renewal of what really matters in what we do!" (Anonymous, personal communication, July 18, 2014).[1]

But *Collecting Collections* did not spring to life fully formed. It began as an informal partnership between two museums: the Guggenheim and the Whitney. The Met came on board in 2003, followed by MoMA in 2004. After some experimentation, we decided that the most valuable resource we could share with educators was not the works in our impressive permanent collections, but the teaching strategies we use to involve visitors in making their own personal connections to works of art. As one former participant commented, "I thought this would be about teaching art, instead it has turned out to be about the art of teaching" (Anonymous, personal communication, July 17, 2015).

These four New York City museums are sometimes perceived as having different teaching philosophies, but as staff members from each museum education department came together and began to discuss teaching methods, we discovered that we were on the same page and in basic agreement about the structure that would yield effective gallery teaching. We all agreed that it was useful to organize gallery tours thematically, facilitate inquiry-based discussions, add relevant contextual information, and include multimodal activities to provide further learning opportunities. We came to realize that what had been construed as separate methodologies were actually differences in style. The team worked together to formulate one cohesive structure that would be flexible enough to allow for different personalities, interests, and content, yet still produce compelling, participatory tours. We shared the belief that the skills we use in the galleries would also be useful and adaptable for the classroom. It is this structure, developed through this long-standing program, that this book seeks to share with both museum and classroom educators.

One of the enormous benefits of the program is that during the week, teachers have the opportunity to participate in gallery experiences facilitated by numerous art museum educators from different museums. This is my favorite part of the week. I get to participate in gallery tours planned and facilitated by my talented colleagues at different museums. Although each art museum educator uses the same planning tool (the Tour Planning Template), each experience is remarkably different allowing each educator to bring their own unique personality, style, and content to the task. The Tour Planning Template, which is introduced in the next chapter, provides a scaffold that is liberating rather than restrictive. It is remarkably flexible while retaining its ability to provide a clear structure around which engaging tours can be fashioned. Although my primary experience is using it in a visual arts context, I have seen it employed successfully using historical, and scientific objects. It is equally as useful in museum galleries and school classrooms. Some of the basic tour components that will be considered in more depth include:

Selecting a Theme: Thematic tours allow the museum educator to curate the gallery experience and tailor it the to the interests and developmental level of the group. Despite the richness and depth of the exhibitions that may be on view, no single exhibition is the focus; rather, the objects selected can span anything that is on view at the museum. Virtual tour providers have even more options, as long as the chosen artworks have a direct connection to the museum. The goal is to select three to five works of art that fall under that thematic umbrella and consider the theme in a variety of ways.

Developing Effective Questions: Once the theme and objects are selected, carefully constructed, open-ended questions are created for each tour stop. They are a cornerstone of gallery teaching. If a question is truly inquiry-based and open-ended, there will be many possible interesting and compelling responses. The use of open-ended questions encourages participants to notice details, look for evidence, and consider new ideas and perspectives.

The Role of Information: Contextual information can be layered into discussions in response to participant observations or questions, with the goal of moving the discussion to a deeper level. If information is provided too early in the conversation, it thwarts wonder and speculation. If inserted too late, it is an afterthought and superfluous. Knowing the right information to provide and at the right moment is an important and acquired skill.

Multimodal Activities: Deep group discussions are wonderful, but there are additional ways to learn. Adding activities that call upon other modalities including writing, drawing, and movement add both variety and new insights to the tour experience.

Although the Tour Planning Template emerged from *Connecting Collections Teacher Institute* for use with K–12 students, it is the planning tool that I, and many of my colleagues, use to create tours across various demographics. As this book demonstrates, the template is applicable to a broad range of audiences.

These basic building blocks, with the addition of a few strategies for connecting the elements, provide the structure for building your own gallery experience. You are free to choose a compelling theme that has relevance to your audience. You may decide to select the most highly regarded highlights from the collection or to focus on lesser-known artists and works that deserve more attention.

The chapters that follow introduce the Tour Planning Template and the decisions and research that go into selecting a fruitful theme, writing open-ended questions, finding relevant information, and developing multimodal activities. The last chapters of this book demonstrate how this basic structure can be adapted for virtual teaching and varied audiences.

According to one *Connecting Collections* participant,

> We came to understand the power of collaborative learning by observing carefully while keeping an open mind; to actively listen to our peers' insights and interpretations; and developed confidence in our ability to find personal meaning in artwork. . . . The patience and enthusiasm of the museum staff, the

excellent orchestration of our group work under their leadership all combined to make our days a turning point in our own quest of instructional excellence. (Marty Merchant, personal communication, 27 July 2006)[2]

NOTES

1. Anonymous quotes in this chapter are excerpted from written evaluations administered at the conclusion of each Connecting Collections Teacher Institute.
2. Portions of this chapter are adapted from Sharon Vatsky, "Connecting Collections: Integrating Modern and Contemporary Art into the Classroom," chapter 9 in *Professional Development in Art Museums: Strategies of Engagement Through Contemporary Art*, edited by Dana Carlisle Kletchka and B. Stephen Carpenter II, National Art Education Association, Alexandria, VA, 2018.

Part II
Planning

3

The Tour Planning Template

After the big buildup, you are no doubt expecting some momentous document to support your tour planning. The Tour Planning Template is actually remarkably simple; it is just a tool for organizing the information you will need to build a successful gallery, virtual, or classroom experience. But lots of thinking and deliberation goes into creating it. I have seen educators struggle over every aspect of creating a tour plan from choosing a theme and selecting tour stops to crafting the exact wording of a question. I have seen them create a full tour plan only to discard it for another idea they think might be more fruitful. Creating a tour plan is truly a creative process. There are lots of moving parts and having a simple tool to assist in organizing the relevant information and strategies is essential. Those who are not passionate about this work cannot imagine the amount of time, energy, and thought that goes into the planning process. When I have finally put the finishing touches on a new tour plan, my emotions move from uncertainty to excitement. I now feel ready and eager to share. I know that a careful plan doesn't ensure a successful tour, but I have done what I can to prepare. I have sometimes likened planning a tour to preparing to have a baby. You go to childbirth classes, practice your breathing, paint the nursery, gather supplies, do everything you can to prepare—once the tour begins (or labor starts), you cannot fully predict how things will go, but you have done what you can to get ready and that preparation will make you more confident and more able to respond, even to the unexpected.

Museum educator Sarah Mostow expressed a similar process and emotional connection with tour planning:

> In education in general, prep is the elephant in the room, in the sense that a lot of preparation probably correlates with great teaching, but no employer could ever ask you to do the hours that are in fact required. It is almost like being an artist in that you are never *not* working. Preparing for upcoming classes is always in my "back brain," and I'm often reviewing—and changing—my plans until the very last minute. When I hit upon a plan I believe in, I feel a sense of calm. I need to trust the artwork and the children and trust the (simple) questions I have prepared.[1]

The Tour Plan Template is where your research and strategies can be thought through so that when you meet the group, full attention can be placed on artful facilitation. The more complete it is the better the chances for a successful group experience. This does not mean that you will be reading or memorizing the plan. You have created it. You have internalized it by thinking through, visualizing, and sometimes testing it out on friends, colleagues, and or family members. In short, it is *your* personal way of teaching. Museum educator Ryan Hill recommends to "Over prepare and then throw it all away."[2] I understand this comment to mean that through the planning process you have internalized what you will need. It belongs to you, you can call upon it, but what happens during the tour will be informed by, but not governed by, that preparation. Although I will rarely refer to it during a tour, except to read an artist's quote or check a date, I usually print out the tour plan and keep with me it on a clipboard for backup. I am pretty old-school. Other educators have it on their phone or iPad.

If you search the internet, you will find many thousands of posted lesson plans nicely packaged and ready to use. I understand the appeal and ease of these prepackaged plans, but I can't imagine using one without significant alteration, not because I am looking to do more work, but because I would feel totally insecure without moving through my own planning process. Yes, I have poached many ideas and activities from other educators, but I always need to think them through and adjust them to my own goals and teaching style. Not everything needs to be unique. Incorporate what is relevant from other educators, but everything needs to be put through your personal internal teaching mechanism. Educators (both museum educators and classroom teachers) are smart and creative. They know their audiences best and can take ideas and make adaptations and adjustments that maximize the strengths of their students/participants.

During the course of the weeklong Connecting Collections teacher institute, each educator works on creating their own tour plan utilizing the Tour Planning Template. They each choose a theme that is relevant to their students, select and sequence works of art, formulate open-ended questions, research relevant information, and create gallery activities. By the conclusion of the program each educator has created a lesson plan that will become part of their curriculum when they return to school. With a few adjustments, this Tour Planning Template can be used to create gallery tours, virtual experiences, or lessons taught in the classroom. It can also be used to create lessons for other curriculum areas.

Combining these tour-building elements enables the educator to create an experience that is unique, flexible, and yet grounded in an underlying structure that can be applied to constructing vastly different lessons and gallery experiences.

A blank Tour Planning Template and an annotated version is provided here that provides references to where you will find further discussion of those aspects of the tour planning process in this book.

TOUR PLANNING TEMPLATE

EDUCATOR: _____

GROUP: _____

THEME: _____

GOALS: _____

ADVANCE ORGANIZER: _____

Object (artwork) Selections: Add a small image (thumbnail) of each work *in the sequence/order* it will be introduced. Depending on the allotted time and group between 3 and 5 tour stops may be included.

TOUR STOP 1

Artist:
Title, Date:
Medium, Dimensions, Museum Collection:

TRANSITION

TOUR STOP 2

Artist:
Title, Date:
Medium, Dimensions, Museum Collection:

TRANSITION

TOUR STOP 3

Artist:
Title, Date:
Medium, Dimensions, Museum Collection:

REFLECTION/WRAP-UP/ CONCLUSION

Open-ended Questions: For *each* artwork write open-ended questions in the sequence/order they will be presented.

1.
2.
3.

Information: Important information about *this* artwork that is related to the tour theme.

-
-
-

MULTIMODAL ACTIVITY:

REFLECTION

ANNOTATED TOUR PLANNING TEMPLATE

Educator: Yep, your name goes here.

Group: Examples: fourth graders studying cities, adult tourists, first-time adult visitors, high school students studying architecture. Any characteristics you can insert will be helpful in focusing your plan.

Theme: Briefly describe how this theme is relevant to participants lives. See chapter 4 for a full discussion of selecting a theme.

Goals: What do you want the group to know or be able to do by the end of the session? (FYI: My goals are never about art historical facts.)

Advance Organizer: See chapter 9 for a discussion of advance organizers.

Navigation (optional): I frequently add my tour route. How will I get from one tour stop to the next? Literally the path we will travel.

Tour Stops: *For each* tour stop include a small image (thumbnail) of each work in the sequence it will be introduced.

Artist (birth-death, nation of birth, lives and works in): You may need a phonetic spelling of the artist's name to aid with pronunciation, especially for non-Western artists. If not familiar to you, practice saying the artist's name.

Title of the work, date, medium, dimensions, museum collection (sometimes called the "tombstone information" or object label)

Open-ended Questions: For *each* artwork write three open-ended questions in the sequence/order they will be presented. (You may not need all of them.) See chapter 6 for a fuller discussion of developing open-ended questions.

1.
2.
3.

Information: Research information that is specific to this particular artwork. See chapter 7 for a discussion of the role of information.

Multimodal Activity: For *each* artwork add an activity other than discussion that focuses on this work. See chapter 8 focusing on developing multimodal gallery activities.

Transition: See chapter 9 for a discussion of adding transitions between tour stops.

Reflection: A time to think back on the tour with the group. See chapter 13 for ways to conclude the tour and consider the experience you have had together.

The components above are repeated and completed for *each* tour stop. Depending on your audience and the allotted time you have with them it is typical to include three to five tour stops on a thematic interactive tour. The primary thing to remember is that the Tour Planning Template provides the opportunity to try out ideas, think things through, and try something new.

NOTES

1. Sarah Mostow, personal correspondence, December 2021. Sarah Mostow is a museum educator at the Solomon R. Guggenheim Museum.
2. Ryan Hill, personal correspondence, December 2021. Ryan Hill is an educator whose career includes a decade at the Hirshhorn Museum in Washington, DC.

4

Choosing a Theme

Creating a theme for your tour is a powerful, organizing device. It allows you to curate the experience and consider everything within the museum including the building itself, the permanent collection, and special exhibitions for possible inclusion in the experience. A theme enables you to travel across exhibitions and consider how artists, over time, have expressed and addressed various big concepts. It also invites visitors to bring the knowledge they bring with them to the task of interpretation.

Although there are other approaches to creating a gallery experience, including exhibition tours where the guide focuses on a single exhibition and the

Figure 4.1. After participants decide on a group, they assemble in a circle so that we can all see the thematic groupings. I seem to be delighted by the "sneaker group."
Photo: Filip Wolak © Solomon R. Guggenheim Foundation, New York. All Rights Reserved

Figure 4.2. The self-named "strappy sandal group." *photo: Filip Wolak © Solomon R. Guggenheim Foundation, New York. All Rights Reserved*

highlights tour where the group stops at the best-known works, the thematic tour offers the educator the ability to consider works that share conceptual similarities but express them in different ways. The educator can tailor the tour to the interests and developmental level of the group by selecting three to five works that fall under a thematic umbrella.

During *Connecting Collections Teacher Institute*, we introduce thematic connections with an icebreaker activity. On the first day of the program, just after the overview and orientation, we ask the group, around fifty people in total, to gather in a large, open space. I provide the following prompt, "Hello and welcome. This week we will be thinking about themes and how they can support your teaching. To begin this process, please take the next two minutes to group yourselves thematically according to the shoes you are wearing. Once you have found your thematic group, discuss the characteristics that you share and what connects you." The next two minutes are buzzing with activity. Everyone looking downward, and a focusing on the attributes of our footwear. People settle on a group, but then may look across the room and see another group that they might want to jump to. Do I affiliate more with the self-named "strappy sandal group" or the "embellishment group"? With the "comfy casual group" or the "ballet flats group"? When time is called, we form a large circle so that our choices can be viewed by all. A spokesperson from each group describes what brought them together. This simple activity gets people talking and thinking about thematic groupings even before they experience a thematic tour in the galleries.

Figure 4.3. Teachers discuss reproductions of artworks and brainstorm possible themes for their lessons. *Center for Arts Education.*

That afternoon we invite the participating teachers to begin the process of building their own thematic tours. Twenty color images of artworks from our collections are printed out on 8.5 x 11-inch paper. Postcards from the museum shop will work equally well. Those images are tacked up, projected, or just laid out on a table with the tombstone information (artist, title, date, etc.) on the back. Participants are then told that they should think of these twelve artwork reproductions as the contents of *their museum.* They are given the task of finding thematic similarities between the works. For this exercise, a thematic grouping includes three works that share a thematic connection. The group then has ten-minutes to generate themes from these twelve works. As the group goes to work, the themes begin to percolate: nature, cities, families, gender, animals, community, signs and symbols, women, solitude, color. The facilitator scribes the themes on a white board or post-it pad.

How many themes can a group think up from just these twelve images? The answer is quite a few. After ten minutes the group has usually generated between twenty and thirty potential themes. I encourage you to try it. It is an exercise in flexible thinking, and by stressing different inherent characteristics, a single work may be used to support multiple themes.

This brainstorming activity will result in numerous thematic options, but not every suggestion has equal potential to provide the foundation for interesting conversations in front of artworks. The next step is to critically consider which themes have the potential to be the most compelling. We look over the brainstormed list and ask, "Which themes can we imagine yielding the most

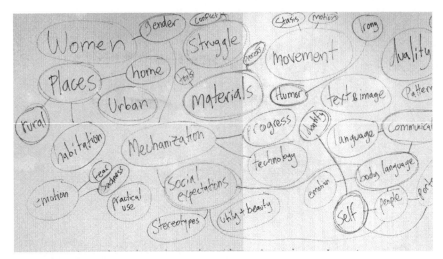

Figure 4.4. Detail from a brainstorming session on possible tour themes.
Sharon Vatsky

fruitful conversations?" It becomes clear that some of the brainstormed responses are stronger than others.

Some are eliminated from the list because they are too specific and personal. I remember doing this exercise with a group of teachers. One educator noticed that three of the works had food references and suggested the theme *diabetes*. This was a brainstorming activity, and diabetes might have been on this educator's mind, but *diabetes* is not a good tour theme. Sometimes an initial thematic concept needs to be tweaked to transform it into a more serviceable one. A graduate student recently came to me with a tour plan based on the proposed theme of *loss and grief*. The artworks she had selected were beautiful, lyrical, and transcendent. We eventually decided that framing the tour with the theme of *memory* would actually open up the dialogue and allow for more open interpretations of the works. The educator needs to carefully consider the broadness or narrowness of the theme as an interpretive frame. If the thematic umbrella is too broad, it will not provide a useful focus and if it is too narrow it will limit conversation and feel like a superimposed constraint.

Some brainstormed suggestions can be made into stronger themes with a bit of modification. The suggested theme of *women* may yield more interesting discussions if it is adjusted to consider *gender roles*. The suggestion of *sadness* as a theme will be stronger if it is broadened to a discussion of *emotions*. These modifications widen the scope of the theme and will spark a more complex range of responses.

I love art teachers. For a good part of my career, I was an art teacher. If there are art teachers in the group it is inevitable that the elements of art, line, shape, form, space, color, texture, be included on the brainstormed list.[1] Unfortunately, the elements of art usually do not make for great themes. One reason is that they apply to the vast majority of artworks, and one purpose in choosing a theme is to narrow the lens. There was a point in my life when, before I even really looked at a work of art, I would begin to interrogate the elements. How had the artist used color to create this mood? How had the space been constructed to create this environment? What I realized is that in my haste to analyze, I was missing the impact of the work. This urge to analyze was actually impeding my ability to enjoy, make meaning, and yes just bask in an encounter with a new work of art. I therefore suggest that before analyzing and breaking a work apart into elements, let's give ourselves time to take in the whole work. The elements of art will come up as the artwork is discussed. A participant may comment about the overall impact of a work. For instance, to the comment, "This work is making me feel edgy (or optimistic, or claustrophobic, or peaceful) the educator can ask, "How has the artist been able to evoke that emotion?" The elements of art will surely be part of the discussion, but they do not make for compelling themes.

In a similar vein, when the twenty images are laid out, someone will nearly always mention that they see specific colors used in multiple reproductions. To our list of potential themes, red, yellow, and blue will be suggested. But imagine the "yellow" tour:

Educator: "Hello everyone. Today we will be looking at works the contain yellow."

Educator: "Here we are at our first work. What do you notice?"

Participant: "I see a patch of yellow in the upper right corner."

Participant: "I see more yellow in the background."

In short, not a particularly scintillating conversation. Imagining how the conversation will play out can provide an important cue to whether a theme will be generative or . . . a dud.

However, I need to add a disclaimer here. I have since encountered a number of exceptions to this rule. On a visit to the Brooklyn Museum, I came across an exhibition titled *Infinite Blue*[2] that featured blue in all its variety, from ancient times to the present day. I learned that in cultures dating back thousands of years, the color blue has often been associated with spirituality, power, status, and beauty. In this exhibition, the color blue became a unifying theme to tell stories of global history, cultural values, technological innovation, and international commerce.

Likewise in 2005, the Guggenheim Museum presented *Russia!* "The most comprehensive exhibition of Russian art outside Russia since the end of the Cold War."[3] In the exhibition, the color red was prominently featured and had multiple meanings including ones related to Russian history, culture, religion, and politics. Red and its multiple meanings within Russian art and history became a rich thematic focus.

Professor and author Olga Hubard recounts a similar experience:

> A few years ago, I participated in a museum education program overseas which was themed, quite simply, "White"—a theme whose potential I was initially skeptical about. The educators led our group through engagements with a series of contemporary Japanese artworks where the color white was conspicuous. The selection of a compelling group of diverse yet like-colored artworks, and the group's responses to these works, brought to life the eloquence and versatility a single color can have. At the conclusion of the program, we all agreed that the color white, encountered in a range of thought-provoking visual contexts, had become a character of sorts, triggering a surprisingly varied range of emotions, ideas, questions, and associations in participants. Needless to say, the success of this program would have been impossible without an extremely thoughtful selection of artworks and without the sensitive, imaginative facilitation of the educators.[4]

Other suggestions for the list of brainstormed themes that I can generally count on being offered are *portraits, landscapes*, and *still lifes*. For the seasoned museumgoer, these painting genres may be a comfortable and familiar references, but for other museum visitors both young and old, these art terms suggest that one might need to be an "art insider" to participate in such an experience.

In 2000, to mark the millennium, the Museum of Modern Art (MoMA) presented the exhibition *Modern Starts: People, Places, Things*. The show deliberately abandoned customary labels. *People* focused on images of the human face and figure, *Places* was dedicated to the interpretation of site, and *Things* focused on the representation of objects. Unlike most exhibitions that are developed by a single department, this exhibit invited all of MoMA's curatorial departments to contribute and offer "provocative juxtapositions, new contexts, and inventive interplays of mediums."[5] This rejection of traditional art labels signaled that you don't need specialized knowledge, or extensive training, to engage with works of art. Providing more accessible, *real-world* themes invites visitors to bring their lived experiences and knowledge to the act of looking at art together. The broad themes of *people, places*, and *things* are more inclusive and inviting than the more traditional art-specific themes of *portraits, landscapes*, and *still lifes*. They signal that your lived experience counts even more than artistic styles, movements, or genres.

The Connecting Collections team has deemed these markers for selecting a theme:

- A universal lens that is relevant to students' lives and classroom content

- Either immediately, or through exploration, is visually evident in the work of art
- Is a concept that can be explored in depth and on many levels
- Provides a common point of connection through which to frame the objects

The act of constructing a gallery experience is a creative process. For me it starts by spending time with the artworks in the galleries. I gravitate to certain works. They percolate (as in the previously described activity) for possible inclusion in a tour. I ask myself which works will yield the most interesting perceptions and conversations. I usually return from this scouting expedition with a number of possibilities to deliberate.

In this book, "Choosing a Theme" and "Object Selection and Sequencing" are separate chapters. In practice, however, these two aspects of tour planning are inexorably connected. The tour theme emerges from the artworks on view. It is not imposed from above. I do not go into the galleries looking to construct a tour about *everyday objects*, but it may turn out to be a connecting thread between artworks that I suspect will be compelling to the group.

For any educator looking for a generative list of thematic possibilities to consider, I recommend visiting the Art21 website https://art21.org/explore/. *Art21* is a long-running PBS television series focusing on contemporary art and artists. Many episodes are based on a thematic model that includes video segments concentrating on five different artists, demonstrating how their work, in vastly different ways, connects to a universal theme. Due to the popularity of their theme-based programs, they have added a web page that offers an impressive number of possibilities.

Over the years, each educator builds a repertoire of themes and supporting works of art that have yielded successful tours. Here are a few themes that I have found helpful in connecting various works of art:

- Places
- Materials and Process
- Identity
- Narrative and Storytelling
- Signs and Symbols
- Making the Everyday Special
- Working from Home (a theme I used frequently during COVID-19 quarantine, focusing on artists who found inspiration in and around their homes)
- Global, Local, Personal (another theme that resonated in the wake of the pandemic and the Black Lives Matter movement when everyone—to greater or lesser degrees—was effected by world events)

Selecting a clear, relatable, inclusive theme and imparting it to the group helps to provide a welcome and invitation to participate. A theme that is too academic or complicated will not put the group at ease. Don't worry that a theme may seem too simple. A simple, understandable theme actually allows you to include more visually and intellectually challenging objects on your tour. "Today we will be looking at several artworks that consider the concept of *home*." The visitor thinks, "*Home*, okay, I know something about that." Be it positive or negative we all have a storehouse of information around the concept and experience of *home*. Participants on the tour will have a better idea of why you may be stopping at one work rather than another and can access their own experiences and expertise around that big idea. Without a theme, some in the group may wonder, "Why is the educator stopping here?"

For a theme to be an effective organizing tool it needs to be used well or it can undermine rather than support the experience. The theme needs to be evident in, and authentic to, the work. It needs to voice the artist's intent and not be the sole invention of the museum educator. I recently participated in a virtual tour. The educator introduced the theme of *power* and asked each participant to share their definition of it. However, as we encountered each work of art, I couldn't see anything in the works that suggested *power*. The artworks were fine, the conversations were fine, but for me the object selections didn't speak to the theme and became not only superfluous, but confusing.

Themes are framing devices that provide a rationale for the works you will stop at during the tour. But interesting works of art are complex and don't come with singular "thematic tags." The educator needs to be transparent about that. The point of a theme is to enable the group to consider how various artists have addressed a big idea across time, style, geography, and medium, but the theme should never limit conversations in front of the artwork. Conducting a thematic tour can be perceived as limiting, but during tours I have facilitated with the theme of *Place* we have also discussed brush strokes, scale, relationships, gesture, perspective, picture frames, composition, color, cracking paint, weather, skin color, gesture, women's roles, and gentrification, to mention only some of the directions that conversations have veered in.

Themes can be an educator's friend if used with thought and care, but detrimental if not carefully considered. As Olga Hubard in her in-depth consideration of thematic tours points out, "Educators who want to honor a work's complexity while also working with a distinct theme might want to lean toward themes that, when paired with a particular work, leave more room for multidimensional investigation."[6] Used judiciously, themes can add unity and coherence to gallery, virtual, and classroom experiences.

NOTES

1. The J. Paul Getty Museum, *Elements of Art*, http://www.getty.edu/education /teachers/building_lessons/elements_art.pdf.
2. Brooklyn Museum, *Infinite Blue*, November 25, 2016–August 4, 2019, https:// www.brooklynmuseum.org/exhibitions/infinite_blue.
3. Solomon R. Guggenheim Museum, *Russia!* September 16, 2005–January 11, 2006, https://www.guggenheim.org/exhibition/russia.
4. Olga Hubard, "What Counts as a Theme in Art Museum Education?" *The Journal of Museum Education*, Vol. 38, No. 1, City Museums and Urban Learning (March 2013), p. 100, Taylor & Francis, Ltd., https://www.jstor.org/stable/43305774, accessed: 20-10-2021 20:41 UTC.
5. John Elderfield, Peter Reed, Mary Chan, Maria del Carmen González, *Modern Starts: People, Places, Things,* Museum of Modern Art, New York,1999, inside cover.
6. Olga Hubard, "Art Museum Education: Facilitating Gallery Experiences," chapter 3, *Interrogating the Thematic Approach*, New York: Palgrave Macmillan, 2015, p. 47.

5

Object Selection and Sequencing

The objects (works of art or artifacts) that you choose to include are the *meat* of your tour. What objects will best support your theme and what is the best order in which to present them? Object selection, like every other part of building and creating a tour, involves personal and subjective choices. Be sure that your selections support the theme, but also look for a variety of perspectives and unexpected ways that the works you include authentically relate to your tour theme. It is also important that you be genuinely curious about and interested in the works you select.

Although well-known works by prominent artists can be crowd-pleasers, this is also an opportunity to introduce a more diverse range of artists and artworks to your group. A gallery educator at the Museum of Modern Art recently shared with me that she had decided to stop including works by Vincent van Gogh and Pablo Picasso in her tour plans. She reasoned that these artists had received more than their share of exposure over the years, and that her group's time would be better spent investigating equally interesting works by lesser-known artists. Visitors cluster around *Starry Night*[1] and *Le Demoiselles d'Avignon*[2] without much prompting, while other works get barely a glance. By not focusing on the museum's "greatest hits," she reasoned that she could devote more time to introducing visitors to women artists and artists of color, who have been marginalized for far too long.

The responsibility to be more inclusive and representative in the selection of artworks is being felt across the nation. In 2020, Yale University announced that it would discontinue offering its introductory art history survey course Introduction to Art History: Renaissance to the Present, citing the impossibility of including all the varied cultural backgrounds that the course's title implies. Considering that my college textbook *History of Art* by H. W. Janson contained not a single woman artist,[3] this change signals that the Western "canon" is being reexamined and acknowledges that the history of art is comprised of not just one, but rather multiple stories.[4]

In the wake of 2020 and the Black Lives Matter movement, more urgent pressures have been placed on our cultural institutions to broaden and diversify the exhibitions and artworks they collect and exhibit. This long-over-due movement toward opening up the traditional art historical canon is happening at every level of the nation's museums. It will take continued dedication to DEAI (Diversity, Equity, Access, and Inclusion) goals over time to achieve greater parity, but the museum educator has the ability to reflect these more inclusive objectives in a very immediate way.

There is growing realization that widening the lens to include more BIPOC (Black, Indigenous, People of Color) and women artists reflects not only a more inclusive, but also a more accurate picture of artistic creativity. However, despite efforts by many museums to mount exhibitions that reflect a broader perspective, recent studies indicate that an estimated 85 percent of artists represented in collections of major museums in the United States are white and 87 percent are men. (This, of course, differs significantly from the US population, which according to census data is 61 percent white and 50.2 percent male.)[5]

Visitors of all ages need to see artists and artworks from cultures outside the European tradition and museum educators can provide content and inspiration to challenge assumptions. We can do that by selecting works that reveal the rich fabric of artists and artistic production locally, nationally, and globally.

In addition to introducing visitors to more diverse artists and works of art, educators are also taking a more nuanced look at works deeply embedded in their collections and examining them from new perspectives. Is there another point of view? Who is missing from this image? What is the power dynamic? Whose voice is, or is not, being recognized and acknowledged? These are questions we can ask to become catalysts for dialogue, revelation, and change.[6] History museums and historic houses are also doing this work and starting conversations that examine their collections from multiple vantage points.[7]

Although I have not made the decision to totally eliminate well-known artists or artworks from my tour plans, I certainly strive to make more diverse and inclusive object selections. A thematic tour is the perfect opportunity to select three to five objects that address the theme from vastly different perspectives, across time periods, geographies, and materials to begin to demonstrate the diversity of creative practice. Contemporary art is truly global and has expanded to include works not only from Europe and North America, but artists from across the globe. These varied histories serve to deepen the museum experience.

Not all works of art are equally good candidates for extended looking and discussion. I may truly love a work, but that doesn't mean it will make for an interesting tour stop. On the other hand, there are some works on view that are such fertile choices, and in such demand, that educators need to carefully schedule their time in front of it, so that everyone gets a turn. One such work that comes to mind was a sculpture shown at the Guggenheim Museum by French Algerian artist Kader Attia; a three-dimensional model of an ancient city sculpted in 770 pounds of couscous—yes, couscous.[8] This work contained many attributes that made it an ideal tour stop. It could contribute to supporting multiple tour themes including *architecture*, *history*, *place*, and *materials and*

Figure 5.1. A group of students discuss *Untitled (Ghardaïa)*, 2009 a work created by Kader Attia using more than 700 pounds of couscous.Kader Attia, Untitled (Ghardaïa), 2009 Couscous, two inkjet prints, and photocopy prints; couscous diameter: 16 feet 4 7/8 inches (500 cm); inkjet prints: 70 7/8 x 39 3/8 inches (180 x 100 cm) and 59 1/16 x 39 3/8 inches (150 x 100 cm); photocopy prints: 11 11/16 x 8 1/4 inches (29.7 x 21 cm) Solomon R. Guggenheim Museum, New York Guggenheim UBS MAP Purchase Fund, 2015 2015.84 © *Kader Attia Photo: Filip Wolak © Solomon R. Guggenheim Foundation, New York. All Rights Reserved*

processes among others. It also appealed to all age groups. The uniqueness of the material was the initial attraction, but as the work was discussed, its symbolic meaning and historical perspective began to surface.

For *Untitled (Ghardaïa)* (2009) Attia modeled the Algerian town of Ghardaïa in couscous, a regional food staple that is more than a thousand years old, originated with the Berber people of North Africa and is now popular worldwide.

The use of couscous as an art medium is symbolic. Although couscous originated in Northern Africa, it is now a popular dish enjoyed around the world, demonstrating how the colonized (Algeria) can have immense cultural impact on the colonizer (France), reversing traditional thinking about the direction of influence.[9] Ghardaïa is located in north-central Algeria in the Sahara Desert, and in addition to its other attributes, couscous also bears a useful resemblance to sand. Most visitors would not have known the artist previous to their visit, but the material, installation, history, and symbolism combine to make for compelling discussions and discoveries.

There is another important quality embedded in this work by Kader Attia—the elements of novelty and surprise. Museums state that they want visitors to have memorable experiences, and of course, educators want their tours to be memorable as well as enjoyable and informative. One way that educators can support that goal is by selecting works that contain an element of the unexpected.

Psychologists have shown that if we experience a novel situation within a familiar context, we will more easily store this event in memory suggesting that adding novelty to our teaching may improve learning and memory. As an example, conjure your best memory of a special birthday. Got it? Then try to remember what happened the day before that birthday. In short, unique events tend to be more memorable than everyday ones. Novelty seems to promote memory, and this scientific finding has the potential to provide educators with a tool for structuring their tours more effectively.[10]

This element of surprise can be demonstrated in many ways, even by selecting seemingly unlikely objects for inclusion. I have witnessed educators facilitate compelling conversations in front of works that I never—in a million years—would have selected. The esteemed educator Rika Burnham chose Robert Rauschenberg's trailblazing *White Painting*,[11] a work six feet tall and more than ten feet across. It is composed of seven panels of uninflected, all white surface, without gesture or modulation, painted with a roller and oil-based house paint. Initially, the group was baffled; it was impossible to consider the work in the traditional ways we are taught to consider artworks. The work was nearly indistinguishable from the bare white walls of the museum, containing none of the traditional art elements like line, shape, color, or texture, that can spark discussion in front of abstract paintings. But with time to look, and tune-in, we began to notice small anomalies, shadows, and the way light played upon the surface. It was a Zen-like lesson in noticing whispers rather than shouts. More than a decade later the experience is lodged in my memory because of Burnham's unorthodox object selection. She challenged and trusted the group in front of a difficult work, and gently coaxed us toward meaning making.

Every educator has their own personal process for selecting objects. Olga Hubard shares hers:

> I pay very close attention to the works I might use, consider my own response to them and imagine the response others might have. When possible, I talk about these works with other people. I research them and think about what aspects might be worth considering as possible areas for discussion. I consider the space (virtual or real) and how I might need to navigate it to support the group's exploration. . . . I think about how a sequence of works might work together, the "story" they might tell as a group. The aspects just mentioned don't necessarily happen in this order, and the planning is not always linear. Depending on the circumstances, I might come up with the theme first and search for works that fit well; other times I consider the works first and consider themes that these works suggest to me.[12]

Museum educator Shannon Murphy describes her planning method:

It's a creative process that unfolds through time. I first need to have my own experiences with the art, and then research the artwork and artist who created the piece(s). I think about the ideas in those artworks and consider my own understanding of them (and my biases). I also consider who is visiting and why? What's going on in the world at that time? What are the other works of art that are on view? I create an introduction to get to know my group and set them up for our experience with art. I'll begin the experience with an object that I think they might like/is relevant/is an easy and crowd-pleasing object to begin with.[13]

Museum educator Sarah Mostow states,

Ideally, the choice of art objects to stop at during a tour will be self-explanatory. A good trick is to include thumbnail images of each artwork in your tour planning document. Just seeing the images side-by-side in a particular order should have a logic of its own. The theme should be self-evident and there should be a sense of "build," which is usually achieved by the last stop exemplifying the theme in a surprising way. For example, a straightforward portrait, a highly expressive portrait, and then a video "portrait" that shows someone's clothing but not their body. The theme is manifest in increasingly complex or abstract ways.[14]

Sometimes beginning a tour with a work by a well-known artist can put the group at ease and provide sense of security. Participants think, "Okay, something familiar, by an artist I have heard of. I'm on solid ground here." This approach allows those on your tour to begin with ideas and images that are more familiar and concrete. Having participated in a lively discussion and built confidence at the beginning of the tour, participants become more willing to tackle works with increasing ambiguity. As you decide on the sequence of your tour stops consider moving from more concrete, figurative works to more abstract or conceptual ones. Once you have the group on board, you can move to more abstract, conceptual, and intellectually challenging works for the subsequent tour stops. The group will join you on this journey to explore more difficult works because they began in familiar territory.

As you build your tour, check that the works you plan to include meet the following guidelines. The works selected for this tour

- relate clearly to the theme;
- are sequenced to allow for a greater understanding of the theme throughout the lesson;
- address the theme in a variety of ways; and
- are developmentally appropriate.

This last bullet point, considering the developmental appropriateness of the objects you select, is important. I have never worked in a children's museum and although many of the works on view are appropriate for all audiences and would receive a "G" rating, for general audiences,[15] the Guggenheim has also exhibited many important works that are not appropriate for younger visitors. I have many stories about the convoluted tour routes that were devised in order to avoid student tour groups from viewing works that depict explicit sexual content or violence. If you are an educator who conducts tours for student groups, you have an extra layer of responsibility. Parents and teachers are trusting you to make informed decisions about the works you focus on. The more you know about your group in advance, the better you can tailor your object selections to their developmental level and interests.

With your theme and object selections finalized and sequenced, you have now established the basic structure for your tour. It is time to begin to consider what will happen in front of each work.

NOTES

1. Vincent van Gogh, *The Starry Night,* Saint Rémy, June 1889, https://www.moma.org/collection/works/79802.
2. Pablo Picasso, *Les Demoiselles d'Avignon,* Paris, June–July 1907, https://www.moma.org/collection/works/79766.
3. H. W. Janson (1913–1982) was a professor of art history at New York University. His textbook *History of Art* sold more than four million copies in fifteen languages. It contained neither the name nor the work of a single woman artist. Women artists wouldn't be included until the 1987 edition. Wikipedia, H. W. Janson, https://en.wikipedia.org/wiki/H._W._Janson.
4. Margaret Hedeman, Matt Kristoffersen, Art History Department to scrap survey course, *Yale Daily News,* January 24, 2020, https://yaledailynews.com/blog/2020/01/24/art-history-department-to-scrap-survey-course/.
5. Eileen Kinsella, "An Estimated 85 Percent of Artists Represented in US Museum Collections Are White, a New Study Claims," Artnet News, February 19, 2019, https://news.artnet.com/market/new-study-shows-us-art-museums-grappling-with-diversity-1467256 or footnote below from original study, C. M. Topaz, B. Klingenberg, D. Turek, B. Heggeseth, P. E., Harris, J. C. Blackwood et al. (2019), "Diversity of artists in major U.S. museums," PLoS ONE 14(3): e0212852. https://doi.org/ 10.1371/journal.pone.0212852, 1, https://journals.plos.org/plosone/article/file?id=10.1371/journal.pone.0212852&type=printable.
6. View the work of Dr. Robert Rock at https://medicine.yale.edu/news-article/reunion-2016-a-look-at-paintings-raises-awareness-in-the-doctor-patient-encounter/.
7. Clint Smith, *How the Word is Passed: A Reckoning with the History of Slavery Across America* (Boston, MA: Little Brown and Company, 2021). The book chronicles the author's visits to historic sites across the United States to examine how the history and legacy of slavery is being addressed.

8. Kader Attia, b. 1970, Dugny, France, *Untitled (Ghardaïa)*, 2009, Couscous, two ink-jet prints and five photocopy prints, couscous diameter: 16 feet 4 7/8 inches (500 cm); inkjet prints: 70 7/8 x 39 3/8 inches (180 x 100 cm) and 59 1/16 x 39 3/8 inches (150 x 100 cm); photocopy prints: 11 11/16 x 8 1/4 inches (29.7 x 21 cm), Solomon R. Guggenheim Museum, New York, Guggenheim UBS MAP Purchase Fund, 2015, 2015.84 © Kader Attia, https://www.guggenheim.org/artwork/34658.

9. But a Storm Is Blowing from Paradise: Contemporary Art of the Middle East and North Africa, Teacher Guide, Kader Attia https://www.guggenheim.org/teaching-materials/but-a-storm-is-blowing-from-paradise-contemporary-art-of-the-middle-east-and-north-africa/kader-attia.

10. Daniela Fenker, Harmut Schütze, "Learning by Surprise: Novelty Enhances Memory. That Fact Has Practical Implications for Educators," *Scientific American*, December 17, 2008, https://www.scientificamerican.com/article/learning-by-surprise/.

11. Robert Rauschenberg, White Painting [seven panel], 1951. Oil on canvas, 72 x 125 x 1 1/2 inches. Collection of the artist, http://pastexhibitions.guggenheim.org/singular_forms/highlights_1a.html., C. M. Topaz, B. Klingenberg, D. Turek, B. Heggeseth, P. E. Harris, J. C. Blackwood, et al. (2019), "Diversity of artists in major U.S. museums," PLoS ONE 14(3): e0212852, https://doi.org/ 10.1371/journal.pone.0212852, https://journals.plos.org/plosone/article/file?id=10.1371/journal.pone.0212852&type=printable.

12. Olga Hubard, personal correspondence, December 2021. Olga Hubard is former director and associate professor of art education at Teachers College, Columbia University, New York.

13. Shannon Murphy, personal correspondence, January 2022. Shannon Murphy is the director of education at the Noguchi Museum, Queens, New York.

14. Sarah Mostow, personal correspondence, January 2022. Sarah Mostow is a youth educator at the Guggenheim Museum.

15. Film Ratings.com, https://www.filmratings.com.

6

Writing and Sequencing Open-Ended Questions

When we began Connecting Collection in 2005, the concept of using inquiry and open-ended questions to encourage students to look more closely and share their perceptions was new to many of the participating teachers. Fast forward to the present day and most teachers who enroll in Connecting Collections are familiar with inquiry-based teaching. Nevertheless, it still takes time, thought, and effort to develop the right questions to ask in front of each work of art.

In writing this chapter I am assuming that most readers will already be familiar with inquiry-based teaching methods and devising open-ended questions. In short, open-ended questions are constructed to solicit multiple visitor responses. Because we each are individuals with different histories, backgrounds, and interests, we will literally look at the same thing and register different responses. This is a wonderful, and illuminating, realization that can happen in front of a work of art. In a world so polarized between pro and con, this or that, we can sit in front of a single work of art and not only have our own viewpoints, but also listen to and appreciate that others are seeing the same thing in their unique way! This external focus on a work of art invites us to share perceptions honestly and openly. Although there may be disagreement, I have always heard it expressed respectfully, frequently with the comment, "I never thought of it that way" or "I didn't see that before." I am reminded of this phenomenon each time I visit a museum with my spouse whose background is in science and engineering. Whereas I first gravitate to the aesthetics of a work, he is much more interested in how it is constructed and installed.

Anyone who has facilitated an inquiry discussion in front of an artwork will attest to these varied responses. In looking at the same work, perhaps a landscape painting, one participant will comment on the bucolic setting, while another will notice the way the paint is applied. Someone else will notice inconsistent shadows while another comments on the artist's choice of colors.

This approach to facilitating discussions in front of works of art has now been generally accepted in museums. Whereas curatorial tours may still be conducted in lecture style, if an educator is facilitating the tour, there is a good chance that an effort will be made to enlist the participants in conversation. But using the Socratic method[1] takes practice. Crafting thoughtful, generative questions and supporting a lively, open-ended discussion is an acquired skill. Without cultivating these skills, a well-presented lecture can be far better than a poorly facilitated inquiry tour.

When I first got to the Guggenheim in 2000, my supervisor handed me a single Xeroxed sheet of paper. There was no attribution or citation that accompanied it, just a set of guidelines on how to check that the questions you were posing to visitors were open-ended. I have only seen it in photocopied form (sometimes grayed out and somewhat askew on the page), but never in print, and so, I will pay tribute here to this well-worn document that provides some very good suggestions.

INQUIRY CHECKLIST

In Your Inquiry, Make Sure You . . .

- Ask questions that do not demand a particular answer, elicit a yes/no answer, or contain answers in them.
- Solicit several responses to each question through (1) wait time and (2) follow-up questions (i.e., Does anyone have something to add? Do others agree/disagree?). Respond positively to a wide range of responses.
- Spend a significant amount of time at the beginning of the discussion eliciting observations and asking for details about the artwork.
- Ask students to back up their interpretations or assertions with evidence from the artwork.
- Determine a theme or teaching objective for your inquiry and select a work or works that support that theme or objective. Ask a limited number of focused questions that lead students toward consideration of that theme or objective.
- Integrate factual information about the work when relevant and available. Know the subject well enough to answer questions when they are asked but feel comfortable saying "I don't know" to a request for facts.

You Might Also Want To . . .

- Call up students' prior knowledge and experiences and ask them to make connections between these ideas and the artwork. Inquire about students' feelings regarding the artwork.
- Design activities and questions for a variety of learning styles—including activities such as writing, drawing, performance, or pair/small group work, or questions that incorporate other sensory modes (such as, What might this painting sound like?).
- Check for understanding during and/or at the end of the inquiry session. Ask students to summarize what they've learned, reflect in writing or verbally, or answer questions that will reveal comprehension.[2]

The suggestions above are solid guidelines for constructing open-ended questions, but my personal litmus test for whether a question is open, or not, is: Do I already have answer(s) to the question in my head? If the answer is yes, then start again. These are the guidelines for constructing open-ended questions that we provide to Connecting Collections participants:

- Questions invite multiple responses
- Encourage close looking and critical thinking
- Support the theme and lesson goals
- Are sequenced from observation to interpretation

If a question is truly open, then I need to also be genuinely interested and welcoming to any and all the responses that I get back. A few years ago, while working with a group of educators in Singapore, we were about to look at a work titled *Love Bed* by Bangladeshi artist Tayeba Begum Lipi (see figures 6.1 and 6.2).[3] In preparation for our encounter with the work, I asked the group, "What are your associations with the word bed?" There were a wide array of responses: rest, comfort, sex, warmth, healing, illness, insomnia, etc. Someone in the group raised his hand and said *vegetable*. For a moment I was caught

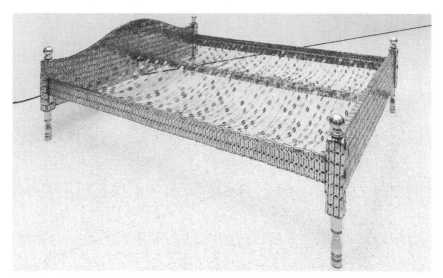

Figure 6.1. Tayeba Begum Lipi. b. 1969, Gaibandha, Bangladesh *Love Bed*, 2012 Stainless steel 31 1/4 x 72 3/4 x 87 inches (79.4 x 184.8 x 221 cm) Solomon R. Guggenheim Museum, New York Guggenheim UBS MAP Purchase Fund, 2012. 2012.153 *Image by the artist, courtesy of Sundaram Tagore Gallery.* © *Tayeba Begum Lipi Photo: Kristopher McKay* © *Solomon R. Guggenheim Foundation, New York. All Rights Reserved.*

off guard. I wondered if I had misheard. I asked, "Could you tell me more?" He clarified that sometimes a person can be so debilitated that they are in a vegetative state. Although not the most politically correct reference, I now

Figure 6.2. *Love Bed*, 2012, detail *Image by the artist, courtesy of Sundaram Tagore Gallery. © Tayeba Begum Lipi Photo: Kristopher McKay © Solomon R. Guggenheim Foundation, New York. All Rights Reserved.*

understood the response. If a question is truly open, sometimes the responses you get back will require additional clarification.

We have all seen the teacher who is seemingly trying to conduct an inquiry-based discussion but soon reveals that this wasn't the case at all. The game instead was, can you guess the answer in my head? The teacher asks a question. When students raise their hands, the teacher calls on them, and to most of the respondents gives an unenthusiastic uh-huh or okay, until they get the answer they were seeking. "Yes!" "Brilliant!" This tactic may work for a short while, but pretty soon the group gets wise to the game and understands that this is *Jeopardy!* and not a discussion or conversation.

A tour stop will usually begin with an invitation to take a deep breath and some time to look closely at the object. After a minute or so I begin with an observation question. My all-time favorite first question in front of a work of art is, "What do you notice?" I much prefer it to "What do you see?" because the word *notice* seems to ask you to be aware of your own perceptions. This question then becomes not just about what you can see or name—a house, a mountain, etc.—but rather where do you gravitate? What holds your interest? Where do you connect?

I am frequently asked how to modify questions for different age groups. One of the benefits of using open-ended questions is that they are *self-leveling.* To the question, "What do you notice?" a fifth grader will respond with their ten or eleven years of experience, whereas an adult will bring their wider view of the world to their reply.

Educator and author Jackie Delamatre notes,

> Questions are critical in modeling how to explore a work of art. When we ask, "What do you notice?" we model for students that their observations are important and meaningful. When we ask, "What more do you notice?" we model that their initial observations are not enough. When we ask, "Where do you see that?" we model that their observations are best grounded in the work. When we ask interpretative questions such as, "What can you guess about this place?" or "How would you describe this person?" we model that their hypotheses are valuable even without a higher degree in art history. When we ask, "What makes you say that?" we remind them to ground their interpretations in observations.[4]

Questions, of course, must be generated in specific relation to the work of art, and so I am reluctant to provide stock questions, but activating *prior knowledge* can be a fertile area of exploration for some works. When we look at something new, we try to relate it to something in our past experience. We bring this prior knowledge to every new encounter and attempt to reconcile and accommodate it into the vast web of knowledge and experience we already have in our memory bank. Visitors come to the museum with a broad range of preexisting knowledge, skills, beliefs, and attitudes, which influence how they will interpret and organize incoming information. How they process and integrate new information will, in turn, affect how they remember, think, apply, and create new knowledge. So, questions that activate prior knowledge like, "What, if anything, does this work remind you of?" can often tap that existing knowledge and bring it to the task of interpreting something new.

Many artworks are ambiguous, that is what makes them art (rather than advertising). There are multiple ways to interpret them and may include passages that defy easy definition or identifications. The conceptual artist Lawrence Weiner stated, "The only art I'm interested in is the art I don't understand right away."[5] As a group discusses these works there may be a tendency to ignore the more nuanced elements and focus on the more apparent or nameable aspects of the work. In instances like this I find the question, "Are you finding anything puzzling about this work?" to be helpful. This question frequently opens the door to discussing a myriad of additional aspects of the artwork that until that point had gone not unnoticed, but unstated. Using the word *puzzling*, rather than a host of other possible alternatives including *confusing*, *mystifying*, or *bewildering* is my word of choice. For me, *puzzling* suggests that we can tackle this together, and subtly implies that this is not a fault within the viewer, but rather a passage that may invite multiple interpretations or even defy solutions all together. We often find that several members in the group have been puzzling over the same thing, and those conversations, where we share our attempts at resolving these questions, can be illuminating, and sometimes downright funny, as we grapple with possibilities and notice the varied ways we interpret the same visual information.

Once you have developed a few questions, test them out. How would you respond to these questions? Try them out on family, friends, and colleagues. The order or sequence in which you ask them also is important. Consider beginning with observation questions that encourage close looking and moving toward questions that invite interpretation. Are your questions generating interesting and varied responses? You may find that changing the wording, even slightly, to include conditional language, can make a difference in the effectiveness of your questions. Compare being asked, "What's going on in this painting?" to "What *might* be going on in this painting?" or "What *do you think might* be going on in this painting?" Adding words like *might, could, may*, suggest that there are multiple interpretations rather than a single definitive answer.

A few years ago, for a professional development session, we brought together the cohort of youth educators at the Guggenheim Museum to discuss what strategies and questions yielded interesting conversations and those that were dead ends. The dead ends are lodged in my memory most clearly.

Two often-used "dead-end" questions that were mentioned are, "What was the artist thinking?" and "What was the artist feeling?" If you can find a quote from the artist that speaks to their intellectual or emotional state of mind while they were creating that work, then certainly add it to the conversation, since direct quotes from artists are frequently the most productive kind of information an educator can provide. Otherwise, we really don't know what the artist was thinking about while making the work. However, the point is not what the artist was thinking or feeling but rather how the artist is evoking a response in the viewer.

Another unproductive, but frequently used, line of questioning involves asking the viewer to imagine the same work if the artist had made different aesthetic choices. "How would this work be different if the colors were brighter (duller, lighter, darker)?" Not only does this question go nowhere, but it is also insulting to the artist and the work. Better to focus on the work we are presented with and consider our response to the work before us rather than to imaginary alterations.

As much as asking open-ended questions can engage a group, this strategy can also be misused and turn into what feels like an interrogation, rather than a conversation. Over the past few decades gallery tours by museum educators have been transformed from lecture-style monologues to more interactive experiences where the visitor's input is valued and key to making meaning together. This transition has been difficult for some, but now that interactivity and inquiry have become standard practice, there is also the possibility that these strategies are being misused. I have seen tour plans with so many questions that the goal seems to have been how many questions can be generated, rather than what questions will lead to the most thoughtful and interesting discussions. As museum educators our goal should not be interactivity for its own sake, but rather creating a space in front of a works of art to slow down, look carefully, think deeply, and share our perceptions. Asking a barrage of questions is counter to that goal.

In their book *Teaching in the Art Museum: Interpretation as Experience*, authors Rika Burnham and Elliott Kai-Kee include a chapter titled "Questioning the Use of Questions"[6] and advocate for the elimination of questions as a teaching strategy with works of art. They make a compelling case by providing examples of all the ways that questioning strategies can go wrong. In place of initiating a dialogue by asking, "What do you notice?" they propose beginning a discussion with, "I invite you to share your thoughts and observations."[7]

I am still an advocate for inquiry-based questions. They make me look and think and focus my attention. As educator and author Laurel Schmidt notes,

Inquiry questions catapult kids out of their La-Z-Boys. Faced with a single substantive question that seems to have lots of answers, their brains kick in like the search engine on a computer. All of a sudden, they think, "What do I know about this?" Signals go out in every direction. Synapses crackle. The hunt is on, and it looks different in every head. One student is searching for facts while another thinks in pictures. Some dredge up personal experiences, others work from logic, or extrapolate from parallel situations. The point is, they're all on task. One good question can produce 200 cranial hits. Inquiry questions create focus, put the brain in gear and keep it there.[8]

Open-ended questions when used thoughtfully and judiciously help you to probe and explore a work of art with a group. As a facilitator, the questions that you ask should be those that you are genuinely curious about. Your interest in hearing multiple responses is how you demonstrate that there is no single right answer, but rather as many answers as the number of participants in your group. In response to thought-provoking questions participants notice details, propose examples, scan their own histories for relevance, look for evidence, and consider ideas, theories, and speculations. This process takes time, but nothing (or just about nothing) beats time spent looking and talking together.

NOTES

1. A method of teaching by question and answer; used by Socrates to elicit truths from his students. The Free Dictionary, https://www.thefreedictionary.com/.
2. If you are the author of this document, please be in touch, I would like to acknowledge you.
3. Tayeba Begum Lipi, b. 1969, Gaibandha, Bangladesh. *Love Bed*, 2012, Stainless steel, 31 1/4 x 72 3/4 x 87 inches (79.4 x 184.8 x 221 cm). Solomon R. Guggenheim Museum, New York Guggenheim UBS MAP Purchase Fund, © Tayeba Begum Lipi. Photo: Kristopher McKay © Solomon R. Guggenheim Museum, New York, https://www.guggenheim.org/artwork/31321.
4. Jackie Delamatre, Questioning the Questioning of Questions, Art Museum Teaching: A Forum for Reflecting on Practice, January 23, 2015, https://artmuseumteaching.com/2015/01/23/questioning-the-questioning-of-questions/.
5. Randy Kennedy, Lawrence Weiner, "Artist Whose Medium Was Language, Dies at 79," *New York Times*, December 7, 2021, B10.
6. Rika Burnham, Elliott Kai-Kee, "Teaching in the Art Museum: Interpretation as Experience," 2011, chapter 6, *Questioning the Use of Questions*, 94–111, J. Paul Getty Trust, Los Angeles, CA.
7. Ibid, 106.
8. Laurel Schmidt, *Classroom Confidential: The 12 Secrets of Great Teachers*, p. 101. Heinemann, Portsmouth, NH © 2004 by Laurel Schmidt.

7

The Role of Information

Just as the selection of a tour theme is inextricably linked to the objects that are included in the tour, the role of information and the open-ended questions you offer for discussion are intimately joined. Although addressed here in separate chapters, the reader should think of these two aspects of tour planning as closely connected.

Because it is so variable, addressing the role of information during a museum experience is, in some ways, the most difficult component of the tour to describe. You can plan your theme, select and sequence the objects, and prepare a series of open-ended questions in advance, but because each experience varies, different information will need to be called upon. Although I can't predict exactly what information will be the most useful, as I monitor the direction of the conversation, I need to consider when the right moment is to add a piece of information. Added too early in the conversation, information can short circuit curiosity. Added too late, it doesn't provide a thought-provoking boost to the discussion.

The Connecting Collections team provides these general guidelines for inserting information into an inquiry-based discussion:

- Information is integrated into the discussion and relevant to the conversation.
- Information supports exploration of the theme.
- Information aligns with the lesson goals.
- Information can take many forms.

But what is the *right* information and what is the *right* moment to insert it into the conversation?

In more lecture-style tours, the educator delivers the information in a single, frequently chronological narrative. I recently attended a virtual talk about the life and work of French Impressionist painter Camille Pissarro (1830-1903). There was no doubt that the lecturer was highly knowledgeable and thoroughly prepared. He even told us the names of all of Pissarro's children. As I write this chapter a few months after the talk, I cannot recall a single name. Why?

Studies have shown that forgetting information is more the norm than retaining it. We are selective with what we decide to keep, since there is only so much storage room in our brains, and we tend to hold on to information that builds on existing areas of interest. Most of us only remember about 5 percent of what we hear during a lecture, suggesting that the lecture is one of the most ineffective methods for learning and retaining information.[1]

Another reason why the names of Pissarro's children have been lost to me is that I must have consciously or subconsciously deemed this information as useless. "Nope, I will never need to rattle off the names of Pissarro's many children, I can take a rest here." This is not relevant to me; no need to pay close attention.

So, how can educators provide information in a way that is perceived as more relevant, rather than just a monologue of facts? For years I have used this simple activity that I call an *object exchange* to demonstrate how careful observation—focusing one's attention on looking—can help to raise the relevancy of information.

We usually do this activity in a classroom setting. It begins with a request: "Please take a moment to look through the belongings you have with you today and find an object that is of personal significance." Here are the directions for the activity:

OBJECT EXCHANGE

1. Each participant is told to work with a partner.
   - They are asked to each select an object that they have with them that holds *personal significance* for them. They are also asked not to discuss that item.
   - They are asked to exchange objects so that they are now holding their partner's item.
   - They each take a minute (time them) to describe the *physical* characteristics of the new object that has been given to them in as much detail as possible, but also asked to avoid *naming* the object. For example, if I am handed a *BIC Pen*, I might begin, "It is primarily made of gray plastic. One end tapers to a point. It is long and cylindrical . . .
   - Have the other partner take a minute to describe the object that has been handed to them.

2. Return the object to its owner.
   - Repeat this process, except that now the person who *owns* the object is asked to take a minute to speak about everything that *cannot* be known about this object from just looking at it.
   - The other partner then does the same.

3. Discussion
   - Bring the group back together and ask them to brainstorm a list of words that describes each of the two interactions they have just experienced. For interaction #1 they usually suggest words like, *observational, empirical, analytical*. For conversation # 2 they may use words like *storytelling, personal, emotional*.
   - Ask the group, "Which interaction did you prefer and why?" The majority of the group will favor interaction # 2.
   - "How are the two conversations related?" The group begins to recognize that the time spent in close observation was essential to making them curious and interested in learning more about the object and its history . . . the information.

This simple exercise demonstrates the power of observation in boosting curiosity and the desire to learn more. It is the reason we begin each new encounter with a work of art with time to slow down, look, and observe.

Although museum educators have sometimes been accused of dumbing down art history by asking visitors to spend time observing, we are not ignoring the informational part of an object, but rather using the power of observation to encourage visitors to wonder and ask their own questions. This is the information that is more likely to "stick."

I think about most art history classes I have taken. The instructor projects a slide of a work of art, tells you the name of the artist, the title, year it was made, and why it is deemed important. *Click*, next slide. It will then be the student's job to memorize the information, restate it on a test . . .and then promptly forget it. When I ask my current graduate students about their art history classes, although there are exceptions, many art history courses are still being taught this way.

It is valuable for educators to have a basic understanding of how we remember information and learn. Everything begins as sensory input from our environment. We have a mechanism to filter out and discard irrelevant or unnecessary data, such as the names of Camille Pissarro's children or the sound of an air conditioner in the background. The very act of paying attention and managing distractions amplifies learning, so beginning with an opportunity for participants to just look at a work of art for a minute or two is a scientifically proven method for making that work more memorable.

This act of observation begins the process of connecting what we are seeing with previously stored memories. We accomplish this by associating new information with knowledge that already exists. Research shows that we can remember things better if we can add the new information in a meaningful, existing context, similar to locating a file that has already been labeled. These preexisting files, or "sticky places," provide us with an area to adjoin new information to what we already know.

Museum visitors do not come as blank slates, but with an abundance of previously acquired knowledge, experiences, interests, and skills. Therefore, questions like, "What aspects of this work, if any, remind you of something you've experienced?" or "What associations do you have with this (subject or artwork)? or "How does this work relate to your experience? How is it different?" are useful in activating prior knowledge and linking new information to our existing knowledgebase.[2]

As an inquiry-based discussion progresses, participants will both notice and question various aspects of the artwork. It is the educator's task to add relevant pieces of information in response to questions and observations. In her book on museum teaching, Olga Hubard suggests that you should "think of the information you hold, as a well-stocked pantry. Though you may have innumerable ingredients, you use only those that make a specific dish tastier."[3] This idea of a well-stocked pantry means that the museum educator needs to be well-prepared and learn about the artist, the work, the process, the materials used, and the historical and geographical context, but only a small amount of the information available will be used during the tour.

To stretch Hubard's food metaphor a bit further, the image that comes to mind for me is building a multilayered sandwich with information added sparingly in response to the way the discussion is going or to questions that arise from the group. It should feel natural, the way you might have a conversation with a friend about a having seen a film or read a book. You are neither front-loading information—providing lots of facts before the group has had a chance to do some careful looking—nor dumping a load of information at the end of the tour stop because you didn't get a chance to impart it. It is also wise to let the group know where the information you are sharing comes from. "I read a recent review and it mentioned that . . ." "I saw a video interview with the artist, and they said . . ." This signals that the information you are sharing is not divinely imparted but available to everyone who is interested in learning more.

It is also okay not to have the information needed to respond to every question. When a question arises that you cannot answer, admit that you are stumped, that you will try to find out more, and get back to the group. Then do it. A follow-up email to the teacher or group leader will be appreciated on many levels. Not only will it provide the missing information, but also make the group feel very special that you remembered their question and took the time to respond. No one knows everything; by making that admission, you are modeling a positive and realistic approach toward learning.

A message that we stress during Connecting Collections is to use restraint when offering information. It is not easy for some teachers to hold back on providing information. Many view imparting information at the very core of their educational role. The Connecting Collections team has devised a few activities to encourage teachers to be more thoughtful about how and when to provide information.

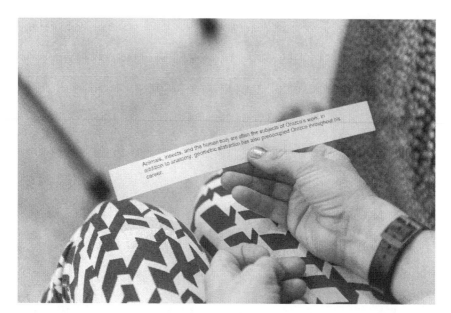

Figure 7.1. An example of an *information strip* that provides a bit of contextual information about the artist and/or the work of art. This strip focuses on a work by the artist Gabriel Orozco.
Photo: Filip Wolak © Solomon R. Guggenheim Foundation, New York. All Rights Reserved.

INFORMATION STRIPS

In preparation for this activity, I select a work of art we will be stopping at and copy the short curatorial essay from the museum's website. I then reformat the essay into separate sentences, print it out, and cut up the essay into strips of paper containing one or two sentences of information (see figure 7.1).

In front of the artwork, before we begin looking at the work together, participants divide into pairs and pick two strips of information about the work we will be viewing together.[4] I tell the group that we will be having an inquiry-based discussion about this work, but *they*, not I, are responsible for inserting the right information at the right moment. The goal is *not* to insert *all* the information on the strips of paper, but to insert the *right* information at the *right* moment. If partners agree on an appropriate moment to insert information that will contribute to the discussion . . . great; they should raise their hands and read the strip of information to the group. If at the end of the discussion you have strips of information that you did not use, that's great too (maybe even better)!

As we reflect on this exercise, we notice that information that directly relates to the work we are looking at is the most useful. Whereas information that references the artists awards, degrees, exhibitions, and associates are the strips of paper that remain in hand.

This exercise is designed to help those who are interested in developing their facilitation skills become more sensitized to what information is relevant to a specific conversation, and what is better left out. After participating in this activity, a teacher approached me privately. She confided, "I really shouldn't have added that piece of information." We both smiled and nodded.

INFORMATION AUCTION

My colleague Emily Rivlin-Nader, manager of Family Programs at the Guggenheim, has devised an activity (see figure 7.2) used in Connecting Collections to demonstrate that other participants, not only the tour leader, may have valuable information that has relevance to interpretation.

In preparation for this activity, Emily creates paddles that are similar to auction paddles. One side has a large question mark printed on it, the other an exclamation point. As the group discusses a work, a participant may raise the "?" side of the paddle to ask the group a question. If anyone has information related to that question, they raise their "!" side of the paddle and respond. This is a vivid demonstration of how the group can build knowledge together, and I have found that participants in the group can sometimes have firsthand, direct knowledge that is more valuable than any research I can do. Here are a few examples:

Figure 7.2. Emily Rivlin-Nadler facilitates an *information auction*.
Photo: Filip Wolak © Solomon R. Guggenheim Foundation, New York. All Rights Reserved.

- I am with a group of adults in front of a work by Sarah Anne Johnson titled *Tree Planting* (2002-2005),[5] an installation comprised of sixty-five photographs that chronicle what has become a rite-of-passage for many Canadians—planting trees in deforested areas of Manitoba. The young adults who participate in these conservation trips work hard, but what keeps them returning, says the artist, is the rewarding sense of community and connection to the land.[6]

  A woman in the group raises her hand. We learn that she is Canadian and has spent several summers participating in this program. She provides us with a vivid account of the experience and adds her firsthand memories to our understanding of the work.

- I am seated in front of Pablo Picasso's painting *Woman Ironing* (1904)[7] with a group of third graders. The students notice how hard the woman in the painting appears to be working and that the iron she is using doesn't have an electric cord. And then, a student raises her hand to say, "When we visit my grandmother in Jamaica, that's how she does her ironing. You need two irons. One that you use, and one heating on the stove." That eight-year-old was now the expert, she had a far greater knowledge about an aspect of the artwork than I did.

- I am facilitating a virtual experience for a group of older adults. The focus of the talk is The Architecture of Frank Lloyd Wright. I show a slide of Wright's Imperial Hotel in Tokyo, which famously withstood "the Great Earthquake of 1923"[8] and was used as a triage center in the wake of catastrophic damage to the city. The storied structure was demolished in 1968. I see an exclamation paddle go up. "Yes, what did you want to add?" "I was married there." The group was then treated to a description of the hotel's architecture . . . and the wedding.

When you hear the word *information* you may think about a boring recitation of facts, but the information used in a tour can take many forms.

BIOGRAPHICAL INFORMATION ABOUT THE ARTIST

I used to deemphasize biographical information, but I have revised my thinking. Some biographical information can make a work more approachable. For younger audiences, inserting a bit of information about the artist's childhood can add a connection. The artist Faith Ringgold was inspired to create her well-known work *Tar Beach*,[9] by her childhood experiences of growing up in Harlem. The architect Frank Gehry has shared that the use of fish-like forms in his designs may be rooted in the vivid childhood memory of the carp that he saw swimming in his grandmother's bathtub that would wind up as the gefilte fish served at Friday night dinner.[10] The revelation that prominent artists were once kids too, can provide an important point of identification.

Sharing the image of the artist can serve a similar purpose. Just like seeing the author's photo on the dustcover of a book provides a connection to the person who wrote it; seeing an image of the artist both personalizes and humanizes them. Museum educator Sarah Mostow shares,

> I like to show students a photograph of the artist. I print this out because I find in our screen-addicted world, one remaining advantage to a museum is that we prioritize original art and human interaction, not technology. The image of the artist is important because it humanizes the work; kids need to know a *person* made this thing. Seeing the age, race, (perceived) gender of the artist is helpful in situating the artist in a social context, and often the details of the place in the photo (a studio, a pet, a hat) etc. help children connect their own life experiences with the work we are discussing."

I need to add a word of caution here. When providing biographical information about the artist, be sure that it is added to support the learning goals and not just as salacious gossip.

Although it may be tempting, it has been scientifically proven that extraneous material, even if interesting, can distract learners.[11] They may remember the piece of gossip instead of more pertinent information.

I recall being in the museum with a group of adults in front of Vincent van Gogh's painting *Mountains at Saint-Rémy* (July 1889).[12] The group was discussing van Gogh's expressive application of paint. A participant raised his hand to contribute, "He cut off his ear." I acknowledged that biographical fact, and the group continued to discuss how the artist had infused every part of the painting with movement and energy. The same participant raised his hand, "He cut off his ear." Clearly this extraneous, but compelling, piece of information was nearly preventing him from focusing on any other aspect of the artwork.

ARTIST QUOTES

Quotes from the artist can provide powerful insights into their inspirations, process, and even frustrations. The artist Vasily Kandinsky wrote of his struggle to resolve a problem he encountered while working on *Painting with White Border* (1913). He states, "It is only over the years that I have learned to exercise patience in such moments and not smash the picture over my knee. Thus, it was not until after nearly five months that . . . it suddenly dawned on me what was missing—the white edge. . . . Since the white edge proved the solution to the picture, I named the whole picture after it."[13] Many people think that if you are an accomplished artist, the work flows from you easily. In this quote, Kandinsky provides a rare glimpse into how difficult the creative process can be. Finding the right quote—one that directly references the tour theme and/or artwork—can add significant insights. Not all artists write about their process, but those who do, whether informative, poetic, or surprising, provide a window into their motivations.

PHOTOGRAPHIC CONTEXTUAL INFORMATION

There are artists who return again and again to painting a particular place. Camille Pissarro (1830-1903) painted the French town of Pontoise in every season; Paul Cézanne (1882-1906) created more than sixty paintings of Mont Sainte-Victoire[14] and Georgia O'Keeffe (1887-1986) focused her work on New Mexico's landscape for decades. These are just a few of the artists who have pursued an ongoing exploration of a singular landscape.

With our ability to instantly call up images on the internet, the educator can provide photographs of these inspirational locales and use them to prompt discussions of how the artist has conveyed their unique vision of this place. In my own teaching, I frequently use a set of photographs that a colleague took on a trip to Paris that documents Édouard Vuillard's *Place Vintimille* (1908-1910). Vuillard found endless fascination in this park that he saw from his Paris apartment window and being able to view this park over the span of a century invariably prompts lively conversations about what has changed and what has stayed essentially the same.

SENSORY MATERIALS

Information can also be provided tactilely. During an exhibition of Russian art, the textures simulated in the eighteenth-century paintings had sumptuous tactile qualities. I was able to get samples of fur, velvet, brocade, satin, lace, gold braid, and tassels to pass around. Although visitors are generally not allowed to touch the sculptures on view,[15] samples of the materials that are used including marble, bronze, steel, and plaster can provide a tactile connection to the artwork.

INFORMATION ABOUT THE ARTIST'S PROCESS

Art materials that relate to the artist's process can provide insight into how the work was made. For instance, viewing a short video focusing about how artist Cai Guo Qiang creates his unique gunpowder drawings provides information much more effectively and dramatically than providing a verbal description.[16]

The enormous resources available on the internet enable you include short interviews with artists, share documentation of their process, and view time lapse installation clips. If strategically used, these additions can prompt dialogue, closer looking, and new insights. But please remember to test out *in the gallery* any videos before your tour to ensure that you have both the volume and connectivity to avoid unpleasant technical glitches. Keep any video segment short, and always use them to prompt further conversations.

There comes a point in every discussion where new information will be needed to get to the next level. That's where your accumulated research about the work will be useful. To build on the direction that the discussion is headed, go to that well of relevant information you have gathered and insert the right story, fact, anecdote, document, photograph, or quote into the conversation. This information will provide the spark for even more thinking and discussion and help make the experience truly memorable.

NOTES

1. Education Corner, https://www.educationcorner.com/the-learning-pyramid.html.
2. Regina G. Richards, "Making It Stick: Memorable Strategies to Enhance Learning." Reading Rockets is based at public television station WETA (Greater Washington Educational Television Association), https://www.readingrockets.org/article/making-it-stick-memorable-strategies-enhance-learning.
3. Olga Hubard, *Art Museum Education: Facilitating Gallery Experiences*, London: Palgrave, MacMillan, 2015, 93. Hubard is director and associate professor of the Program in Art & Art Education at Teachers College, Columbia University
4. The pair is asked to consult and agree about their decision to interject a piece of information into the conversation. We have found this strategy of having them work in pairs provides an important moment of deliberation and discourages "jumping the gun."
5. Sarah Anne Johnson, 2002–2005. *Tree Planting*, 65 photographic works (72 chromogenic prints) overall dimensions variable, Solomon R. Guggenheim Museum, New York https://www.guggenheim.org/artwork/21634.
6. Ibid.
7. Pablo Picasso, 1904. *Woman Ironing*. Oil on canvas, 45 3/4 x 28 3/4 inches (116.2 x 73 cm), Solomon R. Guggenheim Museum, New York, https://www.guggenheim.org/artwork/3417.
8. Imperial Hotel, Tokyo, https://en.wikipedia.org/wiki/Imperial_Hotel,_Tokyo.
9. Faith Ringgold, 1988. *Woman on a Bridge #1 of 5: Tar Beach*, Acrylic paint, canvas, printed fabric, ink, and thread, 74 5/8 x 68 1/2 inches (189.5 x 174 cm), Solomon R. Guggenheim Museum, New York, https://www.guggenheim.org/artwork/3719.
10. Kelsey Campbell-Dollaghan, "Frank Gehry At 83: Still Obsessed with Fish, Fast Company," January 14, 2013, https://www.fastcompany.com/1671622/frank-gehry-at-83-still-obsessed-with-fish.
11. Galen Davis and Marie Norman, Principles of Multimedia Learning, July 19, 2016. A review of educational psychologist Richard Mayer's seminal book *Multimedia Learning*, https://ctl.wiley.com/principles-of-multimedia-learning/.
12. Vincent van Gogh, *Mountains at Saint-Rémy*, July 1889, Oil on canvas, 28 11/16 x 36 1/4 inches (72.8 x 92 cm), Solomon R. Guggenheim Museum, New York, Thannhauser Collection, Gift, Justin K. Thannhauser, 1978, https://www.guggenheim.org/artwork/1491.
13. Vasily Kandinsky, Reminiscences/Three Pictures, 1913, in Kandinsky, *Complete Writings on Art*, edited by Kenneth Lindsay and Peter Vergo (Cambridge, MA: Da Cap Press, 1994), 391.
14. Princeton Art Museum. http://artmuseum.princeton.edu/cezanne-modern/c%C3%A9zanne/mont-sainte-victoire.
15. I add this qualification because I have been on tours for people with low vision and blindness where permission is given to touch the sculptures.
16. Cai Guo-Qiang Creates New Gunpowder Paintings, December 13, 2019, https://www.youtube.com/watch?v=6al_eiTc67M.

8

Multimodal Activities

In 2018, my book *Museum Gallery Activities: A Handbook*[1] was published. Although I am passionate about all parts of museum teaching, I saw a practical need to compile these multimodal activities into one volume to provide educators with both an overview and specific strategies that could be integrated into a myriad of gallery, classroom, and virtual experiences.

Figure 8.1. Many activities can be adapted for in-person or virtual experiences.
Tanya Ahmed © Solomon R. Guggenheim Foundation, New York. All Rights Reserved.

Figure 8.2. Many activities can be adapted for in-person or virtual experiences. *Marjorie Victor*

I am an advocate for gallery activities[2]—the segment of a guided experience in person or virtually where participants *do* something in addition to inquiry-based discussion (see figures 8.1 and 8.2). Participants may be asked to debate a point, take a pose, respond to music, author a brief poem, or do some drawing with the intent of gaining deeper insights and personal connections with a work of art. The gallery activity may be structured so that you work on your own or collaboratively with other members of the group. What joins these activities together is the opportunity to respond to an artwork through modalities other than discussion with the aim of prompting new perceptions and insights. Adding a multimodal activity to a tour stop offers many benefits:

- In keeping with John Dewey's theory of "learning by doing"[3] the structure of the activity can ensure the participation and active involvement of each student.
- The activity can provide an opportunity for students to work together in small groups, where the ideas of each participant can contribute to a collective response and tap the potential of collaborative learning.
- The responsive activity utilizes various sensory modalities adding variety to the lesson and providing nonverbal ways for students to respond and contribute.

- Responsive activities echo psychologist Jerome Bruner's[4] constructivist theory of education that suggests that the instructor should translate information into a format appropriate to the learner's current state of understanding so that the student continually builds upon what they have already learned.

Multimodal gallery (or virtual) activities are sometimes confused with other types of artistic expression, but their goals are quite different. Whereas the intent of artmaking is personal expression, the goal of a gallery activity is to deepen engagement with the work of art or artifact being viewed. An art project may use an artwork by a well-known artist as a springboard or inspiration, but it will quickly move toward focusing on producing an individual creative statement. Other hallmarks of multimodal activities are that they are of relatively short duration (usually 10–15 minutes at most) and use simple, gallery-safe materials such as pencils and paper.

Whenever you are looking at a work of art, whether in original form in a museum, through a virtual platform, or projected reproduction in a classroom, gallery activities have the potential to connect viewers more deeply with the art they are looking at. Everyone is invited to participate at the *same* time. This simultaneous participation means that everyone is engaged in the activity. The goal is not to be "the best," but to respond in your own unique and valid way and contribute to the cumulative process of meaning making.

Although gallery activities are commonly used with younger audiences, I strongly believe that thoughtfully designed gallery activities can and should be incorporated into learning experiences for audiences of all ages and abilities. This doesn't mean that young children and older adults participate in the *same* gallery activities, but rather that developmentally appropriate gallery activities are useful additions across multiple audiences. Active learning is a valid and productive strategy for supporting deeper and more memorable connections to works of art for participants of all ages. Because our brains are programmed to pay attention to the unusual, incorporating drawing, movement, or music helps the information attract our attention and fosters better retention.[5]

So where do gallery activities fit in the Tour Planning Template? In general, a gallery activity can be planned for each artwork. Activities can be as brief as writing down a single word, passing around a touch object, or taking a pose. Other activities may take longer. The length of your tour (class period or online session) and attention span of your group will dictate how long you will focus on each work and devote to each activity.

Although most museum educators will initiate a tour stop with an open-ended conversation before introducing a multimodal activity, an activity can be inserted at any point in a tour stop . . . if there is a rationale for why this is the best moment to introduce this activity.

Adding an activity at the beginning of a tour stop can provide an opportunity to share first impressions.

Activities that might lead off a tour stop

- Write down a single word that comes to mind when you look at this work.
- Create a written list of all the things you notice
- Write down a title you would give to this work.
- Take a moment to sketch a detail from this work that interests you.

These prompts can encourage close observation, be conversation starters, and provide a moment at the beginning of the tour stop to collect one's thoughts.

Activities might be inserted in the middle of a tour stop to respond to a participant's observation or delve more deeply into an artist's process or choice of materials

- Take the pose of the person depicted in the painting/sculpture.
- Choose a brush and create a gestural brush stroke (in the air) that you see in the painting.
- Pass around a touch object that relates to the work.

Inserting an activity in the middle of a tour stop can prompt additional insights and discussions.

Activities at the end of a tour stop can provide a summation and/or springboard for making personal connections to the work

- A collaborative poem
- An annotated drawing
- A written postcard to a friend or relative that shares your experience of this work

Inserting an activity at the end of the tour stop can be an opportunity to consolidate and reflect on what has been seen and learned.

Below is a sampling of multimodal activities with somewhat abridged directions.[6] Where applicable, I have included adaptations for activities that are transferrable to virtual teaching. More about planning and facilitating virtual experiences will be discussed in later chapters, but somewhat to my surprise I have found that many activities, especially those that focus on writing and drawing, can be successfully modified for remote learning.

WRITING ACTIVITIES

CALLOUTS/THOUGHT BUBBLES

For a work of art that contains a depiction(s) of the human figure, distribute a *thought bubble* photocopied on a sheet of paper to each participant. Provide the prompt, "Write down what this character might be thinking or saying." Use visual evidence to support these responses.

FOR VIRTUAL TEACHING

On Zoom, in the chat, participants write what each character might be thinking or saying. Responses to this prompt can also be shared via Zoom Whiteboard, Google Jamboard, Padlet or Miro.[7]

FIRST IMPRESSIONS/LISTING OBSERVATIONS

This activity is unusual in its placement in the inquiry. It is done *before* discussion. Participants, are given two minutes to write a list of all of the things they notice about the work of art. Then, each person, in turn, contributes a single observation without duplication. The goal is to keep adding new observations. To emphasize how much there is to notice, a master list can be created.

FOR VIRTUAL TEACHING

Each participant contributes something from their list. This can be shared individually on Zoom chat or through Zoom Whiteboard, Google Jamboard, Padlet or Miro.

COLLABORATIVE POETRY

Divide the group into smaller cohorts of four to five participants. Each group is given a stack of index cards and a marker. They work together to brainstorm a list of words that relate to the artwork, writing one word per index card. Each group now has a moveable "word bank" from which to compose one line of poetry. When the writing is complete, a representative from each cohort reads their line of poetry aloud to the whole group.

FOR VIRTUAL TEACHING

The whiteboard feature in Zoom can be used in breakout rooms. Groups can collaborate, save their whiteboard, and then return to the larger group to share their writing. The tools are available, but some groups may find the technical interface daunting. The facilitator will need assess the technical know-how of the group or if possible, assign a facilitator in each breakout group. The technology should never overwhelm the focus on the artwork.

Figure 8.3. Marc Chagall, (1887 -1985) *Paris through the Window*, 1913 Oil on canvas 53 9/16 x 55 7/8 inches (136 x 141.9 cm) Solomon R. Guggenheim Museum, New York, Solomon R. Guggenheim Founding Collection, By gift 37.438 *Photo: Ariel Ione Williams © Solomon R. Guggenheim Foundation, New York. All Rights Reserved.*

Figure 8.4. An example of an annotated drawing based on Chagall's painting. *Sharon Vatsky*

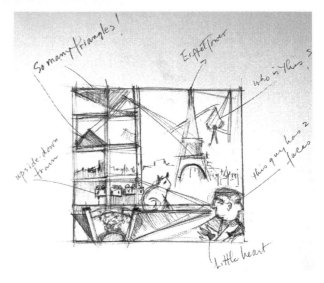

POINT OF VIEW

Take on the point of view of a person pictured in the artwork. Write a brief, first-person, account of what is going on from their perspective.

FOR VIRTUAL TEACHING

Accounts are written on a notepad (paper and pen). Provide ample time to write and revise. Participants are invited to "unmute" and share their writing.

DRAWING ACTIVITIES

ANNOTATED DRAWINGS

Each participant begins by drawing the approximate proportional format of the artwork on a sheet of paper. If you are focusing on a painting, this may look like a rectangle. Leave a wide margin around the rectangle to allow room to insert notes. Create a diagram of the work inside the format. It's fine to spend more time on the areas of the work that attract your attention. In the margins around the drawing jot down things you noticed, discovered, etc. Written notes in the margins may be connected to areas inside the format with arrows. The group then shares their "findings."

FOR VIRTUAL TEACHING

The same directions can be used. Provide approximately five minutes to draw. It is helpful to let the group know how long they have to draw and to set a timer. The sharing focuses on the question, "What did you learn or notice about the work by diagraming and annotating?" Participants may share their drawing, but the main discussion will focus on what was learned through the drawing and writing process.

VIEWFINDERS

Use a viewfinder (a piece of paper or cardboard with a 1" x 1.5" rectangular cutout or an empty 35-mm slide mount). Look through your viewfinder and scan the artwork until you find an area of detail you would like to explore further. Sketch the detail you selected. Round viewfinders can be constructed by rolling a strip of paper or using segments of a cardboard paper towel roll. This works like a spyglass. This activity is most appropriate for visually dense works that can be examined both on the macro and micro level.

MULTISENSORY: SOUND, TOUCH, MOVEMENT

SOUNDSCAPE

Some works of art suggest sounds that might accompany or emanate from them. After discussing an artwork, ask students to find a particular shape, color, or line and create a unique sound that expresses it. "If this artwork could make a sound, what type of sound might it make?" This activity is particularly effective with abstract works. Consider the difference between a sound that might arise from a Mark Rothko (1903-1970) painting versus one by Joan Mitchell (1922-1996); a work by Julie Mehretu (b. 1970) in contrast to one by Agnes Martin (1912-2004). These sounds can be performed together to create a soundscape, or in groups, who have agreed upon and rehearsed their unique sound. The educator can act as the "conductor" pointing to different groups to contribute their particular sound or invite a participant to lead/orchestrate the impromptu composition.

Young people have no trouble making noise in the galleries—adults may need to be encouraged—but it is so much fun when you can liberate a group of adults to make a rousing noise in a museum!

ENGAGING TOUCH OBJECTS

Look closely at a work of art. Discuss the materials and tools that might have been employed to create it and consider how they might have been used. If possible, the educator can provide samples of the tools and materials that were used to create the artwork and invite participants to handle them.

TAKE A POSE

Re-create the pose of a figure in a work of art. While in the position, consider what the person might be thinking, doing, or feeling. Share your ideas.

FOR VIRTUAL TEACHING

During the pandemic, one of the most successful and creative virtual initiatives was launched by the Getty Museum. This project invited us to "get creative with items on hand with the #GettyMuseumChallenge to reenact your favorite art from home."[8] The enormous number of brilliant responses demonstrate that both interest and creativity abound. Although movement activities may not be welcomed by most virtual adult groups, youth and family participants will probably appreciate the invitation to move around.

ARTIST'S PROCESS

Imagine that you are creating this painting. How would you move your body to replicate the artist's brushstrokes?

FOR VIRTUAL TEACHING

This activity is adaptable for online teaching especially for school, youth, and family focused programs.

MOVEMENT WAVE

Pick a shape or line in the artwork and generate a word and corresponding movement to describe it. Take turns sharing your word/movements with the group and discussing which part of the painting inspired it and why.

Below is a list of things to consider when you are creating new gallery activities. You will also notice that I have included more guidelines than I have for other tour components. This is because I have written more extensively about this area of tour planning. In reviewing these guidelines, I was heartened to notice that the considerations that go into planning successful galleries activities are also applicable for virtual experiences, with only some minor modifications. Activities should

- include only gallery safe materials: pencils, colored pencils, and paper, but consider novel ways to use safe materials; for virtual teaching use materials commonly found around the home including pencils, pens, and paper. Imagine everyday materials as art supplies. Consider ways to utilize recycled items and novel ways to use commonly available materials. Let participants know in advance what materials they will need so that they have them nearby.
- relate directly to a work of art/exhibition and should deepen understanding of that work;
- have simple understandable directions;
- be developmentally appropriate;
- be participatory and allow for another level of engagement in addition to discussion;
- be multimodal, including opportunities for writing, movement, drawing, sound, touch objects, etc.;
- be inclusive; all participants are invited to partake in the activity at the same time;
- be tried out by the educator in advance, which is super important;
- support divergent outcomes;
- include some sharing and/or reflection; and
- be fun.

This may seem like a lot of things to think about when creating a gallery activity, but with a bit of practice and experimentation, you will begin to develop a "sixth sense" regarding what will work for each audience. If your activity meets the criteria above, it has a good chance of success.

NOTES

1. Sharon Vatsky, *Museum Gallery Activities: A Handbook* (Lanham, MD: Rowman & Littlefield, 2018).
2. Gallery activities go by many names including multimodal activities, nondiscursive activities, or participatory techniques. I use these terms almost interchangeably in this chapter.
3. John Dewey (1859–1952) was an American philosopher, psychologist, and educational reformer.
4. Jerome S. Bruner (1915–2016) was an influential American psychologist focusing on learning theory and the philosophy of education.
5. Regina G. Richards, Making It Stick: Memorable Strategies to Enhance Learning. Reading Rockets is based at public television station WETA (Greater Washington Educational Television Association), https://www.readingrockets.org/article /making-it-stick-memorable-strategies-enhance-learning.

6. See Sharon Vatsky, Museum Gallery Activities: A Handbook for additional suggestions for and descriptions of gallery activities.
7. Padlet.com and Miro.com are both platforms that allow users to collaborate.
8. The Getty Center and Villa, #GettyMuseumChallenge, https://www.getty.edu /news/getty-artworks-recreated-with-household-items-by-creative-geniuses -theworld-over/.
7. See Sharon Vatsky, *Museum Gallery Activities: A Handbook* for additional suggestions for and descriptions of gallery activities.
8. Padlet.com and Miro.com are both platforms that allow users to collaborate.
9. The Getty Center and Villa, #GettyMuseumChallenge, https://www.getty.edu /news/getty-artworks-recreated-with-household-items-by-creative-geniuses-the -world-over/.

9

Advance Organizers, Transitions, Reflections

The planning part of the process is nearly complete. The bulk of the work is done, but there are still some fine points to consider in putting the finishing touches on your tour plan.

ADVANCE ORGANIZERS

Throughout this book the importance of seeing each visitor as a repository of knowledge and experience has been stressed. This fact is obvious, but nevertheless, sometimes ignored. Each visitor brings their culture, interests, history, knowledge, experiences, and individuality with them to the museum. This is an amazing and rich resource. Think about it. You have the cumulative experience of twenty . . . or so individuals to call upon. The use of an advance organizer helps to bring that wealth of prior knowledge to the museum experience they are about to embark upon.

If you begin to research *advance organizers*, you will notice that they are utilized in all areas of education from early childhood through university studies. They come in many forms. Some are simple, others are quite complex. As applied to museum tour planning, advance organizers are part of an introduction to the tour theme that helps relate what the visitor already knows to the new content they are about to encounter. Making the connection between existing and new information has been proven to increase retention.

Studies of visitors have shown that their museum experiences are more meaningful and better understood if "advance organizers" precede them. Setting the scene for what is to come gives visitors a context for relating to new information. Yes, the educator should provide an introduction to the tour theme, but it is just as important to figure out what strategy will connect the prior knowledge they arrive with, to what's ahead.[1] Utilizing an advance organizer begins to prepare the visitor to consider how the information they already have connects to the tour theme they are about to explore.

What might an advance organizer look like? Let's assume that the upcoming tour will focus on the theme of *Place*. The group is gathered in an orientation or welcoming space outside the art galleries. We have arranged ourselves seated in a circle on gallery stools. As part of the introduction I might say,

> Today we will be focusing on works by artists that depict *places*. Some of the artists we will encounter today became so fascinated by a single place that they returned to it as a subject again and again, sometimes over decades. Before we begin, I would like us to take a moment to visualize a place that is important to each of us. Let's close our eyes, take a deep breath, and try to identify a place of personal significance. It might be a place you encounter every day, a place from your childhood, or a vacation spot. Wherever it is, once you settle on it, try to bring it into focus. What do you see? What sounds do you hear? What is the temperature? What smells are in the air? Take a moment to look around at this recalled place, and when you have clearly retrieved it, breathed it in, and looked around, open your eyes, and return to the group. Would anyone like to share what place came to mind for them?

We hear about a few places. Some people mention having coffee in their kitchen next to a window. Someone else talks about their childhood home. The places are personal and varied. The advance organizer has taken less than five minutes to facilitate. In that time, I hope that the group has begun to connect a personal remembrance of a place to the depictions of places we will be viewing on the tour. We then move to the first tour stop.

If I am planning a tour with the theme of *Identity*, I may begin with this advance organizer. Again, we are seated in a circle on gallery stools. I have distributed index cards and pencils to each participant. "I have selected a few works for us to explore today that are united by the theme of *Identity*. Identity is complex and includes who you are, the way you think about yourself, the way you are viewed by others, and the characteristics that define you. We are all made up of multiple factors that combine in unique ways. Let's take a moment to write down five aspects of our own identity." The group is given a minute to make some notes. I then ask that we go around the circle, sharing one identity factor from the list. Beginning the tour in this manner I hope to highlight the complexity of identity and even activate a bit of empathy for the subjects in the works we will be viewing.

In addition to activating prior knowledge, the advance organizer can help tour participants to feel more connected and prepared for viewing and interpreting the works of art they are about to encounter. Participating in the advance organizer begins to build a connection and comfort level. It should demonstrate that the information and experiences that you have brought with you to the museum will be applicable, relevant, and useful in making personal connections to what you will be seeing.

Just like every other part of tour planning I sometimes struggle with devising an effective advance organizer. For some themes, the advance organizer comes to me in a snap. Other times I draw a blank or agonize over alternatives. At times like these I usually go to a colleague to get their input and advice. It is worth taking the time. Advance organizers can set the tone for your tour and give participants a clearer connection to, and grounding in, what will come next.

TRANSITIONS

Imagine you have just completed a successful tour stop with a group and are getting ready to move to the next work. You could just say, "We're done here. We're moving over there," but let's consider more thoughtful and useful ways to transition from one work to the next.

Transitions are those *bridges* between one work and the next. With some thought and intention these connections between works can add continuity and unity while also building anticipation. Transitions are the mortar between the bricks of your tour.

Local TV news programs have mastered the craft of creating effective (but sometimes overly gimmicky) transitions known as *teasers* in the media industry. They're designed to grab your attention and pique curiosity. Successful ones give just a taste of what's to come.[2] Here's an example: "Next on Channel 5 *Action News*, why the governor says he's not afraid to raise your taxes. . . . Could a hurricane brewing in the Atlantic affect your weekend plans? Channel 5 *Action News* is next."[3]

The goal is to grab attention quickly to keep viewers from changing the channel. They seem simple but writing them is harder than it first appears. While tour transitions don't need to be as sensational as the teasers that are used on the local news, some of the goals are the same—to pique interest about what's coming next.

Transitions are part of crafting productive tours. In her article, "Transitions . . . The Workhorse of a Tour," interpretive botanist Kathy French pointed out that "let's go see the banana," is not a good transition. She suggests that provocative statements, questions, summaries, introductions, and contrasts all make better transitions if concise and to the point.[4]

Effective transitions summarize where you have been and hint at where you are going. They are also a good opportunity to remind the group of the tour theme and how the works you are viewing have both similarities and differences. Because transitions are so specific to the tour stops, it is impossible to provide examples without being specific.

Let's imagine a tour with the theme of *Everyday Objects*. We have just finished looking at one of Joseph Cornell's (1903–1972) three-dimensional box structures.[5] A transition might be, "We have seen how Cornell was able to make everyday objects take on an air of mystery. At our next stop we'll consider how a contemporary artist has used everyday objects to a very different effect."

Or imagine a tour with the theme of *Signs and Symbols*. We have just completed a tour stop at a work by Barbara Kruger (b. 1945).[6] The transition might go something like this: "We have just considered how Kruger uses images from mass media to create new, and sometimes subversive, messages. At our next stop we will look at another artist who also employs signs and symbols."

These transitions summarize what we have seen, reinforce the theme, but also leave our destination open. I don't want to summarize what we will encounter and conclude before we have even gotten there.

Whether you are working in a science, history, or art museum, transitions are part of good tour planning practice. Professional development materials at the Minneapolis Institute of Art state, "Transitions on a tour help link back to the theme, keeping the framework present in visitors' minds. Keep transitions simple to signal the expectation for the group to move."[7]

REFLECTIONS/CONCLUSIONS

It seems intuitive that tours need to have a way to end, but from what I have observed, for a majority of museum or virtual guided experiences, the conclusion is less considered than any other part of the program. The school bus is waiting, and students need get back for lunch, the group took more time at a tour stop than planned or arrived late or took more time at coat check or. . . Whatever the reason, many experiences end without a real conclusion or reflection. But the last five minutes of a tour can be as important as the first five minutes. All too often time runs out before a proper conclusion can be made. It is important for you and the visitor to take a bit of time to wrap things up.

Museum educator Sarah Mostow says, "*Land the plane* at the end of the experience, you need to find a way to bring things to a close. There is no single way to do this, and it is still a challenge for me after fifteen years to find the right words."[8]

This is the moment that I thank the group for their time and participation. I am always truly grateful, because the group has been asked to share, put their ideas out there, and doing that in a new environment requires some bravery. "Thanks for joining me today as we explored how some artists have used *signs and symbols* (or whatever the theme has been) in their work. It has been a pleasure spending time together and hearing your thoughts. Before we disperse, I am curious if there is a moment in the past ninety minutes that stood out for you?" I use this question because it asks each participant to take a quick scan of the experience they have just completed and do a bit of internal self-reflection and evaluation. I expect that there will be different moments recalled, and that's a very positive outcome. I am not interested in whether individuals have learned facts, or key points. My hope is that they made a personal connection to the experience we have shared with the works of art and each other.

The end of a tour is not the time for an "information dump." I have seen educators conclude their tours by reciting all the facts and information they didn't get a chance to share earlier. It is also not the time for a test on what has been learned. I have seen educators end with a question-and-answer session. I would advise against this too. Whether you have just completed an in-person experience or a virtual one, it is generous and appreciated if you offer to stay for a few minutes after the program has finished to answer questions or continue the discussion. Let the people who are done leave but, if possible, hang in there a while for those who may want to continue the dialogue. This suggestion extends to virtual tours as well.

CONCLUSION (AFTER THE CONCLUSION)

Your tour plan is ready. Now comes the even more exciting part . . . using it.

NOTES

1. Nancy Cutler, "Planting Curiosity and Harvesting Interest: Capitalizing on Curiosity", *The Docent Educator*, Autumn 2001, Volume 11, No. 1, https://www.museum-ed.org/planting-curiosity-and-harvesting-interest-capitalizing-on-curiosity/.
2. Glenn Halbrooks, Why Tease Writing Is Critical to a Successful TV Newscast, April 27, 2018, https://www.thebalancecareers.com/why-tease-writing-is-critical-to-a-successful-tv-newscast-2315473.
3. Ibid.
4. Kathy French, "Transitions...The Workhorse of a Tour", *The Docent Educator*, Autumn 1995, Volume 5, No. 1
5. Joseph Cornell (b. 1903, Nyack, New York; d. 1972, Flushing, New York), https://www.guggenheim.org/artwork/artist/joseph-cornell.
6. Barbara Kruger, b. 1945, Newark, New Jersey, https://www.guggenheim.org/artwork/artist/barbara-kruger.
7. Minneapolis Museum of Art, https://artsmia.github.io/tour-toolkit/tour-preparation/transitions/.
8. Sarah Mostow, personal correspondence, December 2021. Sarah Mostow is a museum educator at the Solomon R. Guggenheim Museum.

10

Getting Ready

It's the day of your tour. You have done your prep work and created a complete tour plan, but there are several more steps before you are ready to greet the group in person or virtually.

PACK YOUR BAG

Everything you will need for the next sixty to ninety minutes needs to be packed and ready to go. I usually make a handwritten list of things I will need, which might include the following items: stickers that will be used as name tags a few markers, twenty pencils, index cards, 9" x 12" cardboard or Masonite boards (to serve as a firm backing for writing or drawing), a few erasers, and pencil sharpeners. If a drawing activity is planned, add some drawing paper and colored pencils. Any props or touch materials go into the tote bag as well. You are responsible for preparing and providing all materials that will be needed. I carry a printout of my tour plan on a clipboard. Many educators store their tour plans on their iPhones or iPads as backup or quick reference for artist quotes and facts. I have worked hard on creating that tour plan. Having it with me provides reassurance that I am prepared. I have also loaded a rolling bin filled with gallery stools that will be ready for distribution.

For virtual experiences save your presentation to your desktop so that it is easily accessible. Check your internet connection and silence devices that might cause interruptions.

TIME TRACKER DEVICE

Another crucial piece of equipment to have is a time-telling device. I still wear a watch. I like it because it is less obtrusive than looking at my phone, but most of my colleagues use their cell phones to make sure they keep to their schedule and the group's available time. The same advice holds for virtual experiences—be sure to have a way to check the time. I have noticed that when you are teaching virtually and sharing your screen, the time display that usually appears on the lower right of your computer monitor may not be visible, so always have another option for checking the time close by.

When you are teaching, time can get distorted, both slowing down and speeding up, so having an approximate way to track it is crucial. I usually break down the total time allotment into segments. For example, ten minutes for the introduction, twenty minutes for each tour stop, and five minutes for a reflection. This general timetable provides benchmarks, so if needed, I can adjust my timing along the way.

SILENCE YOUR PHONE

An obvious, but still important, reminder is to silence your phone during the tour.

If you are teaching virtually, especially from home, look around your space. Are there other devices or possible intrusions (kids, pets, vacuum cleaners) that might disrupt your teaching? When I was teaching remotely during summer 2020, I would make a call to the service that mows the lawn asking them not to arrive outside my window during my teaching times. Over the past months we have all gotten more relaxed about the demarcations between our professional and domestic lives. Although the arrival of a cat on your desk or a toddler in the doorway are generally endearing for the audience, these unexpected events can be jarring for the educator.[1]

YOU WILL BE NERVOUS

How do I know this? I know because I have been teaching for decades and I still get nervous before I begin a program. I have never had a major catastrophe—no one has thrown a fit, or staged a rebellion, but I am still never sure of how things will go. I am aware that if I am truly opening up the dialogue to the group, I cannot control the course of the conversation. This possibility is what makes inquiry-based teaching so exciting and rewarding.

Regardless of how much you have prepared, there is the factor of the unknown. How will things go? How will I deal with the unexpected? I have coached scores of students through their first tour. Letting them know that they should expect to be nervous, that I get nervous too, is perhaps the best piece of advice I can provide. If you experience this nervousness, also called stage fright or performance anxiety, you are in good company. Some of the best known and most admired comedians, actors, singers, and athletes also deal with this condition. And in fact, you *are* getting ready for a performance. You will (probably) not be singing or dancing, but you will bring many other skills including your knowledge, empathy, flexibility, intellect, passion, and creativity to the task. Being nervous is natural and normal and maybe even desirable. I tell my students that those nerves signify that you are invested. You care about the outcome. Nervousness is a way of getting ready—all systems are "go."

Facilitating a gallery or virtual experience is a performance. Just like actors getting ready to go on stage, you are getting ready, not only to perform, but to scaffold an interactive experience where the audience participates. This participatory aspect adds an additional layer of the unknown. If you are performing a play or giving a lecture, you can rehearse until you have smoothed out all the kinks, but an interactive program with a group that you are meeting for the first time has a greater level of uncertainty—more like improv. It is not something you cannot perfect through study or memorization.

The more you teach, the more confident you will get in the belief that, despite the nerves, things will work out. After decades of teaching, when I feel nervous, I can look back and remember that I have gotten through these last-minute jitters many times before and had positive outcomes. Fortunately, gallery teaching is not brain surgery. Usually, things go well, or at least okay, and even if they don't you can reassure yourself that no one died. The participants you are working with are usually there by choice and want you to do well. Unfortunately, the tours that have not gone well have lingered in my memory (and pit of my stomach) for months . . . but still . . . no one died. You cannot totally combat feelings of nervousness before a tour, but there are some steps you can take to cope with them:

- Acknowledge that you feel nervous, but nerves should never stop you from doing something. There are all kinds of reasons in life not to continue down a path, but nervousness is not one of them.
- Do what you can to make yourself as physically and emotionally comfortable as possible. Wear something that makes you feel confident. Get a good night's sleep. Make sure that you aren't hungry or thirsty. Although I have no way of calculating the amount of energy expended during a nine-ty-minute gallery or virtual experience, I am always ravenous afterward, which makes me think that this work expends a lot of energy. And of course, a cardinal rule, but one I have never seen stated, "bio break" before you teach. By attending to your own physical and emotional needs prior to the tour, you become more comfortable, authentic, and less self-conscious. You will be present in the moment and be able to focus your full attention on the people you are with.
- Breathe. Take a few deep breathes. Nothing amplifies nerves like low oxygen levels. Deep breathing is one of the best ways to lower stress. When you breathe deeply, it sends a message to your brain and body to calm down.
- Get there early. Another stressor is feeling rushed. Give yourself plenty of extra time to address last minute details or just chill. Even if you know the space well, walk the tour route one more time. Taking this walk provides another way to cope with last minute jitters by adding a bit of exercise. I have also witnessed experienced museum educators being taken by surprise by a closed gallery or a work that was recently deinstalled. A final walk-through can assure that all is where it is supposed to be.
- For virtual experiences there is another layer of potential concern—connectivity. Will the equipment that I am counting on to connect me with

participants work? In the first weeks of the COVID-19 lockdown, I kept getting these anxiety-producing pop-ups stating that "your connection is unstable"; a few times I was knocked off a Zoom call and needed to reconnect in the middle of the program. I decided to invest in upgrading my internet connection. With my internet connection now the vehicle for both my professional and personal linkages to the world, it seemed like a worthwhile investment in lowering my level of preprogram jitters.

I am not trying to minimize the feelings that stage fright can produce, but for many people it can be managed. After a while you will just recognize it and go, "Yep, this is the way I feel before a tour." Dealing with your nerves and learning ways to reduce and manage them will prove helpful in many of life's unavoidably stressful situations, and thankfully the nervousness usually dissipates soon after you meet the group. Unlike your worst expectations, the members of your group are not scowling, but actually appear happy to meet you.

NOTE

1. Kids crash their parent's teleconference call, March 10, 2017, https://www.youtube.com/watch?v=zC9GYxrBZ2Q.

Part III
Facilitation

11

Greeting and Orientation

The first five minutes of your tour are the most important ones.

—Bonnie Pitman, former director of the Dallas Museum of Art[1]

If you work in a museum, it's easy to forget that they can be formidable and intimidating places for first-time visitors. Because the surroundings have become familiar to us, it may be hard to put ourselves in the role of that first-time visitor.

There is even a term for this, *threshold fear*, that acknowledges that there are both physical and programmatic barriers that make it difficult for the uninitiated to experience museums. These concerns, both real and imagined, remain impediments for many potential audiences who remain absent or infrequent visitors.[2] Museum director and author Nina Simon suggests,

> Museum professionals often talk about reaching out to new audiences and helping them break through the threshold fear that can accompany first-time museum visits. And yet for many museum workers it's hard to imagine how someone might feel intimidated or anxious about visiting a museum. If you're a museum person and you want to understand threshold fear, try going somewhere outside your comfort zone. Don't go to a museum. Go to a boxing gym. Go to an uber hip bar. Go to a place of worship that is not your own. Go to a tattoo parlor. Find a place where you feel an incredible urge to bolt out the door the minute you walk in.
>
> Go there alone. See what makes sense and doesn't to you. Consider what intimidates you and what you feel comfortable with. Note the people, areas, or experiences you gravitate to as safe starting points.
>
> And then go back to your own institution and try to see it through that lens. Hold on to your pounding heart and imagine carrying that adrenaline through your own front door.[3]

Please imagine, in your mind's eye, that as a child, you had never been taken to a restaurant or to see a movie. For many of us the rules and protocols for how to participate in public spaces becomes engrained in us early. We experienced and learned them as children so that we barely need to think about them. When you go to a movie theater there are actually many rules that need to be observed: check the starting time for the movie of your choice, buy tickets (I still have trouble with digital ticketing kiosks), maybe get some snacks (eating enormous quantities of popcorn is encouraged, even if you drop some on the floor), find seats in the dark, preferably not too close to the screen, and don't talk during the film or someone will go "Shhh!" When you go to a restaurant you may need to wait in the front to be seated, order from a menu (or from a QR code version), request and pay the check, leave a tip, but many people who grew up going to both restaurants and movie theaters were never taken to museums to learn the various rules that can lessen or alleviate anxiety.

I have taught graduate courses in museum education for more than twenty years. Many of the students have already committed to a career path in museums. The first assignment I give is to write a museum-centric autobiography that begins with their earliest recollections of visiting a museum and includes both positive and negative museum experiences as well as peer and family attitudes toward museums. Not surprisingly, many (but not all) students recall positive and frequent visits with members of their families. They learned early how to visit a museum and that museums were for *them*.

Think about your own emotional state when you are visiting a place you have never been to or embarking on a task you have never tried. What do you need to get oriented, comfortable, and ready to learn? The more these needs are met, and your questions answered, the less anxiety you feel, and the more you will be able to concentrate on the content of the tour. This requisite for establishing comfort is reiterated by Shannon Murphy, the former director of education at the Noguchi Museum.

> I think people need to feel physically comfortable, emotionally welcome, and have a firm understanding of what is about to happen during a gallery experience. I maintain a deep awareness of both my body, and their bodies when we meet. I understand myself as a middle aged, able bodied, cis-gendered, white woman; and I understand the participants in my group based on what they show or tell me. I then establish a style: Do they need me to impress them with my knowledge? Do they need me to talk faster? Slower? Make jokes? I can adjust cultural and learning styles based on what the participant's needs and preferences are, and I'm happy to wear different hats. A style is a way that we're sharing culture, and how we're co-creating an experience with art. I'm always going to tailor the tour to their interests, their bodies, their learning styles, cultural styles, and work on establishing that from the beginning.[4]

In her 2001 essay, longtime museum professional Judy Rand reflects on a rafting trip through the Grand Canyon, which helped her see the needs of the visitor in a new light. She recounts her feelings of frustration and confusion as she engages in a new experience that is out of her comfort zone. She has distilled her realizations into a set of guidelines. I suggest that every museum educator, not only read her essay but also reflect on the times you felt overwhelmed or confused in a new situation. Rand presents a "Visitors' Bill of Rights," that reminds museums, exhibit planners, designers, directors, architects, and evaluators (and I will add educators), to put visitors first.[5]

1. Comfort: "Meet my basic needs."
2. Orientation: "Make it easy for me to find my way around."
3. Welcome/belonging: "Make me feel welcome."
4. Enjoyment: "I want to have fun."
5. Socializing: "I came to spend time with family and friends."
6. Respect: "Accept me for who I am and what I know."
7. Communication: "Help me understand, and let me talk, too."
8. Learning: "I want to learn something new."
9. Choice and Control: "Let me choose; give me some control."
10. Challenge and Confidence: "Give me a challenge I know I can handle."
11. Revitalization: "Help me leave refreshed and restored."

Interactive tours have the potential to meet every one of these requirements. The visitors that opt-in for guided gallery experiences are already seeking out a level of engagement that exceeds the typical visitor. They are committing sixty to ninety minutes of their time and trusting you to deliver a worthwhile experience. They could have chosen the "free-range" version of a visit, but instead have chosen to spend their time with a museum educator. So, you not only have a participant who has made the choice to spend their valuable free time at your institution, perhaps paying a fee to get in the door, but also one that is also willing to commit time to a guided learning experience. You are one lucky educator, but you are also tasked with a major responsibility! Having made the decision to join your tour, what are they hoping for and how can you ensure that it is provided?

In 1943, the psychologist Abraham Maslow (1908-1970) laid out a hierarchy of human behavioral needs and motivations, starting with the most basic of physical needs—shelter, food, water, safety—before advancing to higher-order needs like relationships, curiosity, and self-actualization.[6] In Maslow's hierarchy, the needs on the lower levels must be met before it is possible to fulfill higher-level needs. If the individuals you are working with are physically uncomfortable or emotionally uneasy, it will be difficult for them to focus on anything else including your beautifully constructed tour.

A major factor in determining whether a participatory tour will be successful—or not—is the educator's ability to create a welcoming, inclusive, respectful environment where participants genuinely feel that their ideas, even/ or especially those that are not regular museum goers, are welcomed into the learning space.

The museum educator has a giant task here. You are frequently working with people you are meeting for the first time. They may not have extensive knowledge of visual art or art history and not necessarily be fluent English speakers. Some may have physical impairments or developmental disabilities. The group may include both children and adults, and they will all, no doubt, have various expectations about what constitutes a great museum tour. Nevertheless, it is your job to create an environment for sharing.

Missy Lipsett, an experienced museum educator who facilitates tours for both youth and adult visitors, confided her strategy for welcoming the group:

> To create an interactive exchange between participants during a gallery tour, I have found that it is important to initially nurture a comfortable space. I try to generate this setting by asking participants names, where they are from, what brought them to the museum, if they have been to the museum before, and if so, what they remember. Getting people talking early in a *meet and greet* situation provides an ice breaker that helps participants realize that they are *a group* and that there are commonalities, as well as differences. If appropriate and relevant I sometimes reference what I learn from this initial interaction during the tour. This process of creating a comfortable space as the group gathers is the single most important thing that I can do to initiate an interactive tour.
>
> I follow this same protocol when doing a virtual tour. It is more challenging, since some people turn their cameras off, but there are usually a couple of people who are willing to talk, even if briefly. The virtual tour has the advantage that the people "Zooming in" may already have an affiliation—however loose—to one another. Are they connected to a particular group, company, organization, school, family or social setting? These commonalities can provide some basis for a conversation on which to build.[7]

If you are looking for participation during the tour, this approach will yield much more success than getting twenty minutes into the tour and then asking the group, "What do you think?" Getting participants contributing early begins to *prime* them for the expectation that they will be contributing as the tour continues. The way you respond in these initial encounters may determine the success of your tour. Are you genuinely interested in the answers? Are you welcoming, responsive, and friendly? Consciously or not the participants are "testing the waters" and deciding whether this really is a safe place for them to express their ideas.

There is a good amount of neurological evidence that supports the idea that people who do not feel comfortable cannot learn. Feelings like embarrassment, boredom, or frustration can block the ability to make the necessary brain connections for learning to take place. Participants need reassurance that all responses will be welcomed, valued, and respected.

My first rule of museum education is, "Do no harm." Just as doctors pledge to "do no harm" as part of the Hippocratic Oath, museum educators need to also make this part of their doctrine.[8]

I frequently begin my course in museum education by asking students about their best (and worst) educational experiences. On the front of an index card, I ask them to recall a positive learning experience in one or two sentences. Some focus on a special course or teacher, some on a camp or travel experience. Once they have recalled and written about it, I ask them to turn the index card over and write down some adjectives that describe the *qualities* of that experience. I encourage everyone reading this book to try this exercise! I have kept some of these lists. Students will include words like *challenging*, *experiential*, *skill-building*, *novel*, and *creative*, but just as often use words like *safe*, *comfortable*, *supportive*, and *encouraging*. In short, the learning environment seems to be as, or more, important than the content.

A harsh word or critical response from the educator may be remembered long after the museum visit ends and may taint the possibility of returning and even be generalized to all museums. I observed a group of teens as they discussed a painting. For many in the group it was their first, or one of their first, museum experiences. One teen raised his hand to point at a detail in the painting. Yes, his finger got a bit too close, but the reaction by the tour guide was so out of proportion that I did worry that permanent emotional harm may have been incurred.

Just as negative words and action can impact a tour experience, positive ones can too. The educator needs to be aware that they have the power to harm, they also have the power to be supportive and empathetic. Educator Emily Rivlin Nadler,[9] begins her stroller tours for babies and their caregivers with an acknowledgment that doing any activity with a young child is an accomplishment. She greets the group of exhausted adults and their babies, some sleeping, some fidgeting, some noisy, some contented. "Let's congratulate ourselves on making it out of the house today! We got here! Let's all take a deep breath."[10] This simple statement is empathetic, welcoming, and invites us into a community of adults with babies who have accomplished something difficult and important, that is not always noticed and acknowledged.

NAME TAGS

One of the easiest and most powerful ways to build rapport is to call participants by their name. There are a few educators who have perfected this ability to a high level. Within the course of a ninety-minute tour, educator Rika Burnham would be able to call on group members by name. When anyone responded she would ask them to say their name first, by the end of the session she had memorized the names of all participants and was referring to each by name.

I am not that skilled, but I do have an alternative approach. At the beginning of a tour, before we go into the galleries, I ask each person in the group to write their first name on a plain paper sticker with a Sharpie marker and place it, so that it's visible. For younger visitors I ask their first name and make a sticker for them. I create a name tag for myself as well. We are now able to address one another by name. This can be a small, but powerful, signal and affirmation. As previously mentioned, I ask my museum education graduate students about their best (and worst) educational experiences. As we shared our various remembrances, one student replied, "It was in fourth grade." I asked what was so special about fourth grade? She said, "The teacher knew my name."

VOICE

This should go without saying, but it needs to be noted because I have participated in so many gallery tours (mainly conducted by art historians or curators), where the group needed to strain to hear the presenter. If you have a naturally strong, expressive voice, great, use it, but if your natural voice tends to be on the quieter side, practice raising the volume. At this moment, as we deal with compulsory masking in some public spaces, the strength of your voice is even more important. Assistive listening devices provide one way to magnify the voice of the museum educator, and certainly for hearing impaired audiences they are a must, but they can be detrimental to establishing a truly interactive, democratic interchange of ideas because only one voice is amplified. In this germophobic moment, I doubt we will be seeing them used again—at least for a while.

COMMUNICATION STYLE

Speaking is a personal interaction between you and the audience. You have to care about what you're saying and show it. If you don't care, why should they? Many of the museum educators I consulted for this book mentioned the attributes of warmth, enthusiasm, and authenticity as vital to doing this work.

Sarah Mostow, museum educator, says, "For me teaching in a museum is a privilege. I am happy to be there, and I communicate that to my groups."[11]

Laurel Schmidt, educator and author, said that "the excellent gallery educator exudes a passion for art and enthusiasm for exploring the myriad of ideas that are potentially embedded in any exhibit. This demeanor conveys the message that engaging with art is an important activity than can stimulate the mind and touch your heart. It's something humans have been doing for eons. It can connect us to our past and help us make meaning of the present or look into the future."[12]

Jamie Song, museum educator added, "An excellent gallery educator is engaging—this can take many forms—they can command attention with their demeanor and story-telling, they can offer engaging activities and intriguing questions that call for inquiry and deep thinking, they can also just simply be a great listener."[13]

And from Ryan Hill, museum educator, "If you're not interested or having fun, your participants won't be either."[14]

MUSEUM RULES

Reviewing museum rules is a necessary, but for me, annoying part of the introduction. Especially with young people, I want to excite them by letting them know how much they can do, how cool and enriching this experience can be, rather than starting out on the downer about what they can't and shouldn't do. Yes, younger visitors need to be reminded not to touch or get too close to the artworks, but I have seen this part of the introduction take on way too much emphasis and time. Most students are in the museum for such a short time, it seems a shame to devote a significant part of the visit talking about how their fingerprints can damage things, how the oils on their skin can mar surfaces. I have observed educators who, in my opinion, take much too long elaborating on all the ways that students can harm artworks. It goes something like this: The educator says, "Before we go into the galleries what are some rules that we need to be aware of?" A student raises their hand, "Don't touch the art." Educator, "Yes, we need to remember not to touch and to keep our distance from the art. What else?" A student responds, "No running." "Yes, that's right, what else?" "No yelling." Educator, "Yes, that's right. What else?" "No shoving other kids." Educator, "Yes, that's right, what else?" Student, "No chewing gum." Educator, "Yes, that's right, what else?" In some cases, the discussion of museum rules gets even more protracted suggesting that educators

- Draw on their experience. Have they seen objects that are badly worn from too many fingerprints (e.g., shiny parts on brass and bronze sculptures, greasy stains on stone surfaces, fingerprints and scuff marks on walls)?
- Show them the impact of fingerprints on a surface— pass around a pair of glasses, a mirror, or a piece of metal.
- Refer to their senses. Ask the group to explore traces of perspiration, salt, and oil on their skin.
- Remind them that glass cases might be fragile and unable to withstand the pressure of people leaning against them.[15]

Students' first introduction to visiting a museum becomes all about what they cannot do. Is this really what you want students to remember from their trip to the museum? I much prefer, "We are indoors, so *all* of the indoor rules that you know apply here, but there is one very special additional rule you need to know when you visit an art museum—you cannot touch the art. We experience art with our eyes. If we know that *one* rule, we can visit any art museum in the entire world!" How empowering! You now know the one additional important indoor rule that applies to visiting museums.

In summing up what an introduction and orientation should be, educator and author Joyce Raimondo suggests:

- Say hello and set the tone before you start the program. The aim is for a friendly conversation.
- Tell people at beginning what to expect from the program. Let them know that you want to hear what they think.
- Add humor when appropriate and an informal friendly attitude.
- Have fun! Be fully present and enthusiastic. Show your participants that you are filled with love and joy in your heart for them and the art.
- Being a museum educator is the greatest gift—fill your heart with joy and wonder as you interact with people of all ages and abilities with art at the center. Always be a learner yourself with a "beginner's mind"—curious, humble, embarking on a creative adventure. And know that the work you are doing could change someone's life for the better in ways you cannot even imagine.[16]

NOTES

1. *Extending Connections: A Handbook of Touring Techniques*, Oakland Museum, CA, 1985, p.13. Bonnie Pitman is the current director of Art and Brain Innovations, for the Center for Brain Health at the University of Texas at Dallas
2. Elaine Heumann Gurian, *Threshold Fear, Reshaping Museum Space*, Routledge, 2005, https://www.egurian.com/omnium-gatherum/museum-issues/community/accessibility/threshold-fear.
3. Nina Simon, Come on In and Make Yourself Uncomfortable, Museum 2.0, February 8, 2012, http://museumtwo.blogspot.com/2012/02/come-on-in-and-make-yourself.html.
4. Shannon Murphy, former Director of Education, The Noguchi Museum, Queens, New York. Personal correspondence, January 2022.
5. Judy Rand, 2001. *The 227-Mile Museum or a Visitor's Bill of Rights*. Curator: The Museum Journal 44/1(January 2000): 7-14. http://www.informalscience.org/227-mile-museum-or-why-we-need-visitors-bill-rights.
6. Abraham H. Maslow, July 1943. *A Theory of Human Motivation,*370–396. *Psychological Review* Vol. 50. No. 4. https://docs.google.com/file/d/0B-5-JeCa2Z7hNjZl-NDNhOTEtMWNkYi00YmFhLWI3YjUtMDEyMDJkZDExNWRm/edit.
7. Missy Lipsett, Museum Educator, Solomon R. Guggenheim Museum, personal correspondence, January 2022.
8. Primum non nocere, https://en.wikipedia.org/wiki/Primum_non_nocere.
9. Emily Rivlin-Nadler is the manager of Family Programs at the Solomon R. Guggenheim Museum.
10. Guggenheim Museum stroller tour observation by Allie Beronilla, graduate student, Program in Museum Studies, New York University, November 2021.
11. Sarah Mostow, museum educator, Solomon R. Guggenheim Museum, personal correspondence, January 2022.

12. Laurel Schmidt, educator and author, personal correspondence, February 2022.
13. Jamie Song, museum educator, Metropolitan Museum of Art, personal correspondence, January 2022.
14. Ryan Hill, Educator and Team Member, Empathetic Museum, personal correspondence, January 2022.
15. *The Docent Handbook,* Revised Edition, National Docent Symposium Council, 2017, 7.
16. Joyce Raimondo is the education coordinator at the Pollock-Krasner House and Founding Director of Imagine That! Art Education, personal correspondence, January 2022.

12

Supporting Participation

In the opening minutes with the group, you have

- introduced yourself;
- warmly welcomed them to the museum and provided a brief overview of what's to come;
- asked the participants to briefly introduce themselves (if the group is small);
- distributed name tags and gallery stools;
- introduced the tour theme;
- provided an advance organizer to check that everyone is onboard; and
- for school groups, stashed their coats, backpacks, and lunches and connected with the teacher(s) to confirm that you have shared expectations.

Phew! That's a lot to manage in the opening minutes of an encounter with a totally new group of people!

GETTING COMFORTABLE

You are finally in the gallery and in front of your first tour stop. Adult participants sit on gallery stools. Younger visitors, like camp and school groups, can sit on the floor in front of the works of art they are focusing on. It is thoughtful to provide their teachers and chaperones with gallery stools. For families and intergenerational groups, we may use floor cushions, with gallery stools available as an option.

Some teen groups will sit on the floor, but some will grumble about being treated as kids. I have also seen this result in them lying all over each other. Provide gallery stools if you can. This will greatly enhance their attention, behavior, and treat them as the young adults they are.

If you are young and nondisabled, you may not be aware that some visitors don't have the stamina to participate in a group experience unless they have the option to be seated. The difference between joining or not joining a group tour may be the availability of gallery stools. As writer and museum consultant Steve Tokar observes:

> The governing assumption [in museums] seems to be that the average museum visitor is young, strong, thin, tireless, childless, and possessed of better than perfect vision. Of course, actual museum visitors come in all ages, shapes, energy levels, family sizes, and physical abilities. Some are shepherding boisterous toddlers or slow grandparents or both. Some are pregnant. Many are simply beat and would like nothing more than to sit down and look at a painting or sculpture or video for a while.[1]

Gallery stools are the number one tool of the museum educator. Providing physical comfort will support the possibility of sustained conversations and engagement. Having one has already made the individuals in the group feel special. A participant remarked to me, "I have seen other people with these stools, and now I have one."

I suggest that you have a gallery stool too. Where you position yourself in relationship to the group and the artwork sends a message. Too many educators spend their time walking back and forth in front of the artwork gesturing and pointing. It's distracting to the participants and takes the attention away from the art, where the focus should be.

Jen Oleniczak Brown, former actor, museum educator, author, and founder of The Engaging Educator provides this advice: "Repeat after me, pacing is not effective. I see so many people who think that walking while they talk is a good idea. . . . If you're wandering or constantly moving when you're talking, it's going to be distracting."[2]

There will be times during the gallery experience where you will need to assert yourself as the group leader—but for even more of the experience, learn to make yourself less conspicuous. This ability to make yourself psychologically larger or smaller is important. You are not the star of the show performing with a backdrop of an artwork behind you. The work of art is the star. Although many museum educators have their group seated while they stand, I much prefer to sit down with the group, not because I don't have the energy to stand while facilitating, but because being on the same physical level conveys the message that I am part of this learning community.

VALUING SILENCE

You are now comfortably seated in front of a work of art. What do you do now? Be quiet.

"Silence is necessary," says educator Sarah Mostow. "Allowing time in front of a work for people to adjust their eyes, get comfortable and *look*, is crucial. You can never have that pre-group discussion time back. The initial impressions people form during that first silence will feed the discussion throughout. By allowing silence—by inviting silence—the educator is signaling: this artwork is worthy of close attention. It is valuable. Let's dwell here."[3]

I sometimes liken this convening in front of a work of art to a book group, except we all have access to the entire *book* simultaneously. Instead of needing to reference page numbers, summarize chapters, or describe characters, the entire visual text is available to all of us at the same time.

Participants have already been given a pencil and paper and a hard backing like a piece of cardboard or Masonite. "Let's take a deep breath and focus our attention on this artwork." As a way to extend this moment of silent looking, ask that participants write down some things they notice, the things that are commanding their attention. The importance of writing down a response to the question, "What do you notice about this work?" cannot be over emphasized. Although many museum educators begin their tour stops with this question, it is more typical for the group to begin a conversation by only responding verbally. Then why write?

The process of writing something down is an act of commitment. It is an expression of your individual opinion in direct response to an encounter with a work of art *before* those around you voice their ideas and begin to influence and modify your first and direct impressions. It gives participants on your tour a chance to think before the open-ended discussion of the artwork begins. The thought inside your head is now out in the world—committed to paper. Whether or not you decide to voice your ideas to the tour group in the ensuing conversation, you have formed and recorded independent observations. In the few minutes of looking and writing you have created a small reservoir of independent perceptions and ideas that you can draw from once the discussion begins. This skill of taking in stimuli, processing your ideas about it, and finding ways to clearly express your personal response, is vital to all thoughtful communication.

For some participants, writing down a single word will be an enormous struggle, for others the words and ideas will flow more freely. Our job as educators is to create an environment where varied ideas can be shared, considered, respected, and discussed. One of the big goals of looking together at works of art is getting participants accustomed to digesting their perceptions and expressing their insights in words.

For those educators working with school-aged youth, there is another pragmatic reason for adding writing to your art inquiries. At all levels and subject areas educators are tasked with developing the literacy, language, and writing skills of their students. By regularly asking students to write and talk in response to looking at art, you are helping them to develop language skills and to express their ideas.[4]

You have given the group time to look and jot down some aspects of the artwork that have caught their attention. "Would someone like to share something you noticed?" Hopefully, a member of the group will enthusiastically share an observation, but few people, kids or adults, want to be the first to respond. If your first question is met with total silence . . . wait. This is harder than it sounds.

Lots has been written about the importance of *wait time* in teaching and there has been considerable research demonstrating the benefits of giving people time to think and the positive effects it can have for engagement and learning. In 1972, Mary Budd Rowe coined the phrase *wait time* to describe the period of time between a teacher's question and a student's response. Rowe found that teachers typically wait between .7 seconds and 1.5 seconds before speaking after they have asked a question.[5] Think about that and how it truly disrespects the process of thinking. How can an individual be expected to formulate a thoughtful response to an open-ended question in a second?

When faced with the situation of asking a question and no one immediately responding, educators frequently get unnerved by the lull and resort to compensatory behavior. Instead of being relaxed as participants mull over the question you have asked, you may experience anxiousness. In response to this discomfort, you may be tempted to rephrase the question, or worse, ask another question. Now the group is really confused. Or the educator just might answer the question themselves. That was an easy fix: ask a question and answer it yourself. The trick here is to breathe, appear relaxed—even if you aren't—and give the group time to respond. By waiting you demonstrate by your behavior that it takes time to process thoughts, feelings, and reactions.

As you wait observe the body language of the individuals in the group. It can tell you a great deal about who is willing to respond. Those who avert their eyes and turn, even slightly away from you, are nonverbally communicating "Please don't call on me!" Respect that message. As you scan the group, someone is likely meeting your gaze. It's a fairly good indication that person will be fine with sharing something from their list. When working with school-age groups I have sometimes employed this strategy. After asking an open-ended question I tell the group, "You can respond in two ways. If you have an answer in your mind, but don't want to speak it aloud, raise your hand but only as high as your shoulder. If you have an idea you would like to share with the group, raise your hand high." From my experience just about everyone in the group will raise their hand either partially or fully. This demonstrates that there are many ideas percolating. Begin acknowledging the fully raised hands, you may get some converts as the discussion continues, but you have also acknowledged that students can be thinking and learning, even when not waving their hands in the air.

ACTIVE LISTENING

You have gotten a first response. What next? Listen.

The most critical and powerful aspect of communication is not speaking but listening. Listening shapes speaking. By listening intently and working to understand the thoughts that are being expressed, you demonstrate that you are truly interested in the responses. This, in turn, generates a desire to participate, to be heard and understood.

According to educator and author Laurel Schmidt,

> If you want to create a lively dialogue, work on strengthening your listening skills and practice making sustained eye-contact so that you can be absolutely present when participants are sharing their thoughts. Try not to think of what you want to say next. Just stay in the moment and try to listen to every word because you may hear something surprising or unique that sheds a whole new light on your approach to the art. Don't be afraid to say, "Wow! I never thought about that." And show your emotions. Be passionate even if you've seen the art many times.[6]

More than any other quality, when I asked, "What makes an excellent museum educator?" my colleagues mentioned the ability to listen as the most important skill to cultivate. This sounds easy but can be difficult in a noisy gallery. Participants may have soft voices, foreign accents, make little-known references, or have unfamiliar ways of expressing themselves. But listening is more than hearing. Active listening is demanding work. You need to put aside your expectations, focus, and digest the information that is being shared.

Museum educator Gabriela O'Leary suggests, "Practice listening actively and responding authentically to the contributions participants bring to the experience. Take the time to recognize and honor these contributions to meaning making, validating what participants say and threading connections between the content you are exploring, and the insights participants share."[7]

Educator and author Olga Hubard advises, "Practice listening as attentively and responsibly as possible—to both audiences and artwork. Be genuinely curious about what each encounter will bring."[8]

Museum director Rebecca Shulman recommends, "Really listen. I can't stress listening enough."[9]

Asking for clarification helps you make sure you understand the information the speaker is trying to relay. Did I understand correctly that you are noticing the . . . ? Be sure you aren't interpreting the information and taking too many liberties with someone else's statement and idea. You aren't meant to interpret what's been said or how someone feels or what they think; you are affirming it. You are affirming *them*.[10]

According to educator Sarah Mostow,

> Paraphrasing is one skill all educators must have—the ability to repeat a student's comments in such a way as to leave the conversation open. Even if an educator repeats a comment verbatim ("Juan is noticing that the sky looks stormy 'like it might rain'") there can be different inflections. I try not to imply with my tone "You are saying just what I wanted you to say!" because, again,

that is using kids for a pre-conceived agenda. Instead, my paraphrasing-tone communicates "you are saying something I want to repeat for the group to hear. Let's slow down, look closely, and think more about this comment."[11]

Not every response needs to be repeated or paraphrased, but every response needs to be acknowledged. Some educators, especially those who work with younger audiences express great enthusiasm for every response. Wow! Interesting! Thanks for sharing that! I have also observed effective facilitators who are more subdued in their acknowledgment. What is important is that your reaction be *even*. If you are superexcited about one response and cooler about others, check yourself. Are you fishing around for the answer in your head?

Following that first response, you may decide to probe a bit more? Where do you see that? Why did that catch your attention? Could you tell us more? Or you might turn back to the group and ask if anyone else also had this aspect of the artwork on their list.

Especially with younger audiences, you may get responses where the student/youth is pointing to, rather than describing in words, an area of the artwork that has caught their attention. It is not unusual for adults to do this too, and I confess to it myself. Although it is easier to point at an area of an artwork that you are discussing, I encourage you to develop and model the habit of focusing attention on *words* and gently support participants to do the same. When a participant points to an area of an artwork, you can say, "Can you tell us more about what you are noticing?" By encouraging participants to describe, rather than point, you are supporting the development of verbal communication skills, an attribute highly valued in this culture, and modeling that we can use language to express our ideas.

WHAT ELSE?

You have gotten an answer, but inquiry-based discussions are rooted in the concept that a solid open-ended question should yield multiple, even an infinite, number of responses. Inviting participants to share more thoughts and perceptions emphasizes that you are not looking for a single correct answer, but rather inviting and valuing a diversity of responses. Encouraging multiple answers invites new ideas. And so, to demonstrate that there are additional interesting perceptions to share, turn back to the group and say, "What else?" which is one of the most powerful questions you have. It makes clear that there is no one right answer and that you are genuinely interested in hearing a variety of responses. "What else?" is to gallery teaching what "Yes, and . . ." is to improv and in fact, the two skill sets have much in common. "Yes, and . . ." is a basic premise of improvisational theater. It suggests that a participant should accept what has been stated ("yes") and then expand on the response. This strategy is also used in business to improve brainstorming, communication, and the sharing of ideas.[12] Saying "yes" when a participant shares something they have noticed accepts the comment or observation with a positive confirmation. Then saying "and" invites additional ideas and observations to be shared. Both "What else?" and "Yes, and . . ." can be used as strategies for strengthening communication, facilitating exploration, and creating a supportive group environment.

TURN AND TALK

Asking participants to share their responses with the full group is the most common strategy for facilitating a conversation in front of a work of art, but there are others. Especially for groups that may be reluctant to share with the larger group, *turn and talk* is effective because it turns public space into private space.[13]

In response to an open-ended question, ask the participants to turn to the person next to them and share their thoughts. To be sure that both partners get a chance to speak, remind the group halfway through the allotted period, at the one-minute mark, for a two-minute turn and talk, that it's time for the other person to speak.

I am frequently surprised by the buzz that ensues as soon as a turn and talk begins. There is no way out, you are now one-on-one with another person; you gotta talk, but now it's just to one person, the stakes are lower, the interaction feels more casual and relaxed. Turn and talk can provide an opportunity to try out your ideas. When you call the group back together, you may want to ask, "Who can share something from their turn and talk conversation?" You may be surprised that there is now more willingness to talk to the larger group. Comments may begin with, "*We* talked about . . ." Turn and talk, also known as *partner talk* and *pair share*, is a common classroom strategy, so in addition to making the interaction more intimate, it also utilizes a protocol from the more familiar school classroom environment into the less familiar museum setting.

GETTING BETTER

Inquiry-based teaching is rooted in the idea that collective, shared communication is a valuable way to understand art (and life), but becoming a skilled facilitator takes both practice and experimentation. When you watch a seasoned, skilled, educator you may be tempted to think, "That looks so effortless." But it is not. Understanding, processing, and connecting multiple responses from participants, while being (or appearing to be) calm, receptive, and flexible is challenging work.

Olga Hubard says, "It takes time and practice to learn how to do it. Try out new things, be willing to "fail"—and reflect on how you might do it better next time."[14]

"Don't be afraid to experiment—some things will work, and some things won't, but when lessons fall flat it's okay, it helps you get better in the long run!" says Rebecca Shulman.[15]

Providing visitors with the opportunity to consider, articulate, and process their own thoughts and questions empowers them with a sense of their own knowledge and ownership, toppling the dusty trope that only "art people" can know and comment about art. Sensitizing visitors to the value of their own knowledge encourages them to use and trust that knowledge when looking at art, or considering other issues.

Through experience and experimentation each educator develops their own individual style based on their interests, knowledge, and personality. The best of them practice and hone different approaches and techniques. Educator Jamie Song urges us to

> observe, observe, and again observe others. The great ones, the bad ones, and especially the terrible ones. Pick up their techniques, the know-hows, and what-not-to-dos. See the behaviors of students and participants when an educator does something. Observations allow you to learn from others when the stakes are low for you—and *then* go practice in the field, where you will have good days and bad days, make mistakes, and also have wonderful and powerful, learning experiences.[16]

NOTES

1. Steve Tokar, "Take a Seat, Museum Magazine," September 1, 2008, American Alliance of Museums, https://www.aam-us.org/2008/09/01/take-a-seat/.
2. Jen Oleniczak Brown, *Think on Your Feet: Tips and Tricks to Improve your Impromptu Communication Skills on the Job*, McGraw-Hill, New York, 2020, 216.
3. Sarah Mostow is a museum educator at the Guggenheim Museum, personal communication, January 2022.
4. For more on how looking at and discussing works of art can support language development see Teaching Literacy Through Art, 2002–06, https://www.guggenheim.org/education-research-studies.
5. Mary Budd Rowe "Wait Time: Slowing Down May Be a Way of Speeding Up!" *Journal of Teacher Education* 37, no. 1 (January 1986): 43–50.
6. Laurel Schmidt is an author and educator, personal communication, February 2022.
7. Gabriela O'Leary is a museum educator at the Guggenheim Museum, personal communication, January 2022.
8. Olga Hubard is director and associate professor of art education, Teachers College, Columbia University, personal communication, January 2022.
9. Rebecca Shulman is the former director of the Peoria Children's Museum, personal communication, January 2022.
10. Jen Oleniczak Brown, *Improv[e] using Improv to Find Your . . . Voice, Style, Self*, Balboa Press, Bloomington, IN, 2018, p. 84.
11. Ibid, Sarah Mostow.
12. Yes, and... https://en.wikipedia.org/wiki/Yes,_and...last edited December 8, 2022.

13. "Turn and Talk is a structured discussion that invites students to turn and face a designated partner in order to discuss an idea or question to deepen understanding..." https://goalbookapp.com/toolkit/v/strategy/turn-and-talk.
14. Ibid, Olga Hubard.
15. Ibid, Rebecca Shulman.
16. Jamie Song is a museum educator at the Metropolitan Museum of Art, personal communication, January 2022.

13

Reflection and Evaluation

You have said farewell to your group and thanked them for their participation. They may have even expressed their appreciation by clapping, lingered to speak with you further, or thanked you for the tour.

You feel (check one or more boxes):

Elated
Satisfied
Energized
Exhausted
Relieved
Ambivalent
Confused
Disappointed
Deflated
I'm not good at this
Other

Facilitating a gallery experience for a group is demanding work. For the past sixty to ninety minutes you have been responding to many—sometimes competing—demands.

Museum educator Vas Prabhu asserts,

> When teaching interactively there are so many moving parts and unknowns about how the participants will respond and of course, the pressures of time. I am always thinking about balancing my facilitation, audience participation, interjecting information about artists or art history, and segues that connect one idea to another that will make for a successful gallery or virtual experience.[1]

If you come away from the tour feeling that things *clicked*—it is a truly satisfying feeling. But especially if you are working with new artworks or experimenting with a new activity or line of inquiry, not every first attempt will be a smashing success and that feeling that something fell flat, or even bombed, can resonate in the pit of the stomach. You are not alone. Every museum educator who has tried something new has experienced strategies that have not gone over as hoped, and it is the disappointments rather than the successes that stay with us longest.

Museum educator Sarah Mostow declares,

> A tour is not successful unless *I* feel that it was. (This attitude gives me professional integrity.) The group can be happy, my boss can think it was great, the teacher can complement it . . . but only *I* know if I was able to facilitate a meaningful experience to the best of my ability—or not. I often think about what I could have done better on the subway ride home.[2]

I posed the following question to my colleagues: "Following a gallery or virtual tour how do you reflect upon and learn from the experience?" The educators who responded were in surprising agreement about what happens after a tour, but also had varied methods for reflecting. Some favored an internal review: going through the experience in their mind's eye, some preferred talking things through, while others found note-taking or journaling effective.

A CRITICAL REVIEW

Carolyn Keogh shared,

> I start by just trying to identify what worked and what didn't—what were the moments where participants were visibly excited or engaged? When did it seem like the conversation stalled? After identifying these moments, I'll try to dig deeper and ask myself some open-ended questions: What could have pushed the dialogue to a deeper place? What could be added or tried next time? I always try to reflect keeping the next tour or next program in mind.
>
> With virtual experiences, I'll record the program and make sure to take a look at the chat. If a group is participating in the chat, it's a useful record of engagement and can be a wonderful reflective tool to help map the flow of the experience.[3]

Vas Prabhu responded,

> I document the experience with notes; observing which parts of the lesson worked well and which "lagged." I notice the effect on the teacher/educator and the students. I also call the teacher/educator about the experience. In general, my reflection considers how can I improve my facilitation and how to improve the techniques I am using and finally did my concluding activity and discussion give a satisfying closure, and make participants yearn for more?[4]

TALKING TO OTHERS

For educator Gabriela O'Leary,

> I love the opportunity to debrief on the gallery teaching experience with colleagues. This sometimes happens organically and informally in the museum setting, when colleagues who had all just taught other groups would chat in the studio as we put our materials away, or while waiting for a group to arrive. I find that I am sorely missing this in the virtual world.[5]

Rebecca Shulman says,

> Ideally, I talk to someone (but that's how I process most things). It's even better if they have seen the tour and have feedback for me. I note what worked well and I would want to do again, and what didn't work as well as it could and consider ideas for how it could be better. Write these ideas down somewhere while fresh in your mind![6]

And Shannon Murphy adds, "I like talking with another educator about what happened the most. I also take notes and journal on the lesson plan."[7]

DON'T BEAT YOURSELF UP

Educator Joyce Raimondo says, "Every experience is an opportunity to grow. Don't beat yourself up if you make a mistake. There will always be things to improve upon. That is why being an educator is creative and so much fun."[8]

Olga Hubard shared her approach, "I review how it went in my mind. Sometimes I obsess about things that did not work out as I expected and consider what might account for it and what I might do differently. Sometimes I talk with other people about those concerns. It takes time and practice to learn how to teach in the galleries. Try out new things, be willing to 'fail'—and reflect on how you might do it better next time."[9]

Jamie Song adds, "Don't get bogged down by the mistakes—no two situations will be the same. What worked for one program might not for another. Obviously, take away and learn from each experience, but also be able to dust yourself off and move on."[10]

Museum teaching (and all teaching for that matter) is complicated and delicate work. For those of you who think you just ask, "What do you see?" think again. When you begin to consider the number of elements that go into planning and facilitating a successful tour it truly boggles the mind.

A few years ago, the then manager of the School and Family Programs at the Guggenheim Museum, Mayrav Fisher, implemented a series of professional development workshops with the museum's youth educators. The goal of the sessions was to craft a collaborative reflection tool that could be used as a personal guide for internal reflection and as an evaluation tool for interactive teaching. Over several sessions, the group of approximately fifteen educators worked together to elaborate on the specific criteria that make for successful tour planning and facilitation. After much discussion and many iterations, the group settled on a set of agreed tour goals and objectives. Although designed for school tours, these can be easily adapted for other audiences.

TOUR GOALS

School programs will

- provide a positive, welcoming, and inclusive experience;
- connect experiences to students' lives, curriculum, and exhibitions;
- facilitate open-ended, discovery-based experiences of original art objects in the galleries, including the Guggenheim's architecture;
- offer opportunities for hands-on participation through a variety of activities that address different learning styles;
- strengthen visual literacy, critical thinking skills, and an appreciation for multiple perspectives;
- root experiences in developmentally appropriate content and methodology; and
- include relevant contextual information about art and the museum.

TOUR OBJECTIVES

For tour planning, educators will

- organize tours *thematically*;
- select and sequence objects using solid rationales; and
- design inquiries and prepare materials.

For the actual tour educators will

- upon group arrival, set a positive tone for the tour through an inquiry-based introduction to the museum;
- introduce the goals and theme of the tour through an advance organizer;
- facilitate discussions using open-ended questions that elicit multiple responses and engage students in critical thinking;
- deepen conversations by embedding contextual information organically;
- include activities that further understanding of object and/or theme; and

- at the end of a tour, integrate a summary and reflection of the students' museum experience

For tour reflection educators will

- review tour experience and consider modifications for next time.

The group then went on to iterate a checklist of best practices for each part of the gallery experience. The following list serves as a reminder of the many moving parts that constitute a successful tour.

1. Theme

    - Provides a framework for exploration of deeper concepts
    - Is relevant to the curriculum, student lives, and exhibitions
    - Allows for connections between artists, periods, styles, art objects, etc.

2. Object Selection and Sequence

    - Selection provides opportunities for varied observations and interpretations.
    - Selection has solid rationales for connecting with the theme in new ways.
    - Sequence progresses from simple to complex relationship to the theme.
    - Selection and sequence logistically provide a comfortable experience.

3. Introduction (Greeting)

    - Provides a preview of the museum experience
    - Sets a positive tone through a welcoming demeanor
    - Is well planned and organized
    - Includes stating of museum rules
    - Includes brief inquiry about the museum's architecture

4. Advance Organizer

    - Introduces the goals and theme through question or activity and creates a framework for the tour
    - Helps educators assess student knowledge of the theme

- Relates to student's curriculum, prior knowledge, and personal experience
- Serves as an introduction to inquiry-based methodology

5A. Inquiry (discussion-based exploration)

- Discussion based on a limited number of open-ended questions
- Engages students in critical thinking progressing from observation to interpretation
- Elicits multiple responses and allows ample wait time
- Engages different learning styles

5B. Activity (creation-based exploration)

- Open-ended and provides opportunity for personal choice making
- Allows further exploration by addressing different learning styles
- Developmentally appropriate and scaffolded
- Includes reflection and sharing
- Logistically well organized

6. Contextual Information (introduced by the educator)

- Furthers and deepens understanding of the object
- Organically fits into conversation
- Is followed up by a related open-ended question
- Is developmentally appropriate for attention span and comprehension

7. Transition

- Bridges the object(s) just viewed to the next art object and builds anticipation
- Summarizes or reinforces inquiry conversation
- Encourages further explorations in the time and space between objects
- Check in with students and remind them of plan and theme

8. Summary

- Encourages review of experience
- Relates to the theme or advance organizer
- Is affirming, positive, and open ended
- Encourages continuation or further exploration beyond the museum

9. Reflection

- Review the tour experience and consider what worked and what did not work.
- Brainstorm changes to be implemented next time.
- Share ideas.

If this list looks familiar it may be because the previous chapters have been dedicated to the same goals, objectives, and practices. Reflection is the active process of self-examination. What have we learned? How can we do better? What needs to happen to make this experience more relatable, relevant, current, personal? Staying with those moments of discomfort where things have not gone well is uncomfortable but sometimes fruitful. It may yield new approaches, and ways to better connect to your next group.[11]

A FEW WORDS ABOUT EVALUATION

Throughout this book I have been writing from the perspective of the educator/facilitator. Reflection is, of course, what *you* think about the success or failure of the experience you facilitated, but evaluation puts that determination in the hands of those who have experienced your work: supervisors, teachers, students, and museum visitors. I don't think I have ever read anything written from the perspective of the individual *being* evaluated, rather it is always from the perspective of the evaluator.

We are flooded with evaluations. In some public bathrooms you are asked to press a button to indicate how pleased or disappointed you are with the amenities. After every webinar I attend, a survey form is sure to follow. When I return from my local pharmacy, an email appears asking, "How are we doing?"

If you are like me you only respond to these forms if you are wildly pleased or terribly disappointed. The folks in the middle don't have the intrinsic motivation needed to spend time on completing surveys. And so, if either negative or positive feedback reaches you, take it seriously, be open to it. You may be thinking, "Of course I'd take it seriously," but I have seen educators shrug off criticism and not be willing or able to hear or respond to it.

Most museums include some form of summative evaluation following their programs, but evaluation is only useful if it is *used*. Completed forms and surveys that sit in someone's draw or file cabinet cannot support positive change. I make a habit of reviewing evaluation forms right after the program. Some questions I always pay particularly attention to are:

- Would you participate in this type of program again?
- Would you recommend this program to a friend/colleague?

The comments section of the evaluation form is usually most compelling and surprising. You are getting feedback on what mattered to them. Take it to heart, especially any comments that offer suggestions for improvement.

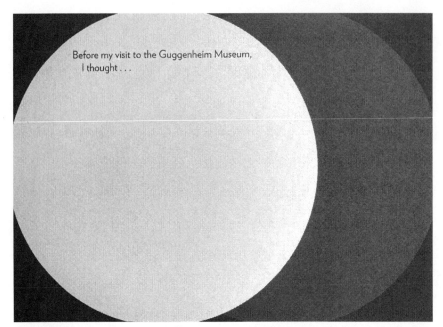

Figure 13.1. Retrospective Evaluation too, front of card.

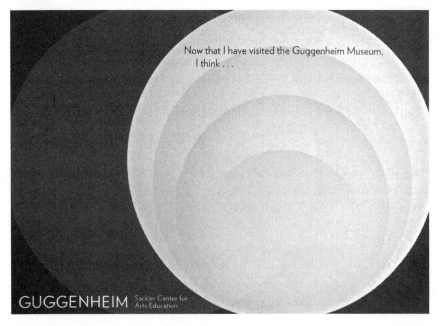

Figure 13.2. Retrospective Evaluation too, back of card.

As a museum educator/facilitator you will encounter evaluation from various perspectives. Each type of feedback holds valuable information.

EVALUATION FROM TEACHERS OF VISITING CLASSES

It is not easy for school-based teachers to take their students on a museum trip. Permission slips, chaperones, transportation, and sometimes justification for how this trip will support classroom curriculum are all part of the many hurdles that need to be negotiated. Schoolteachers frequently come to the museum with clear goals and expectations for what they want from the museum tour. The more you know in advance, the more you can align your tour plan with the teacher's goals. If there is a possibility of connecting with the teacher in advance of the visit you increase your odds of providing an experience that connects and amplifies classroom learning. Evaluation forms are usually emailed to the teacher following the tour. Many times the educator/facilitator doesn't even get to see to the evaluations that are returned. Unless someone has deemed your tour dreadful or spectacular, they will usually be filed away in some digital folder. If the tour met the teacher's expectations, you may not get the emailed survey back at all—however if expectations weren't met, you will probably hear about it.

EVALUATION FROM ADULT TOUR PARTICIPANTS

I have found adult tour participants who hang in there until the end tend to be very kind, positive people who usually adhere to the adage, "If you don't have anything nice to say, don't say anything at all." If you are not meeting their needs/expectations they will find a way to quietly and surreptitiously "peel off" somewhere along the tour route—after all, this is free-choice learning. Those who are with you at the end are usually satisfied. You might even get a smattering of applause. It may be a bit awkward to hand out evaluation forms at this point because you are standing right there, but a short retrospective evaluation can be useful here. Give people "space" to respond—don't hover. This evaluation, based on a thinking protocol developed by Project Zero, Harvard Graduate School of Education, asks only two questions.[12] One side of the card states, "Before my visit to the _____ museum I thought . . ." and the flipside prompts, "Now that I have visited the _____museum, I think . . ." This routine can help to identify how a tour participant's ideas and attitudes may have changed. The responses to these two prompts are as much for the participant as for the educator, helping to focus on how much the "needle has moved" . . . or not (see figures 13.1 and 13.2).

In using this protocol with teens, many of the "before" cards expressed expectations of boredom, disinterest, anxiety, and concerns about feeling out of place, whereas the actual visit was experienced as "fun" and "interesting." One student wrote, "I had been worried and confused about being able to understand what the artist way trying to portray. Now that I have visited, I realize the artwork's true beauty. This experience has helped me understand that there is

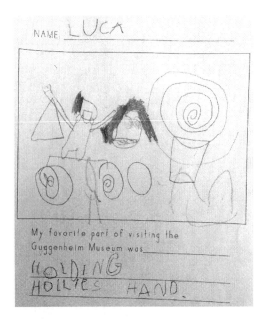

NAME LUCA

My favorite part of visiting the Guggenheim Museum was
HOLDING HOLLIES HAND.

Figure 13.3. Evaluation form by Luca, Holding Hollie's Hand *Sharon Vatsky*

more to art than what meets the eye and there is a whole world of art beyond European. I have never been the type to go to art exhibits, but from now on I definitely will. I might even become a regular at the Guggenheim."[13]

EVALUATION FROM KIDS

These are my favorites. Just about no one asks kids what they think about a school tour or program, but their responses may be the most candid. My colleague Carolyn Keogh[14] decided to ask the kids that participated in a summer course for their feedback, rather than the more traditional route of asking parents or teachers. The responses led to some programmatic adjustments. The consensus opinion was that the program fulfilled expectations, but that better snacks were needed. The comment section included some specific suggestions for snack upgrades.

An example of useful (and heartwarming) feedback came from a young visitor named Luca (see figure 13.3). Luca's drawing includes several details that demonstrate his attentive response to the Guggenheim's Frank Lloyd Wright architecture, including spirals and a triangle. (The museum is designed around a spiral ramp and many of the museum's light fixtures and even a staircase are triangular.) The drawing also depicts a small full-figure with outstretched arms, Luca, and a large floating head belonging to Holly Ecker, the museum educator who facilitated this tour. I had this feedback form pinned to my office bulletin board for years. It's a reminder that sometimes it is not the objects on view that make the most lasting impressions. For Luca, when asked what his favorite part of the visit was, he responded, "Holding Hollie's hand."

EVALUATION/FEEDBACK FROM YOUR SUPERVISOR

I have observed and provided post-tour feedback to dozens of educators. No matter how you approach it, this process is stressful on both sides. Providing individual feedback to educators requires time, attention, and sensitivity. No one likes to be judged. I try to give one-on-one feedback immediately after the tour, beginning with the question, "How do *you* think it went?" I have found that most educators are pretty honest and reflective in their assessments, but if there is dissonance between what the educator describes and what I observed, this is cause for concern. Once we discuss their reflection points, I begin by recounting the positive aspects I observed. For any places that could use improvement, I try to get the educator to think about how they might revise their approach. I ask them to reflect on any parts of the tour that might be improved upon and any thoughts they have for making adjustments." Interestingly, it is frequently the most accomplished educators who are the hardest on themselves and the ones that need to focus on improving their skills that are sometimes cavalier in the face of less than stellar feedback. For educators who need additional help with developing their skills, we usually articulate the areas that need attention and schedule another observation in a few weeks. No gallery experience is perfect, but each one offers the possibility to learn and grow.

KEEP IT SHORT

Many of us have received an emailed evaluation survey and opened it with the intention of doing a good deed by completing it. As you begin to fill in the blanks, you realize that this is much more of a project than you had bargained for. Long forms don't necessarily provide more useful information, and the longer the form, the greater the risk it won't be returned. In Connecting Collections the evaluation form we send out at the conclusion of the program has been condensed to just six targeted questions. Figure out what you want to learn and focus on how to get that feedback with the briefest possible form.

One of the shortest and most successful museum evaluation tools was only five words long but enabled visitors to recount and share memorable aspects of their visit. The Museum of Modern Art (MoMA) developed an interactive, open-ended response strategy called the "I went to MoMA and . . ." Project where visitors leave their mark using the museum's preprinted notecards. The experiment resulted in an amazing collection of replies and information. Many of them can be viewed on the project's website.[15]

NOTES

1. Vas Prabhu is an independent museum educator. Personal communication, February 2022.
2. Sarah Mostow is a museum educator at the Guggenheim Museum. Personal communication December 2021.
3. Carolyn Keogh is the former Manager of School and Youth Programs at the Guggenheim Museum. She is currently Director of Education & Public Programs at the Olana Partnership. Personal communication, January 2022.
4. Vas Prabhu is an independent museum educator. Personal communication, February 2022.
5. Gabriela O'Leary is a museum educator at the Guggenheim Museum. Personal communication, February 2022.

6. Rebecca Shulman is the former director of the Peoria Children's Museum.
7. Shannon Murphy is the former director of education at the Noguchi Museum, Queens, NY. Personal communication January 2022.
8. Joyce Raimondo is the education coordinator at the Pollock-Krasner House and Founding Director of Imagine That! Art Education. Personal correspondence, January2022.
9. Olga Hubard is director and associate professor of arts education, Teachers College, Columbia University. Personal communication, January 2022.
10. Jamie Song is a museum educator at the Metropolitan Museum of Art. Personal communication January 2022.
11. Randi Korn, *Intentional Practice for Museums: A Guide for Maximizing Impact*, Rowman and Littlefield, Lanham MD, 2018, 67.
12. A thinking routine from Project Zero, Harvard Graduate School of Education I Used to Think... Now I Think..., http://www.pz.harvard.edu/sites/default/files/I%20Used%20to%20Think%20-%20Now%20I%20Think_1.pdf.
13. Anonymous, Stuyvesant High School student after visiting *Art and China after 1989: Theater of the World* exhibition at the Solomon R. Guggenheim Museum, January 2018.
14. Carolyn Keogh is the former Manager of School and Youth Programs at the Guggenheim. She is currently Director of Education & Public Programs at the Olana Partnership.
15. Brigitta Bungard, Jocelyn Meinhardt, December 7, 2011, "I went to MoMA and...": It's Back! https://www.moma.org/explore/inside_out/2011/12/07/i-went-to-moma-and-it-s-back/.

Part IV

Adapting the Tour Planning Template for Diverse Audiences

14

Audience at the Center

ADAPTING THE TOUR PLANNING TEMPLATE FOR VARIED AUDIENCES

There is a ton of research available on who visits museums—and even on who doesn't. It is all interesting, but will it help you on that 2:00 pm tour? Nope (figure 14.1).

Traditionally, audiences have been categorized by demographics, school groups, families, older adults, tourists, etc. More recently, museum researchers John Falk and Lynn Dierking have segmented audiences into five identity groups determined by their motivations to visit museums including explorers, facilitators,

Figure 14.1. The 2:00 pm daily tour gathers in the rotunda of the Guggenheim Museum. *Filip Wolak © Solomon R. Guggenheim Foundation, New York. All Rights Reserved.*

professionals/hobbyists, experience seekers, and rechargers.[1] These groupings may be useful for the marketing or visitor experience departments, but they are of limited use to the museum educator. Researching your audience(s) is different from *knowing* them. However, there is a way that museum educators can learn more about the various audiences they work with, and it is surprisingly simple and intuitive. You can talk with them.

A true delight in writing this book has been the opportunity to invite several museum education professionals, who have spent years getting to know a particular audience segment, to contribute chapters. Over the years, they have experimented with various strategies, accommodations, and methodologies, but what struck me most about reading their contributions to this book, is that each educator seems to employ a simple yet direct strategy to better know the audience they work with. *They speak with them.*

Francesca Rosenberg who directs the well-regarded *Meet Me* initiative at the Museum of Modern Art, which focuses on providing programming for individuals with Alzheimer's disease and their caretakers, has spent decades getting to know this audience. Even with that deep understanding of what might be expected, Francesca shared that as each group settles in at the beginning of a museum tour, she informally goes around, greets each group member, and welcomes them. Dementia can manifest in many ways. This initial one-on-one interaction provides her with a sense of who is in the group, and their ability to engage, while also putting the group at ease.

As you might imagine, stroller tours that focus on young children and their caregivers can take a bit of time to coalesce. A young visitor might arrive at the museum requiring a diaper change or snack before heading into the galleries. When leading these tours, Emily Rivlin-Nadler who manages family and youth programs at the Guggenheim, takes those initial moments to ask, "How was your trip to the museum today?" The response can provide cues that can, almost intuitively, help the educator make small adjustments in tone.

As the group gathers take those first few minutes to have a brief welcome. Even this abbreviated interaction can provide a bit of comfort and connection. "Have you visited the museum before?" "Where are you visiting from?" Remember that just as you are trying to *size up* your audience, they are checking you out as well. People join public tours because they are interested in learning *and* personal connection. These moments before the tour formally begins can be used to create a sense of affiliation and provide you with information about who is in the group. You may be able to weave this casual conversation into the experience as the tour unfolds, demonstrating that you were listening, not just filling time.

Melanie Adsit, former senior manager of youth, family and inclusion initiatives has overseen the Guggenheim for the All program that provides museum experiences for students on the autism spectrum. She frequently says, "If you know one person with autism, you know one person with autism." It's difficult to generalize, so she has built a three-part program that includes a previsit meeting at the school, a visit to the museum, and a follow-up lesson back at the school. The previsit session provides an orientation for the students within the accustomed school setting, giving them a preview of what to expect when they visit the museum. They also meet the *same* two educators who will facilitate their museum experience, creating a bridge of familiarity between the previsit and museum visit. Meeting the students in their school environment also gives the museum educators a better understanding of the group and how to design the museum visit for maximum engagement.

Even with this previsit experience Melanie reminds us that "the introduction to a lesson is the museum educator's chance to learn about their students— their communication styles, preferences, strengths, dislikes, discomforts, and responses to the new space. During this introductory period, it is essential for the museum educator to remain flexible about their plan for the lesson and to use their powers of observation to see where adjustments should be made."[2]

In their chapters, both Queena Ko and Lisa Mazzola, who work with school audiences, discuss the importance of being in touch with the teacher in advance of the museum visit. Although it takes an extra level of commitment to have this initial phone or email conversation, the rewards are enormous. The teacher knows the class well and can provide information on what themes and activities will be most engaging.

I am sometimes asked whether it may spoil the surprise if students know what to expect at the museum. My response is that the more students know about the museum visit in advance, the better and deeper the learning experience will be. Advertisers have long understood this concept. Providing a preview can serve as an enticement and way to enhance interest. They produce coming attractions, movie trailers, and sneak peeks designed to whet the appetite.

This previsit conversation with the teacher also has the potential to link classroom learning with the outside world. Students often feel that what they learn in school has little relevance to the real world. By speaking with the teacher, the museum educator can select a theme and tour stops that reinforce school curricula. You can work with the teacher so that students can show off their knowledge during the visit. They can shine.

Personally, one of the most compelling examples of how a preview can pique interest came in 2001 just after the World Trade Center attacks. All school trips were halted, and school buses were restricted from traveling over bridges. I was working on a pilot program focusing on using videoconferencing to introduce the Guggenheim Museum to wider audiences—an early precursor of today's ubiquitous explosion in remote learning. I provided orientations to a school in Schenectady, New York, approximately three hours north of the museum.[3] The students and their intrepid teachers became so intrigued with Frank Lloyd Wright's architecture, that as soon as the restrictions were lifted, they embarked on the long drive to experience the museum in person. Now that remote access is so prevalent, there is even greater possibility of providing a previsit orientation in advance of the museum visit.

Karen Bergman, who oversees the Mind's Eye program for adults with blindness and low vision, has taken these communication efforts a step further. Many of the Mind's Eye participants are *regulars* who participate in Guggenheim programs, either in person or remotely, several times a year. Since Karen is sighted, she frequently consults with members of this loyal and dedicated community to ensure that the programs offered are on target. She says, "It's important to listen to your audience and develop programs in collaboration with them and in response to their actual requests as opposed to their imagined needs."[4]

In speaking with educators about resources they use to help them plan more accessible audience-centered experiences, several mentioned the value of utilizing the Universal Design for Learning Guidelines (UDL) as a blueprint for creating inclusive lessons.[5] It's website states, "Universal Design for Learning (UDL) is a framework to improve and optimize teaching and learning for all people based on scientific insights into how humans learn. . . . The UDL Guidelines offer a set of concrete suggestions that can be applied to any discipline or domain to ensure that all learners can access and participate in meaningful, challenging, learning opportunities."[6] Although used widely in classrooms, UDL is equally applicable to museum learning. UDL is a way of thinking that can guide the museum educator in planning and facilitating experiences. It puts the unique learner at the center, focusing on process over product and valuing continual growth, reflection, and lifelong learning.

Museum educators work with diverse audiences. To do this responsibly and effectively each of us needs to examine and understand our own unique set of cultural perspectives, beliefs, and yes, biases. Of course, each visitor also arrives at the museum with their own identity and cultural lens. They have formed a perspective on the world based on aspects of their race, social class, gender, language, sexual orientation, nationality, religion, or ability . . . just as you have.

Museums have only recently begun to examine and acknowledge their histories that have frequently been steeped in bias and inequality. In many museums, it is the education department staff that have been most willing to be more reflective, change the dominant narrative, and be more inclusive and equitable. We aspire to planning and facilitating experiences that reflect many backgrounds and allow us to connect across cultures. We need to value and affirm the varied experiences and perspectives that visitors bring, whether they be connected to racial/cultural background, language, disability or other, as essential assets and resources for learning.

This book focuses on guided museum tours, but those experiences cannot be separated from the rest of the museum visit. Creating an inclusive museum environment for all visitors should be the ultimate goal. Guided groups encounter other frontline staff, so it is important that all museum workers are offered professional development training in sensitivity and awareness techniques that promote inclusiveness and access. Those interactions need to be as welcoming as their time with you.

One strategy that proved effective at the Guggenheim Museum was a series of joint trainings for the visitor experience, security, and education departments (the "frontline" departments that interact directly with visitors). We realized that to effectively collaborate in the galleries and provide visitors with positive experiences, we needed to know each other better, but in many cases, we were strangers. We might pass each other in the hallway and nod, but that was frequently the extent of our interactions.

The heads of the three departments invited staff to come together for a series of trainings. The goal of the initial meeting was more like a mixer, designed to support the creation of personal connections. There were about fifty staff members in attendance. One activity was based on the notion of *speed dating*.[7] We sat on gallery stools, face-to-face, in two concentric circles. The organizers had devised some general "get to know you" questions: "What do you like to do when you are not working at the museum? "What is your favorite spot in the museum and why?" "What are three things I should know about you?" When a question was read aloud, you had a minute each to share your response with the person across from you. At the end of the exchange, the participant in the outside circle moved over one seat so that everyone now had a new partner. Then another conversation prompt was given. Over the course of thirty minutes everyone had met and spoken with twelve staff members outside their department. We learned a bit about each other and connected on a personal level. This simple activity had enormous benefits. When an educator brought a group into a gallery, there was now a good chance that they knew a bit about the security staff member stationed there and could better collaborate to provide a supportive learning environment. The feedback from this training indicated that it had a positive impact on intradepartment communications. Subsequent trainings focused on specific characteristics of different audiences so that all staff could be aware of what to expect and how to be welcoming and accommodating to visitors with various needs. Museums can demonstrate their commitment to inclusivity by providing all museum staff, especially those dealing directly with the public, with training that ensures a safe welcoming environment for all visitors.

Each of the following chapters focuses on a specific museum audience and describes how a museum educator has adapted the Tour Planning Template to provide an optimized learning experience. These are, of course, examples and by no means the full extent of possibilities. Getting a better understanding of your audience(s) doesn't come without work. It takes time to build personal connections and open communication, but when educators "use both universal design as well as object-centered and inquiry-based learning, the result often-times is accessible programs for all visitors."[8]

NOTES

1. Lynn D. Dierking and John H. Falk, 2013, *The Museum Experience Revisited*, Left Coast Press, Inc., Walnut Creek, CA, 47–49.
2. Melanie Adsit, Adapting the Tour Plan Template for Students on the Autism Spectrum, see chapter 16.
3. Sharon Vatsky, 2008, *From Concept to Conference: Developing a Distance Learning Lesson Using a Museum/School Collaboration Model*, published in Video Conferencing Technology in K-12 Instruction: Best Practices and Trends, Information Science Reference, Hershey, New York, 70–79.
4. Karen Bergman, Adapting the Tour Planning Template for Adults Who are Blind or Have Low Vision, see chapter 20.
5. The UDL Guidelines, https://udlguidelines.cast.org/.
6. About Universal Design for Learning, https://www.cast.org/impact/universal -design-for-learning-udl.
7. Merriam Webster dictionary defines speed dating as "an event at which each participant converses individually with all the prospective partners for a few minutes in order to select those with whom dates are desired," https://www.merriam-webster .com/dictionary/speed%20dating.
8. Katie Stringer, "Accessibility in Museum Education: Universal Design, Programs, and Real Solutions for Museums," in *The Manual of Museum Learning*, Second Edition, ed. Brad King and Barry Lord, (Lanham, MD: Rowman and Littlefield, 2016), 186.

15

Adapting the Tour Planning Template for School Tours

Queena Ko

For many people, their first memory of stepping inside a museum harkens back to a class field trip. This creates a major assignment for the museum educator to provide a positive experience that may be recalled in the future. Whenever someone suggests, "How about visiting a museum?" either a positive experience will come to mind, where ideas were accepted, respected, and acknowledged, or a negative one that recalls boredom and discomfort. This is a significant responsibility that requires planning, communication, flexibility, and facilitation.

My preparation for a one-hour long school tour follows a modified Tour Planning Template and includes three to four tour stops and one long art-making activity. At the first artwork, I focus on inquiry-based discussion, the second or third artwork reinforces the theme with an art-making activity, and the final artwork applies what we have learned to a larger context. As a youth educator, I know that even within an established outline, there are many unpredictable dynamics at play.

Although educators receive some information about the group in advance of a tour, circumstances vary from class to class. Every field trip also involves factors that cannot be controlled. Despite one's best planning, an educator cannot anticipate late buses, traffic delays, or the urgent need for a bathroom or snack break. A seasoned educator knows that flexibility is a priority when planning for K–12 audiences. Not all surprises can be anticipated, but there are steps the museum educator can take during the preparation process to (hopefully) avoid some of them. If possible, it is advantageous to communicate with the teacher who has scheduled the tour in via email, phone call, or Zoom in advance of the visit. Here's an example of a previsit email that an educator might send:

Subject: Your Guided Visit at the Whitney Museum on 4/26/22
Dear Teacher,

I am the educator who will be facilitating your Guided Visit at The Whitney Museum of American Art on Tuesday, April 26, 10:00 a.m.–11:00 a.m. During a school group tour, we typically look closely at 3–4 artworks in the galleries and engage in guided discussion and hands-on drawing or writing activities along the way.

- To plan for your visit, please email me back with responses to the following questions:
- Are there any artworks, artists, or specific ties to your curriculum that you are hoping to touch upon during our tour?
- Do any of your students have mobility issues, sensory challenges, or accessibility needs that I should be aware of in advance of the tour?
- What teaching strategies work best to engage all learners in your class?

Looking forward,
School Programs Educator
Whitney Museum of American Art

These are excerpts taken from teacher replies to a previsit email:

We have been studying the wire sculpture work of [Alexander] Calder . . . the class has even created their own wire "Circus" so it would be nice to see that work. My class is a fourth grade gifted and talented class who really loves narrative stories. The class overall is very well-behaved and very inquisitive. They ask tons of questions and sometimes talk over each other. In terms of management, it really helps to remind them to be mindful of not interrupting adults or other students in the middle [of] talking and to wait until an appropriate pause to ask their questions or make a statement. Generally, in the classroom we raise hands to respond. It might also be helpful and necessary in the galleries.

This is my sophomore computer graphics class. We have spent a lot of time on the design of type, logos, and photo manipulation . . . we will look at how artists support their message through layout, color, and impact. It's ok if we do not touch much on this, though. To be honest, I am open to whichever pieces you think will spark some deep looking and critical thinking. Open ended [sic] questions are of course a great way for them to engage, but I find that when I leave them too broad, they often take tangents. So, I will follow up broad questions with a more pointed one. I have a few students that feel like they really cannot draw and can shut down if that is the only option, so I often incorporate list making of observations as well as sketching or very low stakes drawing."

As you can see from these two detailed responses, an educator can learn a lot about the students, curriculum content, and the teacher's classroom management style from a brief reply to a previsit email. Previsit emails are a great way to learn about the personality of the group so that the educator can adapt the tour plan accordingly.

On the day of the visit, it's a good idea to check in again with the adults that accompany the group. A simple assessment question that I often ask teachers, chaperones, and students upon a school group's arrival is, "How was your journey to the museum?" The answer to this question tells me a lot about the group and their current physical, mental, and emotional states. If the group says they have just spent three hours stuck in traffic on a school bus, it might be wise to start by gathering the group in a large circle to synchronize with a few breathing or mindfulness exercises before starting in on tour content. Group management is critical to the success of your museum tour!

Spending ten to fifteen minutes at the beginning of the tour to check in, introduce yourself calmly, and center your group makes a huge difference. This step is especially important for kindergarten and first grade groups, as these young learners are museum newcomers. For this age group, I often spend extra time introducing museum rules in a patient and reassuring manner. Instead of "Don't touch the artwork!" an educator can say, "Please remember to keep your hands to yourself as artworks are fragile." Museum educators are always aware of their dual responsibility to protect the group, and to protect the artworks.

Facilitation of school group tours at the Whitney Museum of American Art are guided by four themes that school groups can select when booking a guided visit at the museum: Artist as Observer, Artist as Storyteller, Artist as Experimenter, and Artist as Critic. The rationale behind these artistcentric themes is included as a mission statement on the Whitney website: "Artists' ideas are at the center of Whitney School Programs. We ask K–12 students to think like artists and challenge them to be critical observers of their world. Through the careful examination of artists' ideas, materials, and processes, students consider the multi-faceted role that artists play in American culture and society."[1] The theme provides the framework that guides educators in object selection and in formulating open-ended questions. Take the theme "Artist as Observer" for example. When assigned this theme, a logical choice is to build a tour around the skill of observation, to ask students to consider how artists look closely to represent what they see. A subtheme used frequently at the Whitney is "Artist as Observer: Places" and a successful object sequence with this subtheme might include artworks like Charles Demuth's *My Egypt* (1927), which depicts an industrial grain elevator from Demuth's hometown in Lancaster, Pennsylvania, or Archibald John Motley Jr.'s *Getting' Religion* (1948), a painting of a night scene in the South Side neighborhood of Chicago, where the artist lived when he was a child.[2] Open-ended questions that would accompany this theme might include: "What do you see in this place?" "How did the artist choose to depict this place?" "Why do you think the artist might have chosen to portray this place, in this way?" The museum visit can be an ideal place for students to practice using artworks as primary sources, citing visual evidence, and elaborating on their thinking process. The "Artist as . . ." framework gives students the opportunity to think critically and explore ideas from an artist's point of view.

In recent years, schools have had increased emphasis on social and emotional learning (SEL) in classrooms as a way to cultivate knowledge, skills, and attitudes crucial to student development. According to CASEL, the Collaborative for Academic, Social, and Emotional Learning, core competencies in SEL include self-awareness and social awareness.[3] The four "Artist as . . . " themes in the context of a gallery tour encourages students to articulate their own observations, while gaining a broad understanding of different perspectives by listening to their classmates' ideas. The process of inquiry also allows for comparisons and contrasts between artworks created over a span of time periods, cultures, and historical, social, and political contexts. Putting yourself in another's shoes is an important exercise in empathy, giving young learners the agency to maintain a positive dynamic in the classroom and take responsibility for creating equitable and caring communities.

The theme "Artist as Storyteller" allows ample room for students to practice observation and exercise their imaginations. I'll often modify the Tour Planning Template by adding a more in-depth advance organizer that introduces key terms and builds shared understanding of the theme. This strategy is particularly successful for elementary school groups (grades K–6) as it creates opportunities to connect the museum visit to classroom content that students are already familiar with: "Our theme for today is storytelling. All stories have characters. What is a character? Can you think of a character you know from a book, movie, or cartoon? Artists can also include characters in drawings and paintings. In our artworks today, let's look closely at the characters to see what we can discover about the story." A thoughtful advance organizer lays the foundation for artwork sequencing and inquiry that supports deeper personal connections with the theme.

The mixed media work *Portals* by Njideka Akunyili Crosby (2016) is a great first stop on a storytelling tour as it allows for in-depth character study.[4] The artwork is a seventeen-foot-long diptych that includes a larger-than-life painted self-portrait of the artist sitting at a table next to collaged photographs of her family and figures from her place of birth in Nigeria. Discussions at this artwork can begin by asking students to focus on the central figure and physically embody what they see: "What do you notice about this character?" "What do you notice about the pose or facial expression?" "Can you copy the pose or facial expression with your own face and body?" "Based on what we see, what do you think this person might be thinking or feeling?""

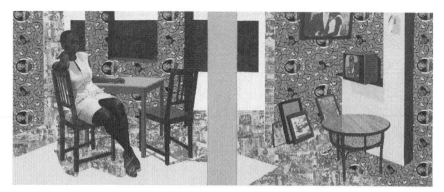

Figure 15.1 Njideka Akunyili Crosby (b. 1983) *Portals*, 2016. Acrylic, solvent transfer, collage of fabric and paper, and colored pencil on paper. Overall: 83 5/8 × 206 in. (212.4 × 523.2 cm). Purchase, with funds from the Jacques and Natasha Gelman Foundation. Inv.: 2016.93a-b. *Digital image Whitney Museum of American Art / Licensed by Scala © Njideka Akunyili Crosby*

Incorporating movement activities in inquiry helps this age group ground their experiences in their own bodies. This tour theme can be adapted for middle school and high school students (grades 6–12). For middle school youth exploring self-expression and identity, sharing information about the artist's biography or artistic process can be a great point of connection. With *Portals*, I often tell students that Akunyili Crosby emigrated from Nigeria to the United States when she was sixteen years old, and that she incorporated images from her family albums into the painting using a photo transfer process. As a follow-up the educator might ask students how this biographical information relates to the title of the work, which references the dual identities that Akunyili holds, and her desire for her artwork to act as a portal to another time and place. This inquiry sequence can also be modified for high school students by broadening the context to include information about the permanent collection at the Whitney Museum of American Art, which includes over twenty-five thousand works created by more than 3,700 American artists during the twentieth and twenty-first centuries. Akunyili Crosby's work (which was purchased by the Whitney in 2016) reflects the ethos of new acquisitions and the museum's interest in broadening the range of voices and stories represented in American art.

Despite the flexibility of the "Artist as . . ." framework, not every theme can be adapted for every age group. "Artist as Critic" is a theme most suited for high school or college-age students who are ready to grapple with the role of critique within art. Critique challenges students to be curious, construct their own meaning, and express their own point of view. This framework is especially compatible with special exhibitions such as the Whitney Biennial shows with a historical focus such as *An Incomplete History of Protest: Selections from the Whitney's Collection, 1940-2017* (August 18, 2017–August 27, 2018). This exhibition of artworks from the Whitney's collection examined how "artists from the 1940s to the present have confronted the political and social issues of their day."[5] Included in this exhibition was Melvin Edwards's sculptural installation *Pyramid Up and Down Pyramid*, originally constructed in 1969 and refabricated in 2017.[6] Edwards's piece is ideal for exploring critique in the context of a museum. *Pyramid Up and Down Pyramid* is a room-sized installation of barbed wire extending between a dividing partition wall and the adjoining gallery walls. The piece is divided into two: on one side of the partition wall, lengths of stretched barbed wire visually create steps that ascend, on the other, steps that descend. I've had students question the choice of barbed wire: Is it meant to protect? Or imprison? And the symbolism of displaying an inverted pyramid: What goes up must come down? But most meaningfully, students often reflect on the significance of this installation in the context of the date of when it was originally made. Melvin Edwards, an African American artist born in Houston, Texas, created this work shortly after he moved to New York City in 1967 and exhibited the work during a solo exhibition at the Whitney Museum in the 1970s. This was a time when very few Black artists were exhibited in major museums, and has resonance now, as artists of color continue to be underrepresented by museum institutions. To structure a conversation that allows for complexity and nuance within critique, I modify my tour plan to include the opportunity for individual exploration, choice, and discovery alongside focused inquiry. I invite students to individually look at this artwork and experience the installation from different angles. This time alone gives students the space to independently formulate ideas about the work before being asked to share back their observations with the group in a *low-stakes* environment. An example of a low-stakes share-back is an activity using sticky notes on which students jot down brief, anonymous thoughts. This activity invites all students in the group to participate, especially those that are less comfortable sharing aloud. Sticky notes are also useful for collective reflection. They can be organized communally on the gallery floor, moved around, and rearranged.

"Artist as Critic" is a useful framework for encouraging students to contemplate various perspectives and practice peer debate and discussion. I often end these in-depth inquiries by asking students to reconsider the artwork. Do we notice anything new after spending time observing and discussing? By asking students to articulate how initial impressions of the artwork might have shifted, they are more likely to remember and recognize that opinions can change over time. Art can serve as a catalyst for changing perspectives about history, politics, gender, and race in American life and culture.

The need for flexibility as a youth educator applies to in-person, virtual, and hybrid museum tours. In 2020, despite the ongoing COVID-19 pandemic, the Whitney Museum of American Art taught nineteen thousand students from 158 different schools, completing 970 online lessons. Virtual tours make the museum more accessible to students across the nation and globe, and for schools without the resources for in-person group visits to a museum. A standard virtual museum tour for school groups at the Whitney in 2022 was hosted on Zoom or Google Meet, and includes slides prepared on Google Slides, PowerPoint, PDF, or other digital platforms that enable the addition of text and images. Although online lessons at the Whitney follow the same structure of inquiry discussion paired with multimodal activities, I'll typically pare down my Tour Planning Template to include two or three works of art, as opposed to the three or four works of art that we might view in the museum galleries. I also tend to decrease the number of open-ended questions, as it takes more time to lead a group discussion online. Virtual tours also offer more flexibility for incorporating first-hand sources such as quotes and artist interviews, along with supplemental materials available online including artist websites, museum audio guides, or videos of exhibition walkthroughs. The slideshow format makes it easy for educators to include an artist headshot and studio process images. Including more contextual information provides students with a better sense of how, where, and when the artist lived, offering a more holistic view (of the *who*, *what*, *when*, *where*, and *why*) of the artwork. The disadvantage of virtual tours is that students aren't able to experience the materiality of the artwork, especially the dimensions and scale, and how it looks within the space in which it is shown. This is particularly evident with sculpture and installation artworks. With these mediums, it is important to incorporate gallery views, as well as 360-degree and detail images of the artwork.

Remote teaching comes with its own set of unexpected challenges. Students may be individually logging on from home, or on personal devices without camera or microphone access. Students may be gathered together in the classroom and can encounter technical difficulties including audio feedback or inadequate image resolution. In preparation for virtual tours, it's a good strategy to be as clear and concise as possible during the tour planning phase. It's helpful to write out inquiry questions in advance of the tour and to include preplanned questions as text on certain slides. When adding contextual information in the form of text or multimedia files, including animated transitions so not all of the information on the slide is visible at once, creates visual difference and incorporates natural pauses when pacing an inquiry sequence. I've also found that successful virtual activities are often ones that encourage students to get up and look away from the screen. For example, if we are looking at a painting depicting a city landscape, I might ask students to look outside their window and tell me what they see before comparing their point of view to the perspective of the artist or artwork. Or when looking at an abstract sculpture, I might ask students to stand up and move their bodies to create a curved line, or an organic shape, or a balanced pose, before returning to the screen to investigate the composition of the three-dimensional form.

Creating social connections and interactions online can be especially difficult. On a virtual platform, there is less room to build organic conversation. Using physical cues that students can easily repeat on their own video cameras such as "respond with a thumbs up if you agree" or "point to the screen if you see what I see" helps to create shared meaning making throughout a virtual tour. Lastly, a virtual tour allows for a wider selection of artists and artworks. Educators are no longer limited by the artworks currently on view in the galleries; they have free reign to include lesser-known artworks in museum's collections, even those that are fragile and rarely shown. Virtual tours provide an opportunity for educators to select artists that have been historically marginalized and excluded and introduce young learners to a greater diversity of voices that might resonate with their own.

The Tour Planning Template is a valuable tool for reflection in both gallery and online tours. When reflecting on a lesson that falls flat, I usually conclude that it isn't because I haven't prepared enough, but because I wasn't flexible enough with my tour planning. I might have tried to include too many artworks, spent too long on an inquiry, or chosen artworks that were too similar. The written tour plan helps me evaluate what might have gone wrong and how I can improve. The Tour Planning Template is a document that I can tweak and adjust to learn from my mistakes. Sometimes an artwork just doesn't lead to a rich discussion. That's okay! There is no need to scrap my whole tour. I can just replace that artwork with a better fit for the sequence. Sometimes I discover a better way to phrase questions for an in-depth inquiry, or a clearer way to deliver instructions for a complex activity. That's an opportunity to go back to my tour plan and add notes on how I can continually make my teaching better. As a youth educator, I use my tour plan to continually grow, learn, and adapt for our young audiences.

A flexible, supportive educator can provide the space for students to share their ideas in a new setting. It is a big responsibility for a museum educator to create affirming experiences for young audiences. Through thoughtful tour planning, an educator can cultivate an environment in which students feel welcomed and create positive memories that have lasting impact beyond the duration of the museum tour.

NOTES

1. Whitney Museum of American Art, https://whitney.org/education/k-12/school-programs/themes.
2. Whitney Museum of American Art, https://whitney.org/collection/works/635; Whitney Museum of American Art, https://whitney.org/collection/works/47460.
3. What is the CASEL Framework? https://casel.org/fundamentals-of-sel/what-is-the-casel-framework/.
4. Njideka Akunyili Crosby, *Portals*, 2016, Whitney Museum of American Art, https://whitney.org/collection/works/48677.
5. *An Incomplete History of Protest: Selections from the Whitney's Collection, 1940–2017, Whitney Museum of American Art,* https://whitney.org/exhibitions/an-incomplete-history-of-protest#exhibition-about.
6. Melvin Edwards, https://www.alexandergray.com/news-events/melvin-edwards105.

16

Adapting the Tour Planning Template for Students on the Autism Spectrum

Melanie Adsit and Jackie Delamatre

Museum education programs provide opportunities for inspiration, creativity, and expression for all learners. However, for students on the autism spectrum, the museum itself can create unexpected barriers. Museums can be crowded, noisy, and full of unfamiliar stimuli, which can be disconcerting, if not overwhelming. Open-ended questions used by museum educators can sometimes be too "wide open" for more concrete thinkers. The strategies outlined in this chapter can be used to devise inclusive museum programs for all learners but can be particularly helpful when working with students with autism. By creating museum experiences that are designed to accommodate a wide range of learners, educators can remove barriers that limit access and offer learning opportunities for all.

The Guggenheim for All program began in 2008 at the request of Guggenheim educators who taught school programs at the museum. Many classes that included students on the autism spectrum were visiting the museum on school tours, and the museum's education team felt the need to learn more in order to best engage these students and help them feel welcome and comfortable during their visit. The following strategies were devised from action research in the museum and feedback from students, teachers, and parents in the local autism community.[1]

When designing museum programs, it is useful to keep in mind that students with autism often

- benefit from clear lesson structures and clear communication;
- are most comfortable when given advance notice of what to expect with no surprises;
- have specific sensory needs;
- benefit from support in socialization and communication; and
- have interests and strengths that are powerful motivators.

Museum tours can maximize engagement for students on the spectrum by tapping into their natural interests and strengths through student-centered discussions and multimodal activities. Many students on the spectrum have passionate interests, abilities, and knowledge to share. The inquiry-based and student-centered practices used by museum educators can give these students a chance to share these skills with teachers and classmates and let their abilities shine in the museum.

PLANNING A MUSEUM EXPERIENCE FOR STUDENTS ON THE AUTISM SPECTRUM

Education programs in the museum often are "one and done" field trips or family events. Museum educators may have limited or no contact with students prior to the program and only very basic knowledge of their specific needs and abilities. While this provides a challenge for museum educators working with any population, this poses additional challenges when crafting programs for students on the spectrum who have an incredibly diverse range of skills and abilities and very specific individual educational and behavioral needs. Museum educators are charged with the difficult task of creating a program that is appropriate and meaningful for students despite their limited knowledge of the individuals themselves.

To address this, museum educators should try to connect with students and/or teachers/caregivers in advance of the museum visit. The goals of this previsit connection are

- to help students, teachers, and parents become comfortable with and prepared for what is going to happen in the museum; and
- to allow museum educators an opportunity to gather information on the needs and abilities of individual participants.

These contact points can take many forms. A school tour can benefit from an in-person previsit or a virtual visit in the classroom in advance of the museum visit. If this is not possible, an email exchange with teachers or a pre-program survey distributed to program participants can also be used to gather this information.

Connecting before the museum visit helps museum educators and students establish familiarity and rapport and set the groundwork for success in the galleries. This can be achieved via telephone or email, but communication before a museum program can be tricky. Teachers may not be available to discuss their students or may be short on time. There may be privacy restrictions on what information can be provided. Information may not always be accurate, and teachers or parents may have little experience predicting how the children will respond in a museum environment.

Ideally, the museum educator(s) will be able to visit the classroom or conduct a virtual lesson with students before their trip to the museum. This previsit is a chance for museum educators to meet participants in a familiar environment and prepare them for what to expect on their visit by:

- sharing concrete information about the museum, where it is located, how long it will take to get there, and what to expect during the experience; and
- conducting a brief activity or guided discussion that is similar in structure to what students will do in the museum. This gives students a chance to practice new processes and think about themes or ideas without the challenges presented by an unfamiliar space.

Museum educators should work to establish rapport with students and be very observant during this previsit lesson. They can learn much about students' communication styles, preferences, dislikes, and relationships that will prove useful during the museum visit. One educator recalled a meeting a student in their previsit who had a particular interest in elevators. She made certain to share information about the museum's elevators during the previsit and incorporate a ride on the museum's elevator into the tour. This served as a powerful motivator for the student to visit a new and unfamiliar place and engage with the building's architecture in a way that aligned with his interests. In another instance, a previsit questionnaire alerted the museum educators that one student was incredibly scared of dogs, even in images or reproduction. The educator was then able to modify their tour, and remove a segment that included a sculpture of a realistic dog! By finding out information about student interests and stressors beforehand, educators can leverage these interests and avoid unpleasant surprises while in the museum.

If it is not possible to arrange a previsit lesson, the educator can share information about the museum with the group and gather information about the students via email, phone, or survey.

The museum can send its *social narrative* (or social story) in the form of a PDF or slide show.[2] A social narrative is a document that describes what students can expect during the museum visit using photographs, symbols, and simple text. The social narrative shares important details about how students will travel to the museum, the museum environment, the agenda, and museum norms and conventions, like not touching the art objects or sitting on the floor or a stool while learning. For students with autism, receiving this detailed information beforehand can be a critical part of helping them feel comfortable in a new space.

To gather information before the museum visit, teachers or parents can be contacted by telephone, email, or survey. Consider asking versions of the following questions:

- How do your students prefer to communicate? Do they use communication boards or other augmentative and alternative communication devices?
- Do your students have specific sensory sensitivities that we should know about? If so, what strategies or accommodations do you use to address them?
- What strategies are used in your classroom to support attention and engagement (e.g., fidget tools, call-and-response techniques, sketchbooks for doodling, repetition/reinforcement of ideas)?[3]
- What excites and engages your students? Do they have interests that would be helpful for us to know about?
- What are your students' dislikes or fears? Are there any triggers or topics to avoid?

FACILITATING A MUSEUM EXPERIENCE FOR STUDENTS WITH AUTISM

After careful planning and communication, the students are finally at the museum. How the museum educator manages and responds to the group will determine the success of the experience. During the museum visit, consider the following:

- **Give clear expectations for behavior.** Museum rules should be stated simply, clearly, and positively. Instead of saying students shouldn't run, tell them they should walk slowly and carefully. Instead of saying, "No touching," tell students instead, "We do not touch the art in the museum. There are certain things that we can touch. I will show you what they are. If you have a question whether something can be touched, please ask."
- **Offer support for communication, attention, or sensory needs.** Make communication boards, fidget tools, floorplans, touch objects, noise-canceling headphones, or stools available to students who need them. Allow students to choose which supports they would prefer. Make all supports available to all students to avoid singling out specific individuals.
- **Provide ample notice and clear expectations before shifts and transitions.** Let students know a minute or so ahead of time that you will be moving to a new gallery or transitioning to a new object or activity. For example, an educator might say, "In one minute we are going to finish this drawing and walk together to another space. Take one more minute to finish up your drawing."

- **Help students stay regulated.** Despite the educator's best efforts, students may feel overwhelmed. If a student is having difficulty, the educator should try to understand what is causing the issue and remove the offending stimulus or provide a calming alternative. Some options include fidget tools, sketchbooks for doodling/drawing, rhythmic movement, or deep breathing exercises. Often, the best strategy is to help the student leave the challenging environment and get to a sensory break area. The museum should have a safe, quiet, sensory-friendly space available that students can visit as needed. They can return to the group when they are ready.

The introduction to a museum tour is another chance for educators to learn about students' communication styles, preferences, strengths, dislikes, discomforts, and responses to the new space. During the introduction, it is essential for the museum educator to remain flexible about their plan for the lesson and notice where adjustments should be made. Key parts of the introduction include:

- **Share names and greetings.** Welcoming each student individually and providing name tags is important so that students can be addressed by name. The educator should interact briefly with each student to learn more about them and how they communicate and process information. Guggenheim educators often introduce themselves to each student and ask each student to share or spell their name for the name tag. This could also take the form of a brainstorm or icebreaker related to the lesson (e.g., asking students to share or say their name and their favorite color). During this interaction, educators can learn about each students' communication style and how much processing time they may need. The educator can then adjust the conversation accordingly throughout the tour.
- **Share a visual schedule.** A visual schedule is a representation of what will happen during the museum visit. It should be shared and reviewed with the group at the outset to help students know what to expect. Visual schedules reduce anxiety by providing a sense of control and knowledge of what comes next. This schedule does not need to include many specific details but rather provide a basic overview of the activities. It can include a simple floorplan to show the tour route or bullet points that provide this information in both short text and pictures.
- **Identify sensory friendly spaces.** Let teachers and students know that there are sensory-friendly spaces available if they need to "take a break." Show teachers and students how to get to these spaces if needed and allow students the option to leave the tour with an adult and rejoin the group when they are ready. Sensory maps can be provided to help people unfamiliar with the museum navigate these spaces.
- **Reassess the plan.** Educators should plan more options for tour stops and multimodal activities than needed so that they can select which will work

best. These initial conversations can provide important clues to which art-works and activities are best suited for the group.

SUPPORTING PARTICIPATION IN GUIDED DISCUSSION

In museum education lessons, educators pose a series of open-ended questions that ask students to practice the skills of observation and interpretation. These open-ended questions are intended to help students construct knowledge by making connections between what they see and their prior knowledge while building shared meanings with each other. Successful discussions with students with autism use many of the same methods including validating multiple interpretations and encouraging students to elaborate on their comments. However, what works for some students may not work for all. Students with autism may need to engage in discussion using varied modalities. To support students during a guided discussion, educators can do the following:

- **Connect to students' interests and experiences to make the discussion relevant.** Use concrete examples to explain abstract concepts. Provide examples from life, television shows, movies, and books that students know and enjoy.
- **Share developmentally appropriate information.** Do not make assumptions about students' intellectual or cognitive abilities based on their communication or behavior styles. Many students with autism who do not speak have excellent receptive language skills and cognitive ability. However, it is common for adults to "speak down" to them based on inaccurate assumptions. One student told his museum educator, "I like this museum because I'm a teenager and here you treat me like I'm a teenager."
- **Use a mix of open-ended and closed-ended questions.** The educator might pose the question, "What do you see?" and follow-up with a more specific question such as "What colors do you see?" Closed-ended questions with an opportunity for kinesthetic response like "Point to a circle that you see" can allow a wider range of students to participate. Another useful strategy is to "take a vote" or ask for a show of hands, such as, "How many of you think this person looks sad? Raise your hand if you do." This approach supports participation by students who may not communicate using spoken language.
- **Include touch objects and props** to increase interest and reinforce concepts. Having a piece of marble to touch when looking at a marble sculpture or a touchable example of an object depicted in a painting can help students connect to works of art through tactile senses.
- **Allow for "think time".** After posing a question, allow three to five seconds before repeating or restating the question. Instead of calling on the first person whose hand goes up, wait for others and explain why you are waiting. This can help support students who may need more time to process information.

Figure 16.1. Museum educator Jodi Messina leads a Guggenheim for All school program. After discussing the painting *Several Circles*, 1926, by Vasily Kandinsky, students take turns placing circles to create a collaborative collage. *Filip Wolak © Solomon R. Guggenheim Foundation, New York. All Rights Reserved.*

- **Model complex thought processes.** Provide a concrete example of an answer to a complex question and be explicit about how you got there. For example, after asking, "What would you like to do if you could visit the place we see in this painting?" the educator might say, "If I could visit this place, I'd walk over the bridge in the lower right corner and go for a swim in the river because it looks like a hot day. What would you do?"
- **Present written information and instructions both verbally and visually**. Make sure that visuals and text are clear, legible, and concise. Use a clear sans serif font such as Arial, in at least 14-point black. Use simple pictures or illustrations whenever possible.
- **Offer multiple ways for students to communicate their ideas.** They may want to express their thoughts through a thumbs up or thumbs down, a show of hands, pointing, or through writing, drawing, or movement. Students can match what they see in a work of art to images on a communication board, a scavenger hunt, or a reproduction.
- **Use sentence starters to scaffold communication.** If asking, "What animals do you see?" some students may benefit from being provided with the start of the sentence: "I see . . . "

ADAPTING MULTIMODAL ACTIVITIES

One of the key elements of museum education is hands-on exploration. Many students construct knowledge best when they can engage with ideas and objects kinesthetically, rather than just verbally. Students with autism may benefit from hands-on learning even more than neurotypical students but may not have previous experience with art materials and techniques. To support students during hands-on activities, educators can

- **Develop activities that can be personalized** and contextualized to students' lives. Allow students to make their own choices regarding content and change or adapt the project based on their interests.
- **Provide both visual and verbal instructions** for an activity and break the instructions down into a clear step-by-step process. Break steps into manageable "chunks" rather than giving all steps at one time. Move on to the next "chunk" when the previous one has been completed. Provide written instructions that can be revisited throughout the lesson to help students remember the steps in the process.
- **Model or demonstrate the activity** rather than just explaining. Show each step in the process with a brief demonstration. Be sure to provide opportunities for students to ask questions about the process before jumping in.
- **Allow students to participate through varied modalities** including visual, auditory, kinesthetic. Some students may prefer to connect to artworks through movement rather than through speech. Kinesthetic activities can include taking the pose of a figure in a painting, finding a shape in an artwork and duplicating it with their hands, or pretending to hold a paintbrush to imagine how the artist made the brushstrokes. These activities encourage close looking and focus while allowing for communication and expression that is not dependent on spoken language.
- Allow students to explore and experiment with materials for a short time before asking them to create. This can help them to get comfortable with unfamiliar materials before beginning their creative work.
- **Use visual timers or time checks** during artmaking sessions so that students are not surprised when they end. Remind students that they can continue to work on the activity after the tour is completed.

CONCLUSIONS AND FOLLOW-UP

The end of the museum visit is a time to review what happened and give everyone a chance to share what they learned, liked, or are proud of. As always, the educator should keep the conversation clear and specific. They should provide opportunities for students to see each other's work. Encourage students to comment on each other's work by sharing something they liked or a question they have about another student's work.

Allow time to share and reflect on what students have made. This is an opportunity for socialization and communication. Students who may not communicate readily through spoken language may be inspired to share about something they created and are proud of. Students can be prompted with a sentence starter such as, "I drew a . . ." Learning is an ongoing process and what students take away from a museum experience evolves even after they have left the museum. As museum researchers John Falk and Lynn Dierking have stated,

> Ironically, understanding learning from museums requires understanding not only what happens while visitors are within the walls of the museum, but equally important, what happens to these people after they leave. Subsequent experiences, some reinforcing and others not, dramatically contribute to what someone ultimately learns from the museum.[4]

Following up on a museum visit can be just as important as the visit itself. For students on the autism spectrum, this can help provide time needed to process new experiences. Ideally, museum educators can provide a follow up visit to the classroom to engage in reflection and artmaking. This visit is another opportunity to reinforce ideas and themes and to ask students to reflect about what they learned, when back in the relatively quiet, familiar classroom setting. Alternatively, the museum can provide postvisit activities for classroom teachers to implement at school or follow-up activities for students to take home. This can extend engagement and learning beyond the trip itself.

Despite the sensory and social difficulties the museum environment may present, museum tours can be adjusted to meet the needs and support the abilities of students on the autism spectrum. Educators working with school groups will undoubtedly encounter students with autism in their classes but may not feel that they have the knowledge or training to successfully support these students. It is important for educators to remember that the inclusive practices used to support students on the spectrum can enhance participation for a wide range of learners. By providing clear structure and expectations, supporting student needs, and working to leverage students' own interests and abilities, educators can create a supportive and welcoming environment for not only students on the autism spectrum, but for all students visiting the museum.

NOTES

1. Much of the content for this chapter is adapted from the Guggenheim for All toolkit, a free online digital resource for museums wishing to create or refine their offerings for visitors with autism and sensory sensitivities.   To access the GFA toolkit, please visit https://www.guggenheim.org/accessibility/guggenheim-for-all/toolkit.
2. Social stories are based on the work of Carol Gray. To learn more about social stories, visit https://carolgraysocialstories.com. The Guggenheim's social narrative can be found at visiting The Guggenheim: A social narrative for visiting the museum, https://www.guggenheim.org/wp-content/uploads/2022/02/guggenheim-for-all-social-narrative-in-person-visits-20220216.pdf.

3. Fidget tools are small hand-held objects that can help with focus, attention, calming, and active listening.
4. J. H. Falk and L. D. Dierking (2018). *Learning from Museums*. Lanham, MD: Rowman & Littlefield, 66.

17

Adapting the Tour Planning Template for Social-Emotional Learning

Lisa Mazzola

I am visiting a classroom of New York City high school students. Our attention is focused on a projected image of a young girl seated on a chair. The work titled *Almerisa, Asylum Center, Leiden, The Netherlands, March 14, 1994* (see figure 17.1), is by the Dutch artist Rineke Dijkstra. I have just asked them to "tell me what you notice." There is a long pause, the room is silent, but just when I begin to lose hope that a brave student will venture a first response, I notice that a lone hand is raised. "I have something to say, but if I tell you, it will give it all away." I assure the student that their observations and thoughts are welcome. The student goes on. "She is sad and isolated, her feet dangling on a chair that is too big for her, she doesn't feel firmly on the ground." I ask others what they think, and comments start popcorning around the room. These students have a lot to say about how the subject, a six-year-old girl, might be feeling and why. Their comments demonstrate the power and potential that art has to invite us to consider the feelings and emotions of others and the universal need for connection and belonging.

My journey to investigate this potential began in April 2019. Through a con-fluence of events, I found myself with two colleagues in New Delhi, India, attend-ing the launch of SEE (Social, Emotional, and Ethical) Learning, a K–12 education program developed by Emory University's Center for Contemplative Science and Compassion-Based Ethics, in collaboration with His Holiness, the Dalai Lama. My colleagues and I had a shared interest in exploring how we could use artworks and our museum-based teaching strategies as tools for social-emo-tional learning (SEL) with the K–12 teachers and students we work with at The Museum of Modern Art (MoMA). Attending this conference provided the op-

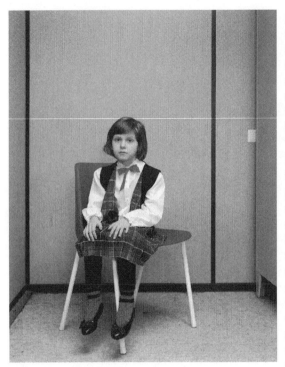

Figure 17.1. Rineke Dijkstra
Almerisa, Asylum Center Leiden, Leiden, the
Netherlands, March 14, 1994 Chromogenic print
37 x 29-1/2 in. / 94 x 75 cm *Courtesy of the artist and
Marian Goodman Gallery Copyright: Rineke Dijkstra*

portunity to gain insights and hear the experiences of leaders in the field. One of the sessions was led by a group of K–12 teachers and students who shared their experiences with the SEE Learning curriculum. The students came from humble backgrounds, yet they spoke of their experience with grace and confidence. It was such an engaging presentation that I wanted to learn more. I noticed that the same students were hosting a poster session about the work at their school, located in a village just outside Dharamasala. I decided to pay them a visit. As part of their display, they included student artworks that were connected to SEE Learning lessons. The students and their principal took great pride in sharing the work and talking about their process. It was a heartfelt moment, but what struck me most about our conversation was how much it mirrored the types of conversations we have in the galleries at MoMA. The ideas we shared, the vocabulary we used were all in alignment with my museum teaching experience, with the added layer of students sharing the thoughts and emotions that arose for them. I found myself feeling a sense of empathy and connection with these young people I had just met. It got me thinking about how the work we do as museum educators could support this type of learning.[1]

What I didn't know was that less than a year later, a series of global events would increase the need and interest in developing resilience, empathy, and compassion among other core SEL skills. The coronavirus pandemic required all of us to develop strategies for teaching and learning in new and unprecedented ways. And for K–12 schools it led to a renewed focus on SEL. I felt grateful to have begun this journey, but suddenly the stakes felt even higher.

Schools, homes, and community organizations such as museums can all play a role in supporting the well-being of people of all ages. The topic of art and health was at the forefront during the pandemic. Museum educator and researcher, Jackie Armstrong writes about engaging with artworks and how the creative process can impact well-being. "The ability to be in front of an artwork and notice the details allows one to be in the moment and aligns with the same mindfulness skills that can help manage stress. The desire to express oneself creatively relates to a need to feel seen, heard, and understood. Together these things support resilience and emotional well-being, and help people feel more in control, even during times of chaos and uncertainty."[2] What I am drawn to in SEL is its ability to integrate wellness techniques for the students' overall well-being, but also how it can be used as a means to create a sense of community during your time together. Although the benefits of SEL and SEL and the arts are well researched, we wanted to further educate ourselves before moving forward. We turned to leaders in the field including Daniel Golemann, whose seminal work on emotional intelligence has informed SEL curriculum worldwide. Goleman helped establish the Collaborative for Academic, Social, and Emotional Learning (CASEL). CASEL defines SEL as "the process through which all young people and adults acquire and apply the knowledge, skills, and attitudes to develop healthy identities, manage emotions and achieve personal and collective goals, feel and show empathy for others, establish and maintain supportive relationships, and make responsible and caring decisions."[3] The CASEL framework helped us understand the relationship between the five core competencies within the different contexts we live in. These competencies are:

- **Self-Awareness:** The abilities to understand one's own emotions, thoughts, and values and how they influence behavior across contexts.
- **Social Awareness:** The abilities to understand the perspectives of and empathize with others, including those from diverse backgrounds, cultures, and contexts.
- **Self-Management:** The abilities to manage one's emotions, thoughts, and behaviors effectively in different situations and to achieve goals and aspirations.
- **Relationship Skills:** The abilities to establish and maintain healthy and supportive relationships and to effectively navigate settings with diverse individuals and groups.
- **Responsible Decision-Making:** The abilities to make caring and constructive choices about personal behavior and social interactions across diverse situations.[4]

The MoMA school and teacher programs team revisited the SEE Learning curriculum, which affirmed what we learned from CASEL. SEE Learning is centered around three distinct aspects, what they term "dimensions":

self-awareness, compassion, and engagement.[5] They delve deeply into each one as it relates to the domains of the personal, social, and system. The two methodologies are similar, but each provides a unique perspective. Both models emphasize the interconnectedness of the competencies across domains and contexts and include resources and strategies to support teachers in developing their SEL skills.

Facilitating SEL-focused art engagements require self-awareness. Planning and preparation are key to a successful lesson, and even more so in this context. The better prepared you feel, the more present and grounded you will likely be on the day of your lesson. When working with a K–12 group, speaking with the cooperating teacher in advance of lesson planning is standard practice. Only a few years ago the main request from teachers who were bringing students to MoMA was to connect the visit with a curriculum area (e.g., English language learning or social studies). There is a growing awareness and interest in using the museum visit as a platform for SEL. In some cases, it is the individual teacher's interest in supporting student well-being. In others, school leaders ask teachers to integrate SEL into their instruction. This is all helpful for museum educators who seek partners in this work. As with any lesson, it is important to listen to the teacher's goals and have a shared understanding of how the lesson will unfold. This conversation invites the teacher to share their SEL goals (if they have them) and ask specific questions about their students. If the teacher confides that their students have a hard time expressing themselves or their emotions verbally, but are very expressive when writing or drawing, then my planning will take that into account and include opportunities for students to draw and write. The conversation is your opportunity to get an understanding of the teacher's needs regarding SEL, while also setting boundaries.

If you are working with a K-12 group that has not specifically outlined SEL skills as a goal, but you would like to include them, plan to have a conversation with the teacher to let them know how you are planning to weave SEL into the lesson. You don't have to share SEL specific language but could simply state that in addition to the goals you have both outlined, you would like to support students' well-being by including moments of slow looking and quiet contemplation. Or convey that through guided close looking of three to four artworks students will have the opportunity to engage in and/or deepen compassion practices by considering the perspectives of others."

Following my conversation with the teacher, I begin my lesson planning by asking myself a series of questions. This process is consistent with my usual approach, with the addition of the following questions:

- What SEL skills are most relevant for this class?
- How can I connect these SEL skills to lesson content?
- What artwork(s) will best support these goals and be accessible to the students?

- How can questions and activities be structured to connect to SEL skills?
- How will I ensure that students feel safe to share?
- How will I need to adjust my questioning and facilitation strategies?

The answers to these questions guide my thinking and provide a way to scaffold my ideas. The skills I focus on are determined in conversation with the cooperating teacher, but I also want to integrate the SEL skills into a broader theme that will also connect with the artworks. For example: A ubiquitous and accessible museum tour theme is *Identity*. It is broad enough to allow students to consider a range of relevant topics (cultural, personal, social, geographic) that align with school curriculum, access students' lived experiences, and are also pervasive within visual art. One example of a theme that I teach to combine art and SEL is: "Art and Identity: How do visual artists consider the perspectives of others in their work?" My lesson goals reflect the SEL competencies in relation to the theme. For example, students will:

- Identify aspects of personal and social identity in themselves and others
- Consider the perspectives of, and empathize with others, including those from diverse backgrounds, cultures, and contexts.
- Connect to and understand their own emotions and thoughts
- Recognize strengths in others

Other examples of themes that can connect art and SEL are: [6]

- Color and memory
- Connecting with community
- Depicting hope
- Reflecting on everyday moments

Each of these themes can be an independent focus, or as in the previous example, can connect with another concept depending on the needs and goals of the group. Some examples of ways to adjust the themes to meet these needs include:

- Artist Process: Color and memory
- Art and Social Issues: Connecting with communities
- Artist as Advocate: Depicting hope
- Art and Society: Reflecting on everyday moments

In planning an SEL focused gallery experience, my process closely parallels the methodology described in this book. Following the Tour Planning Template, I decide on a theme, and then narrow down the artwork selections. It is important that sufficient information is available about the selected works, so I favor works that have supporting information, in the artist' voice whenever possible. This research phase can be time consuming, but it is also crucial. It is important to be true to the intent of the work and not assign thoughts and beliefs that are not intrinsic to the artist's intent. Another consideration is developmental appropriateness. The artwork must be accessible to the students and ideally will not give rise to any negative emotions. How a work is perceived is not entirely within our control, as we all have our own subjective view, but I do my best when making choices, and in some cases will share them with the teacher ahead of time.

An example of an artwork that works well with the theme of *Art and Identity* and *Art and SEL* is mentioned at the beginning of this chapter. Dutch artist Rineke Dijkstra first photographed Almerisa Sehric, a Bosnian girl whose family had relocated to Amsterdam as part of a project documenting refugee children. The first photograph was taken when Almerisa was six years old. She continued to photograph her, making eight photographs over eleven years. The series documents Almerisa's development from childhood through adolescence and into adulthood. As part of the lesson, I would share information about both the artist and her subject including this quote from the artist. "I first met her in 1995, in an Asylum Seeker Center in Leiden, the Netherlands, where I was working on a series of portraits of children of refugees. I met her parents, and they told me that they were refugees from Bosnia, where they escaped from the war, and they just arrived in Holland two weeks earlier after they roamed around in Europe for about six months. I was photographing another kid, and Almerisa was watching me as I was photographing this other kid, and suddenly she started to cry, and I ask her, well, what's wrong, what's the matter? And she said, I also want to be photographed. And I said, well, do you have a nice dress? And she said, yes, sure. And so, 20 minutes later she came back in this outfit. And I think because she has just cried before, she looked a bit sad and silent, which I think makes this picture special. One thing I really like in the pictures of Almerisa, if you look at the third picture, the moment that she gets grounded in the Netherlands, her feet also reach the ground. And you can see how Almerisa is changing, transforming from a child into a young woman in the way she dresses, but also in her attitude, you can see how she's adapting to West European culture." [7]

Through this series Dijkstra conveys both the vulnerabilities and strengths of Almerisa, providing a strong connection to the goals for the lesson. Students are often able to connect with this artwork without any information, just using their observation skills. Stating things like, "In the first photograph, she (Almerisa) is sitting on a chair with her feet dangling and she doesn't look stable." And "In the later photograph, the chair is getting sturdier, and she looks more stable, like she is growing up." This is just one example of an artwork, there are many others I could choose to support this lesson.

To help meet the needs of students who might feel less comfortable sharing verbally, I might include a writing activity. Providing printed reproductions of the series with comic book "thought bubbles" added creates an opportunity for the students to take Almerisa's perspective. Students then write what they believe Almerisa might be thinking, using visual evidence to support their interpretations.

Once the object selections are made, I can consider their sequence, and develop questions and activities. I will keep referencing the tour planning template, to make sure I am in alignment with my goals. I often go back and review my lesson plan multiple times to make sure I am on track. Then walk the actual path with my lesson in hand, playing it out in my mind. I find that walking the tour route, processing, and observing the artworks is both meditative and grounding. At the end of this process, I can tick all the boxes and move forward to facilitating the lesson knowing that I have done my best planning.

Figure 17.2. Rineke Dijkstra
Almerisa, Zoetermeer, the Netherlands, January 4, 2008 Chromogenic print 37 x 29-1/2 in. / 94 x 75 cm
Courtesy of the artist and Marian Goodman Gallery
Copyright: Rineke Dijkstra

As previously mentioned, a critical part of engaging in SEL practices is being conscious of your own mindset. Gallery teaching requires the facilitator to be present and self-aware, even more so when you plan to engage others in inquiry around topics that relate to emotional states. To prepare myself, I like to take part in a grounding exercise right before I teach. I seek out a quiet space where I can spend five to ten minutes sitting still, focusing on nothing but my breath. This enables me to take stock of how I am feeling on that day. Am I feeling excited but nervous? Do I have any other thoughts that I am struggling with? It also gives me the space to remind myself of my intention for the lesson, which is to support the students (and teachers), and create an environment where they can learn, connect, and have fun. A grounding exercise is a subtle but powerful tool. It may seem awkward or strange at first, but over time this ritual becomes familiar and reassuring.

To be most effective, I like to create a safe and nurturing space for the lesson. You can set some basic guidelines to create an environment where students authentically engage with each other and can have conversations around sensitive topics with honesty, respect, and generosity. You can ask students to give you a "thumbs up" to show they agree. I also provide options for participation by letting them know, "If something doesn't feel right for you, take a moment to check-in with yourself and then rejoin the conversation." Or "You can sit quietly in front of the artwork with your eyes open, or closed, whatever feels best to you."

To introduce the theme and the ideas we will explore through the artworks, I often include an ice breaker that serves as a form of resourcing, which is a technique used to help regulate the nervous system. I ask the students to, "Remember a time when someone was kind to you. What are some of the words they said or things they did? How did that make you feel?" I will give students the opportunity to share, but it is not required. After eliciting some responses and sharing more about what we will do during our time together, I will also let them know that if at any point during the lesson something doesn't feel right, they can always return to this memory of kindness they experienced.

When students are sharing thoughts and emotions, it is important that they feel heard and understood. I make sure to use clarifying language when I restate their responses such as, What I am hearing is ...? or "Tell me if I have this right?" Throughout the lesson I allow more time between questions to give students (and myself) extra time to consider the questions and response of others. Consider ways to share your perspective appropriately and thoughtfully with students to connect with them and model empathic listening (SEL). "Have you had an experience like Almerisa's where you felt unsure or vulnerable? Having these thoughts and feelings is what connects us all as humans." Leave the students with something that inspires positive thinking by ending the lesson with an optimistic closure. "What is one thing about your visit that you are excited to share with a friend or family member?" Inviting students to consider their emotions can be very therapeutic but is not therapy, nor is it your role to be a therapist.

The same planning process can be used for virtual experiences, but the content and facilitation need to be adapted to the constraints of remote learning. It is, of course, imperative that works be selected that can be easily understood on a computer monitor or tablet. If you are working with a group of students, it is likely that some may choose to have their cameras off, or you are being projected onto a classroom Smartboard. In either case, you will want to prepare yourself for not being able to see students' facial expressions which we often rely upon to gauge their level of engagement or comfort. You can use the chat feature to accommodate students who are less comfortable speaking aloud. It can be a little tricky to follow everything at once, but you can allow extra time to pause and read through the chat.

Following the lesson, it is important to allow time for reflection. Similar to my preparation for most tours, I like to sit quietly for a moment, gather myself and check in on how I am feeling. I often find that my adrenaline and cortisol levels are elevated after teaching, so I like to have a drink of water, sit for a moment, and connect with myself. Students will often share their reactions to the lesson during your time together, so it is rare that you will have no sense of how things went, but you can journal or turn to a colleague to share your experience for feedback. I have had experiences where I felt the lesson I have taught was not successful–usually because the students were not as talkative as I had hoped. Over the years I have learned that you can't assume that students are not connecting or learning just because they're not talking.

If you do encounter a troubling moment, as we all have, it is important to allow yourself time to process, consider alternative solutions, and then move on with greater insight and understanding. The impact of your social emotional learning strategies might not be immediately evident, but as with all museum teaching, have faith in the process and approach it with a sense of curiosity and joy.

NOTES

1. I was joined by my MoMA colleagues Francis Estrada and Larissa Raphael. Together we develop SEL based lessons and resources at MoMA. I am grateful for their collaboration and collegiality.
2. Jackie Armstrong, Artful Practices for Wellbeing (MoMA Magazine, May 18, 20020). https://www.moma.org/magazine/articles/322.
3. Collaborative for Academic, Social, and Emotional Learning (CASEL). Fundamentals of SEL. https://casel.org/fundamentals-of-sel/.
4. Collaborative for Academic, Social, and Emotional Learning (CASEL). What is the CASEL Framework? https://casel.org/fundamentals-of-sel/what-is-the-casel-framework/.
5. The SEE Learning Companion (Emory University, 2019). Chapter 2, page 19
6. Francis Estrada, Lisa Mazzola, Larissa Raphael. The Museum of Modern Art. Weekly Lessons. https://www.moma.org/research-and-learning/teachers/weekly-lessons#art-and-social-emotional-learning.
7. Audio from the playlist Collection 1970s–Today, https://www.moma.org/collection/works/100526.

18

Adapting the Tour Planning Template for Family Tours

Emily Rivlin-Nadler

Families live in routines. The best museum experiences allow a family to break away from those routines, encounter something totally new, explore and learn together, and see one another in a new light.

The modern, or contemporary, art museum may not be the first destination that comes to mind for a family outing. An art museum can seem like a daunting place to visit with children: there are no dinosaurs, the "no touching" rule needs to be enforced, and changing exhibitions make it hard to know what to expect when visiting. Although it might not be the first destination considered for a family field trip, it can be a satisfying and important place to visit and participating in a guided experience can address many of these concerns (although, not usually the absence of dinosaurs).

When we think about *family audiences*, we usually envision an intergenerational group that comes to the museum together and are already well-known to one another. Most families operate in highly defined roles and know one another in very set ways: X is the baby of the family, T is the bossy older child, Y is the playful grandfather, Q is the busy mother. When I plan museum experiences for these audiences, I like to find ways to change and expand set family dynamics.

To plan a family experience using the tour planning tools outlined in this book, I try to ground every decision with a single goal in mind. The primary goal for the tour is focused on the participants feeling comfortable and empowered to make personal connections to one another and the art and artists on view. The Family has come to the museum today, primarily, to spend *time together*. Toward that end my planning includes the following considerations:

- Everyone in the family group will participate. Although some families come to the museum with the expectation that the adults will watch the kids have an experience, the tour is designed for *all* family members to contribute.
- This is a level learning field. My goal is that everyone in the group will encounter something novel and learn something new.
- *Everyone* in the group will have the chance to *learn from and about one another* in a new way.
- This experience will provide tools that build comfort in exploring art as a group even after our time together ends.

THEME AND QUESTIONS

I lean toward themes that invite connections to lived experiences. This allows the group to share new ideas and observations with one another. Almost any theme can support this goal with the right set of questions. For example, for a tour with the theme *Place*, I might begin with a more representational work and start with observation questions so that we build an agreed sense of what the depicted place is like: What do you see? What might this place sound like? Where in this picture might you want to hang out for a little while? Why?

By beginning with these general observation questions, I am also modeling the types of questions adults can ask their kids in front of any work of art. The rich conversation that most often follows from even these open-ended questions demonstrates that you do not need a deep well of art history knowledge to start a conversation about art. Kids are ready to jump in, look closely, and share their thoughts.

The discussion builds toward a related question that invites sharing within the family group. The question invites families to build on shared experiences they have had together or introduce memories they might have otherwise never recalled or discussed:

- Describe your favorite view out a window of your home and how it changes throughout the year.
- What is something special about your home that you think no one else has noticed?
- Talk to someone in your family about the most crowded place you've ever been
- Where is your favorite place to go for quiet time?

OBJECT SELECTION

Sometimes a well-meaning museum curator will warn me that an upcoming exhibit might not be the best fit for family audiences. I go into that meeting expecting the artworks to be filled with sex, drugs, and rock and roll. Instead, I find that the works are just not immediately understandable because of a range of attributes such as being conceptual, abstract, made from nontraditional materials, complex in their meaning, or created by artists who are not house-hold names.

These types of works are actually the best for family programs because they level the playing field for deep engagement and learning. Both the adults and kids in the family enter the experience knowing exactly the same amount about the works, and that might be . . . nothing.

When considering a work that might feel challenging for some, connecting the work to the tour theme can provide a "toe-hold," or orientation point, to use while looking together. Just knowing that we will talk about this work in relation to the theme provides a path along what might otherwise feel like sheer cliff-side. Knowing the theme can help family members feel more grounded in their looking and more comfortable in approaching the unfamiliar.

This comfort-building is mostly provided for the benefit of the adults in the group. Kids are far more open to the unfamiliar (as long as they feel safe and supported). It is not uncommon for the youngest members of the group to take the lead and surprise and teach the adults when viewing unfamiliar works.

Although it may seem counterintuitive, I can include artworks with more challenging subject matter in planning a family experience than when planning a school tour. The fact that children are together with their caregivers and not in a school setting allows for the inclusion of works that touch on potentially sensitive issues. When planning for school groups, we need to navigate around content that parents might not want their children to encounter without them. In a family setting, each family can make the decision about how much they wish to engage with any aspect of the work in a more intimate and thought-ful way. To leave space for that to happen, I include opportunities for more independent conversations and activity time for families to work more privately.

INFORMATION

In considering what information might be useful to include, I think about what would be meaningful in the context of the overall goal of making personal connections to members of their family and to the artist whose work we are viewing. It is a reminder that artists are human beings, communicating across space and time through their art. It can sometimes seem like the art on view in a museum dropped from the sky or that the artists chosen are superhuman in some way. Sharing a photo of the artist (especially at work), a description of their process, and relevant quotes can help provide an understanding of them as people.

The planning process includes research on the artwork and the artist, dates, history, anecdotes, art movements, etc. I keep all of this in my "back pocket," knowing that I will need at least some of these facts for side conversations with the adults in the group during art-making activities or while traveling between tour stops. I find that it is best to wait until someone asks a question before introducing information. These questions demonstrate an interest in learning more and focus on what is individually meaningful. Front loading information to the entire group early in the conversation only creates a distraction.

Information given at the right moment can bring a hesitant adult more fully on board with the experience and confirm their previous knowledge. "Yes! You are right, Édouard Vuillard *is* depicting Paris in this work".[1] The addition of information can also complicate a knee-jerk or dismissive response to an artwork. To the comment, "This just looks like child's play" the educator can disclose that "the Japanese artists of the Gutai movement of the fifties and sixties were focusing on playful ways of making art. They were responding to the military rule of their country during World War II, so 'play' became an important statement about personal freedom."[2]

MULTIMODAL ACTIVITIES

Family tours are activity heavy. Intergenerational groups are, by definition, demographically diverse. In a single group you are working with a wide variety of ages, abilities, and comfort levels. Hands-on activities in a variety of modalities allow for engagement that moves past the verbal back and forth of inquiry, which is not everyone's strength.

As discussed in chapter 8, activities can be introduced at any point during the tour and can even replace a close-looking or reflection question. Information about process can also be introduced in a more hands-on way through activities that feature how the artist works or materials they have used.

For example, before we see even one work of art, I may challenge participants to experiment with an element of the artist's process. Some challenge prompts might be:

- Draw a place that is important to you from memory.
- Create a composition using only straight lines.
- Draw someone in your group in motion.

Once participants have puzzled through a challenge as an artist themselves, they can compare their experience to the "solutions" the artist on view is showing. It starts our conversation with a bit more experience and layered understanding.

Activities are also important to family tours because they support and highlight the goals of being together and learning from one another. All activities feature a collaborative element, where family groups are either directly working together or building on what each are doing. Creating activities that invite adult engagement helps to set the expectation that this is a moment for everyone in the group to work together. It is not a time where the kids participate, and the adults wander around the museum.

When invited into an art-making activity, many adults will shut down and claim, "Oh no thanks, I'm not an artist." Since we might be taking people outside their art-making comfort zone, I include warmup activities that involve "deskilling" so that no one feels that they need to be an accomplished artist to participate. Deskilling activities require no previous experience for full partic-ipation and deliberately eliminate tools that some adults might be proficient with. Examples are taking away scissors and creating torn paper collages; intro-ducing *blind* gesture or contour drawings where you are not allowed to look at your paper; drawing with your nondominant hand; or using an unconventional material or process. Focusing on the process and not the product opens up a more inclusive space for intergenerational play and discovery.

VIRTUAL FAMILY TOURS

Spending time with family has taken on new meanings during the COVID-19 pandemic. As a parent of two young children, I know that while the quantity of time spent together skyrocketed, the quality was very different. I was rarely *just* with my kids. I was with them and working, or with them and doubling as their classroom teacher. Many of us were also isolated and cut off from our extended families. From my own experience, I could envision how virtual fam-ily programs could provide unique time together beyond another video call or while multitasking.

The family tour model transferred surprisingly well to the virtual space. Families that were together in the same physical space were able to talk and collaborate in the same ways that they could at the museum. However, the real gift of the virtual tours was the ability to connect families who were not able to be together physically. Despite being oceans apart, grandparents were able to join their children and grandchildren for these shared experiences. Cousins on oppo-site sides of the country would make faces at each other from their Zoom screens.

The thematically-based tour structure held up well as a virtual tour frame-work with some adjustments. At the museum, I usually plan three or four tour stops that each include looking, discussion, and activities. I quickly learned that virtual tours worked better when we separated the looking and discussion segments from the activities. Working within a theme we would spend the first half of our time gathering inspiration through conversation about related artworks and artists in the museum's collection. An extended amount of time was then available for participants to create their own artistic responses. During these experiences I could highlight more works of art than at the mu-seum, usually between five and eight pieces.

Everyone joining the experience from their own home allowed for a higher level of personal connection than we can achieve in the museum space. People could bring personal objects into their art making. During a tour with the theme of *home* we thought about our homes as a combined portrait of the people who live there. I invited participants to create a portrait of a loved one using objects from their home inspired by the artist Dahn Vo.[3] The results were immensely personal. One nine-year-old from California created an homage to his grand-mother who joined the program from England. His creation was made from the actual books they were reading "together" during quarantine, layered with children's books that had belonged to his mom and read across generations. The emotional response of the participants to this project made a colleague of mine joke that we should measure the success of all programs by how many grandmothers we can make "happy cry." It was exciting to see that we could build space for real connections, even outside the museum.

Whether at the museum or at home, encountering the unexpected with our familiar family members allows for these magical moments to broaden our understanding of each other and our shared world. A well-designed guided tour experience is crucial because it gives families that unique (and fun) time together while also offering them the tools to continue their lifelong conversation with one another through art.

NOTES

1. Édouard Vuillard, 1909–1910. *Place Vintimille.* Distemper on brown Kraft paper, mounted to canvas, two panels, left panel: 78 3/4 x 27 9/16 inches (200.1 x 70 cm); right panel: 78 13/16 x 27 9/16 inches (200.2 x 70 cm), Solomon R. Guggenheim Museum, NY, Thannhauser Collection, Gift, Justin K. Thannhauser, 1978, https://www.guggenheim.org/artwork/4166.
2. *Gutai: Splendid Playground,* February 15–May 8, 2013, Solomon R. Guggenheim Museum, NY, https://www.guggenheim.org/exhibition/gutai-splendid-playground.
3. *Dahn Vo: Take My Breath Away*, February 9–May 9, 2018, Solomon R. Guggenheim Museum, NY, https://www.guggenheim.org/exhibition/danh-vo.

19

Adapting the Tour Planning Template for Virtual Tours for Adults

Sharon Vatsky

The reality of the COVID-19 pandemic dawned on all of us differently. One day we were going about our daily routines and then "poof," everything changed in an instant. In early March 2020, I sat in an administrative meeting at the Guggenheim where it was announced that there was a possibility that all New York City museums might be required to shut down. I thought, "I cannot even imagine that" and then very soon after we were all instructed to pack up and head home.

Although, initially, we believed the shutdown would last only a few weeks, the education department at the Guggenheim Museum began to look for ways to morph and reimagine its offerings. Other museums across the nation and the world were also scrambling to figure out next steps. Within weeks our programs moved from in-person to the virtual realm, and I was tasked with facilitating virtual adult programming for our varied audiences.

Fortunately, I had previous experience teaching online. For several years I had been working with a nonprofit organization, Selfhelp, whose mission is "helping older adults and vulnerable populations live with independence and dignity."[1] Since 2010, Selfhelp's acclaimed Virtual Senior Center (VSC) has provided virtual interactive, real-time classes where older adults can hear, see, and talk with each other. Over forty classes are offered each week ranging from art history to current events to museum tours to weight training. This groundbreaking program effectively reduces social isolation by creating social networks and connecting participants to each other and to the larger world.

One of my favorite program titles is, "You Can't Sleep, I Can't Sleep Either!" Of course, this program offers tips for getting and staying asleep, but more importantly it provides a supportive forum for talking and connecting.

I had been offering exhibition-related talks to VSC members for several years, and had gained some familiarity with facilitating online programs, but providing virtual programming during 2020 became a major part of my responsibilities. Since the museum's members could not visit in person, virtual programs became a way of retaining membership and staying in touch. Virtual programs became the primary point of connection between the museum and its multiple audiences.

After an extended education department-wide meeting we issued a press release that outlined the guiding principles that would inform our programming efforts:

THE GUGGENHEIM EDUCATION PROGRAMMING GOES DIGITAL IN RESPONSE TO COVID-19

Like many arts and cultural institutions, the Guggenheim has had to temporarily close its doors as a result of the global pandemic. However, we remain committed to providing shared experiences that harness the transformative power of art. We listened to our community and heard the following three priorities as a call to action:

1. Help people find connection through art during this time of isolation
2. Support educators and parents across the globe
3. Sustain the vibrant programs that serve our existing audiences[2]

Museums across the nation and the world were asking the same question. How will we be able to stay in touch with our audiences? What we soon discovered was that, in addition to those who had made in-person visits, there were totally new audiences out there. To our initial surprise, people were joining our programs from across the globe and from (literally) around the corner. Some had heard about the Guggenheim and its extensive art collection but had never visited. Others fondly remembered their in-person visits and were eager, in this time of isolation, to be reconnected with a familiar institution.

One of the basic tenents of the Guggenheim Museum's in-person experiences is that they are interactive. Observation, discussion, and participation are hallmarks. This philosophy was the starting point for all our remote offerings as well. As we experimented with various approaches for facilitating participatory online programs, we began to devise strategies that would support participatory virtual tours. Several weeks into the launch of our digital programs we were receiving positive responses from our target audiences.

> It was a nice way to stay engaged with art and to stay connected with the Guggenheim during an otherwise socially isolated time. Being "with" people from all over the country, and world, was remarkable! Although I've been to the Guggenheim and taken the architecture tour in person, I still learned many new things.

> The program was presented in an informative and professional way. There was time for comments and questions, which was much appreciated. It was like being at the Guggenheim with a personal guide to help you to further understand the artists intent and additionally their background which informed much of their work. I look forward to attending other programs in the future.

> I was a bit nervous about the participatory element: How would it be managed with such a large group? Would I be put on the spot? But it was such an enriching part of the session! And so different from the other online programs I have attended which have basically been lecture-based.

> The presentation was excellent and there was a good balance between host and participant conversation. I enjoyed the comparisons and extra bits of information that were provided. I've been missing the museum space, so this was a great way to feel connected again![3]

Of course, these are some of the most glowing reviews, but they do point toward some of the factors that support positive outcomes. Many align perfectly with planning and facilitating in-person experiences, but some are quite different.

PLANNING

With a few adjustments, the Tour Planning Template, the primary organizing theme of this book outlined in chapter 3, also works for planning online experiences. Virtual experiences are still organized around themes. In fact, selecting the program theme becomes even more important when the theme also serves as the program title and a marketing tool. Trying to keep the themes relevant to the current moment such as, *Working from Home: Artists Who Found Inspiration in Their Immediate Environment*, used our home-based work situations to relate content to current events. *The Guggenheim Museum Through the Eyes of Cartoonists, Illustrators and Artists*, depended on the popularity of programs related to the museum's unique architecture while adding a new perspective and a bit of fun.

Planning virtual tours provides the opportunity to include works from the entire collection, not only those that are on view in the galleries.[4] These expanded artwork options result in programs that explore a wide variety of topics from a series titled *Global Themes* that includes international artists exploring political and social issues, to *A Taste of the Guggenheim* that focuses on works that have food as subject matter.

Some educators have adapted quickly to the virtual realm, others have found online teaching less satisfying, but all agree that the planning process for virtual programs takes more time. When working in-person, in front of real works of art, considering three works during an hour-long tour seems comfortable, but a compelling virtual tour cannot not rely on only three images. Participants are looking at a reproduction on a computer screen, a picture of a picture of a picture, and it cannot be considered in the same way as an in-person encounter with a work of art. A virtual program requires additional contextual information in visual form. Adding an *installation shot* showing the artwork as it is seen when on view in the museum, an image of the artist, artwork details, a short video of the artist speaking, all add layers of context that partially compensate for not being there in person. Most importantly it is imperative to use best possible reproduction(s) of the artwork positioned as large as possible on the slide template. When posing an open-ended question, it is easier for the group to contemplate and respond to the question when it is written out on a slide. So, presenting a single work of art usually includes several supporting slides. Researching and crafting these presentations takes time.

The good news is that facilitating virtual programs that focus on visual art actually hit a learning sweet spot. If your presentation consists mainly of images, and you will be supporting it with a narrative and discussion, according to Richard Mayer, one of the most influential educational researchers, optimal learning occurs when visual and verbal materials are presented together simultaneously. It has been scientifically proven that we can learn more deeply from words and pictures together than we can from just words alone.[5]

Mayer's research provides several principles that can be applied to designing presentations to support learning. Many seem like common sense, yet I have seen so many presentations that fail to heed his findings. He advocates for:

- Focusing the presentation on the essential material and eliminating everything else that be a could distraction (such as decorative templates, background music, or needless animations). With the wealth of presentation templates available it may seem tempting to select something jazzy and colorful. Unfortunately, this may distract learners from what you want them to concentrate on.
- Minimizing the use of text during narrated presentations. When the educator includes text on-screen, while they are talking, they risk overwhelming their learners with trying to resolve the differences between paying attention to the spoken word or the printed text. Narrating over a slide with printed text creates a cognitive dissonance that can interfere with learning.

- Using a more relaxed tone and less formal language during an online lesson can positively impact learning. Thus, educators should use an approachable, conversational style. When facilitating online programs Mayer encourages the use of contractions as well as first and second person ("I," "you," "we," "our," etc.).
- Including an image of the educator as a "talking head" during a multimedia presentation doesn't *necessarily* improve learning outcomes. You don't add value by showing your face during a narrated presentation. Consider including your face only when there are no words or pictures on the screen, or when you wish to speak to or engage with the group directly.[6]

Nothing can replace in-person encounters with works of art but looking at art on a computer monitor can have its rewards. In 2020, Kent Monkman's monumental paintings *Welcoming the Newcomers* (2019) and *Resurgence of the People* (2019) were on view in the Great Hall of the Metropolitan Museum of Art.[7] These enormous, complicated works were hung high on the walls at the busy crossroads of the bustling museum. I visited them several times, pausing and looking up while visitors whizzed past. The paintings were fascinating, but there was so much to take in and process.

During Connecting Collections 2021, which was held virtually, Zev Slurzberg, the managing educator for School and Educator Programs at the Met, focused on these works during an online inquiry. As Zev led us through a series of open-ended questions, with the paintings on the computer monitor in front of me, I was able to make sense of the narrative and relationship of the figures in a way that hadn't happen during the in-person visit. It wasn't the same as seeing the original artwork, but viewing the work on a computer monitor allowed me to look at and process the imagery in a slower, more thoughtful way.

FACILITATION

A STABLE INTERNET CONNECTION

While teaching my first few virtual programs, I would occasionally get a pop-up on my monitor informing me that my internet connection was unstable, and I was even bounced off a Zoom call in the middle of a program . . . yikes! I was able to rejoin, but that experience prompted me to contact my cable company. My cable connection was now my lifeline to the outside world.

If you participate in online programs, you realize that you are not the only one who has experienced technical difficulties. I am always secretly reassured when I see others experiencing technical glitches, even some high-profile digital gurus. If you are not a digital native, you tend to blame yourself for all technical problems. "Did *I* do something to cause this?" I have however noticed that those raised with newer technologies blame the technology, not themselves, when something goes awry. That said, reliable equipment is important.

SAY HELLO

Many programs begin with a PowerPoint slide on the screen, but if you are facilitating a participatory program, it is more welcoming to begin by introducing yourself, welcoming everyone, and providing a brief overview of your plan. For many adult audiences (but not all), asking participants to type their first name and where they are calling in from in the chat, provides an initial personal connection and something to do as you wait for the whole group to join.

Remind the group that they are muted, but that you welcome their questions. I usually say, "If your question pertains to a specific slide, unmute yourself and ask your question. If the question is more general, we can address it at the end of the talk. Feel free to use the chat so that we can see your questions and comments."

CAMERAS ON, CAMERA OFF

As an educator, I feel reassured when I can see that there are actual people, rather than black rectangles, on the other end. I prefer that people have their cameras on, but people may be joining from places they prefer we don't see. They may be driving, or have childcare responsibilities, or just not want to be on camera. I learned early not to insist that cameras be turned on. A colleague was facilitating a program. One of the participants who had her camera off chimed in with a comment. The facilitator asked, "Can you put your camera on?" The participant answered, "I am at the hospital in labor, so I really prefer to keep my camera off." That one interaction was enough to teach me not to ask that all cameras be turned on. I recently joined a virtual talk where the facilitator greeted the group by saying, "We are delighted you are joining us. Feel free to have your camera on or off. Do whatever works for you." I immediately felt at ease.

THE CHAT FEATURE IS YOUR FRIEND

In the virtual realm, asking participants to unmute themselves to respond directly to a posed question is frequently met by silence. In the galleries you may be able to rely on eye contact or body language to identify who is okay with speaking. In the virtual realm those cues are unavailable. Fortunately, if you are teaching on Zoom, the chat feature provides a way for the group to respond to your questions and even to one another.

The chat scaffolds participation by providing a safe intermediate step. After asking the group to respond to an open-ended question by typing a response in the chat, scroll down the responses, acknowledge them—even reading some, or all of them, aloud. When and if you come to a response that is more ambiguous, you might say, "I see you mentioned_____, can you tell us a bit more about that?" The chat has become the bridge between participant and facilitator, between typing a response and speaking to the group. Monitoring the chat during a presentation takes a bit of experience. If you are fortunate enough to have someone assisting you, they can alert you to the activity in the chat, but most of the time most of us are flying solo.

There are many other applications that will allow participants to share their responses including, Zoom Whiteboard, Jamboard, Miro, MURAL, and Padlet, but some thought needs to go into matching the application with the audience. If the application requires a level of technical know-how that is outside the participant's comfort level, you will need to devote significant time during your presentation to introducing those skills, or you will lose some participants along the way.

THE RIGHT AMOUNT OF PARTICIPATION

Adults who join live virtual museum programming may or may not want to be active participants in the program. Some will keep their cameras off; that's fine. Some want to listen in silently or multitask, for example making dinner while learning something new. Another segment will want the immediacy, involvement, and interaction that a live event offers. This is truly free choice learning. Each virtual program for adults will include a range of expectations and levels of interest in participation. It is the educator's job to encourage dialogue from those who are eager to engage by genuinely welcoming responses, while also signaling that it's fine to hang back and listen in.

Occasionally, I have encountered online sessions where a single individual dominates the conversation and prevents the discussion from being inclusive. The nature of online programs requires that the educator take more of the lead than in in-person experiences. Intervals for participation need to be more deliberately inserted into the tour plan. For me, during an in-person experience I would estimate that 80 percent of the input is from the group. Although I do not have an empirical measurement, I would guess that participation is cut at least in half for most virtual experiences. The medium is different and requires an adjustment for what is right and comfortable in this realm of communication.

A while back I joined an online session hoping to familiarize myself with something new. I had intended to hang back, listen in, and in that way learn more about the topic. A few minutes into the program we were given a scenario and put into small group breakout rooms for ten minutes to come up with some possible solutions. Not what I had bargained for. I can almost hear what went on in the planning session. "We want this program to be *really* interactive. Let's get them working in small groups right away." I pressed *leave session*. Breakout rooms can be a great tool, allowing participants to work in small groups or even have *pair share* conversations, but these tools are best utilized after some trust, familiarity, and shared goals have been established.

MULTIMODAL ACTIVITIES

Many multimodal activities discussed in chapter 8 can be adapted for the digital realm. To avoid disrupting the flow of the lesson, be sure to let participants know in advance if they will need to have any materials, like paper and pencils, close by. Although not all multimodal activities can be adapted for virtual facilitation, many can, with writing and drawing activities being the easiest to adapt for virtual teaching.

Some participants report that they enjoy participating in multimodal activities even more on remote platforms because of the privacy it affords. The drawing and writing you do in response to an artwork is yours alone unless you choose to share it with the group.

The Guggenheim Museum recently reported that virtual courses that focus on artmaking are now their most popular adult offerings and virtual programs for youth also highlight "hands-on opportunities for children to explore the museum from home with their parents and caregivers."[8]

FREE OR FEE?

According to Culture Track, an organization dedicated to researching the most pressing challenges facing cultural institutions, the majority of virtual participants, nearly 70 percent, value free access to digital content. However, there is a smaller percentage who are willing to pay for programming.[9] That group mentioned multiple factors that influence their willingness to pay for programming including

- excitement about the topic/theme;
- interest in an individual artist or speaker/presenter;
- reasonable pricing; and
- live programming with comfortable participation methods.

The message seems to be that it is not impossible to monetize virtual programming, but if you plan to charge, make it special: more intimate, more topical, more compelling.

Before wrapping up this chapter I want to share a program structure that deviates from the Tour Planning Template. In 2020, when we found ourselves in quarantine at home and separated from one another, it occurred to me that although we might be isolated from the people we most care about, we were now surrounded nearly 24/7 by the objects that were most near and dear to us. As discussed in chapter 7 (The Role of Information), I had frequently introduced groups to the physical and contextual resonance of art objects through an activity that I referred to as an "Object Exchange." During the height of the COVID-19 pandemic, the familiar objects around us became all the more important. I wanted to find a more democratic and inclusive format and so the lesson Objects Tell Stories (see below), which prioritizes objects imbued with emotions and history, evolved and was facilitated with teens, colleagues, students, older adults, and families. Once you do it, its value is self-evident. Give it a try.

OBJECTS TELL STORIES

Program Description: An hour-long program that enables us to share objects we hold dear while connecting to one another.

Museum educators work from the premise that objects hold significant and multiple meanings. This applies to master works by famous artists, heirlooms passed down from generation to generation, and the everyday objects that surround us. Objects hold our history, connect us to culture, and stir our emotions. As we spend more time in our homes let's take a look at some of the objects we value, explore their secrets, their stories, and how they can connect us to others.

Select an object from your home that holds personal significance for you. Have that object close by so that you can share it with the group. Please know that you will be asked to speak, participate, learn, and have fun together.

Program length: 1 hour
Optimum # of participants: twenty or fewer
Process/Facilitation:

- Each member of the group will have a chance to share their object one at a time. Initially, the owner of the object DOES NOT talk about the object they have selected, they show it to the camera. Other participants write down something that they notice about the object in the Zoom chat box—its color, material, shape, etc. We describe qualities of the object without naming it.
- After about a minute, the facilitator reads the list of words from the chat box. For example, a ballpoint pen might provoke the descriptions long, round, one end tapers, most of it is plastic with a metal tip, etc.
- Then, the person who owns the object tells us everything that cannot be known about this object by just looking at it (two minutes or less).
- We continue until everyone in the group has had a chance to show their object and share it.
- The last few minutes are used for reflection about the experience.

One of the most positive discoveries for museums in the wake of the COVID-19 pandemic is that there *is* an online audience interested in their programming. Adults want to connect with museum content even if they can't visit in person. Teachers want their students to be able to access museums from their classrooms, families search for rich educational experiences, those not able to visit in person because of geography, monetary resources, or physical capacity still want to connect with museums.

These findings suggest that even as museums return to more normalized operations, a portion of museum programming for adult audiences should continue in the digital realm. When those who have participated in online cultural programming are asked, "What did you get out of doing online arts or culture activities?" The top five responses were:

- 49 percent said fun
- 47 percent said learning something new
- 43 percent said relaxation
- 30 percent said connection with others
- 28 percent broaden my perspective[10]

These seem like very good reasons for museums to keep digital programming alive.

NOTES

1. Selfhelp Virtual Senior Center, https://www.vscm.selfhelp.net/.
2. The Guggenheim Education Programming Goes Digital in Response to COVID-19, Press release, April 10, 2020, https://www.guggenheim.org/news/the-guggenheim-education-programming-goes-digital-in-response-to-covid-19.
3. Quotes are from evaluation forms submitted anonymously by program participants, compiled by Laili Amighi, associate manager, Public Programs, Solomon R. Guggenheim Museum, July 2020.
4. Collection Online, featuring over 1,700 artworks by more than 625 artists, the Collection Online presents a searchable database of selected artworks from the Guggenheim's permanent collection of approximately 8,000 artworks, https://www.guggenheim.org/collection-online.
5. Richard Mayer's Cognitive Theory of Multimedia Learning, https://www.mheducation.ca/blog/richard-mayers-cognitive-theory-of-multimedia-learning.
6. Galen Davis and Marie Norman, Principles of Multimedia Learning, July 19, 2016, https://ctl.wiley.com/principles-of-multimedia-learning/.
7. The Metropolitan Museum of Art, Kent Monkman, mistikôsiwak (*Wooden Boat People*), https://www.metmuseum.org/exhibitions/listings/2019/great-hall-commission-kent-monkman.
8. Distance Learning Programs for Students and Families at the Guggenheim Museum, https://www.guggenheim.org/press-release/distance-learning-programs-for-students-and-families-at-the-guggenheim-museum.
9. Culture Track, CCTT-Key-Findings-from-Wave-2.pdf, slide 20.
10. Ibid., slide18.

20

Adapting the Tour Planning Template for Adults Who Are Blind or Have Low Vision

Karen Bergman

I'm asked surprisingly often why someone who is blind would choose to visit an art museum. I recently asked our Mind's Eye program participants to share why they attend our programs at the Solomon R. Guggenheim Museum and received the following immediate responses:

- "Whether we are blind or sighted, art stimulates imagination. This program is about cultivating imagination."
- "Visual art is a small part of it. It's about the artist, political environment, and materials used."
- "For those of us who have had vision and loved art, this gives understanding of new pieces."
- "It's about sharing experiences. We have different levels of vision—for example, some see color, and some don't. There is a spectrum of experience and through sharing, we all experience so much."
- "It's about taking the time, being respectful to the art and the artist by really diving into the artwork."
- "Everyone's perspective brings us closer and closer to what the work is and together we gain a greater understanding of it."
- "It's about listening."
- "All the different perspectives add understanding, and sometimes confusion—but isn't that what the artist wants?"

Since its pilot in 2008, the Mind's Eye program[1] for adult participants who are blind or have low vision has been a two-hour museum gallery program

Figure 20.1. A Mind's Eye participant touches a raffia grass skirt similar to the material in a nearby sculpture in the exhibition *Simone Leigh: Loophole of Retreat. Filip Wolak © Solomon R. Guggenheim Foundation, New York. All Rights Reserved.*

rooted in verbal description, conversation, sensory experience, and creative practice. When planning these tours, I begin with the methodology explained in this book, using an advance organizer, selecting a few objects for stops, and preparing open-ended questions. An additional foundational element of our programs is verbal description, or a verbal delivery of visual observation that enables listeners to form an image in their mind's eye. Verbal descriptions generally begin with standard information about the work (artist, title, date, dimensions, medium), followed by an overview of the work's subject, form, colors, and textures. The description might focus on style or technique. (Recorded verbal descriptions are available on the Guggenheim's website,[2] and Art Beyond Sight provides in-depth resources for writing verbal descriptions.)[3]

Foregrounding a program with verbal descriptions provides access to visual content and lays the foundation for our shared conversation. I have found that beginning with a very detailed verbal description can confuse or lose listeners quickly. Worse, it can limit listener's imaginative engagement with the work. Starting with a brief description, and then scaffolding onto it, invites follow-up questions based on aspects of the work that pique participants' curiosity. After offering a brief but carefully considered verbal description, I then ask the audience questions such as:

- What can I clarify about the description?
- Is there anything that you'd like to add to the description?
- Would anyone like to share their initial thoughts, comments, or questions?
- What do you experience or take from this work?

By providing broad description and then following participants' points of interest, we forego a linearly constructed experience and instead discover the work communally through collaboration. The educator's role is to organize participants' observations cohesively and respond by sharing additional information and interpretation surrounding the artwork at hand.

Sensory experience is an essential programming component for this audience. Tactile objects can provide further insight into artworks being described. Touch objects can be crafted to express basic composition and identification of forms. When preparing these, however, seek to express elements of the work beyond simple outlines. Texture can be a rich element to explore with tactile objects. Consider how additional aspects of a work could be revealed in complex and nuanced ways (see Figure 20.1 not 201.1).

Tactile objects are also an exciting opportunity for collaboration:

- Ask exhibiting artists if they have material tests or small-scale models they are willing to share.
- Ask conservation teams for material tests and other tactile resources.

- Ask exhibition teams for any unused installation pieces; a leftover section of rope from Maren Hassinger's *Untitled* (1972/2020)[4] allowed participants to engage directly with the work's material.

Beyond touch, other sensory experience can be incorporated. Music can be played that relates to the work, but keep in mind that this should not be an arbitrary choice. Play a song when specifically relevant. For example, sharing examples of polyphonic music after noting the title of Perle Fine's abstract work *Polyphonic*[5] provided additional insight and ignited further conversation about the painting.

We generally bring iPads or other tablets into the gallery with high resolution images so participants can view the artwork at close range, enlarge specific details, and view it with greater contrast.

Offering responsive art activities is an effective way to encourage creative practice. A wooden stylus can be used to draw on scratch-foam board[6] to create embossed tactile drawings (see figure 20.2). Sculptural 3-D exploration can be done with quick-drying clay in a separate workshop or classroom space.[7] Whenever making responsive artwork, state the purpose of the activity. For the exhibition *Marking Time: Process in Minimal Abstraction*,[8] an exhibition that focused on various approaches to mark-making, we did various drawing activities on paper with graphite sticks and noted, "These activities are not about the finished product, but about being aware of your arm's weight and movement while drawing." In one workshop, we featured David Hammons's work *Close Your Eyes and See Black*.[9] After discussing the content and printing method, we responded through art as participants explored various modes of making their own body prints through tracing or stamping. I have found that attendees are more comfortable participating when it's clearly stated that the intent is to explore materials and process.

When preparing for a tour, it's important to spend significant time with the artwork. I often begin by asking myself what I notice first. Then, I try to:

look from afar;
look at the surface up close;
list and describe all the materials, colors, and textures I notice;
describe the subject matter;
sit with it;
draw the work; and
ask myself where my eye went and why. Did it rest, and where?

When I think I've seen it all, I take another minute to see what else can be discovered.

During this process work to identify visual bias. Take time to correct defaults or assumptions about the gender, race, or age of a person represented. (A great resource for standardizing descriptions is the Cooper Hewitt's *Guidelines*

Figure 20.2. A Mind's Eye participant creates a tactile drawing using a stylus on foam. Ink can be applied on these embossed drawings to create relief prints.
Filip Wolak © Solomon R. Guggenheim Foundation, New York. All Rights Reserved.

for *Visual Description*[10]). Even though visual experience is inherently subjective, aim to keep descriptions objective! And even when my descriptions are objective, I often find that participants jump in with questions about my subjective experience, such as, "Are the muddy colors you're describing ugly?" "How does it make you feel?" Participants often want to engage with my own emotional and aesthetic reaction.

It can be challenging to describe an artwork in a way that honors it. When it's an abstract work, I avoid describing shapes as identifiable forms. In one program I stated, "The yellow triangle tapers and bends" and a participant added, "Like a heavy slice of cheese pizza." Sometimes participants welcome descriptions that connect to an identifiable shape. I prefer to leave space open so that even if representational forms emerge, the connections are made by participants themselves as they construct images in their mind. For example, Vasily Kandinsky's *Several Circles*[11] could be described simply as colorful circles of various sizes, some overlapping, against a black background. Without drawing my own connections to the natural world, participants identified their own references: bubbles, a microscopic organism, planets orbiting and colliding, and a pupil within an eye (the small black circle within a larger circle).

When selecting artworks, at times I naturally gravitate toward certain works that may seem more straightforward to describe, like a representational oil on canvas portrait as opposed to an abstract sculpture made of multiple materials. However, limiting the object selection does not provide an equitable experience.

Push to select a true diversity of works. When finding an artwork particularly challenging to describe, lean into that and ask, "What can I further clarify?" "What's not making sense?" "What can be added to the description?" Take additional time while preparing for the tour to identify what about the work is challenging to describe, and if relevant, share that with the group during the tour.

In the museum, we offer two program sessions per month with different timing options. The afternoon program is offered during public hours when the museum is buzzing with activity. Participants can take additional time to explore the exhibitions on their own following the tour's completion. The evening session accommodates traditional nine-to-five jobs and offers a quieter, more intimate after-hours experience when the museum is closed to the public. In a two-hour program, we generally feature six to eight artworks in the gallery. It's best to prepare extra works in case the pace moves quickly, as well as plan for alternate ways to wrap up a tour if a longer discussion leads to skipping the final work(s). Conversation can be unpredictable; good preparation allows you to be flexible and enjoy the ride.

When we took our programs online in March 2020 due to COVID-19, we found many unexpected benefits to the online format. Zoom allows participants to join via web link or dial-in phone number. High resolution images displayed on screen can be augmented with participants' own devices and preferred settings. Multiple options for program times allowed participants to join live from across the globe. Along with these practical aspects, virtual tours provide the opportunity to share a greater diversity of voices by featuring artworks not currently on view, many by artists that have been historically excluded.

While the in-gallery tactile experience was initially lost in the virtual space, it became easier to feature other sensory elements. Virtual tours allow the possibility of sharing:

- Voices: audio clips artists reflecting on their own work, curators discussing the work, etc.
- Music: related to a time period of the work's making or the scene depicted, a musical response to an artwork, a song relevant to an artwork's title, etc.
- Videos: of artworks themselves, of artists working, etc. If the video does not have embedded audio description, prepare an audio description.

The opportunity to share audio and video on virtual tours can add important contextual information.

Following a gallery or virtual tour, it's important to take some time to learn from the experience. I generally begin a self-reflection by asking

- What could I have done better?

- Where did participants join the conversation? Where did they seem to hold back?
- Where could I have provided more space for conversation? Where could I have jumped in to move the conversation along?

More importantly, process the experience with participants. Ask them what could be done better through feedback forms and in conversation. What do they want from these programs? During the early unknowns of the COVID-19 pandemic, many people felt isolated and fearful. As individuals who navigate the world through touch, some Mind's Eye participants expressed their particular vulnerability and asked if programs could be offered more frequently. We began conference calls to discuss a single artwork from the museum's collection. These calls continue each week and provide an intimate community space. It's important to listen to your audience and develop programs in collaboration with them and in response to their actual requests as opposed to their imagined needs.

In the initial move to virtual formats, the program pillar of tactile experience was lost. However, it soon dawned on me that, at home, each participant has a wealth of resources at their fingertips! It just takes some thoughtfulness and creativity to facilitate a program that can utilize these resources. For one virtual program, I gave a verbal description of *Untitled (Black Felt)*,[12] a work by Robert Morris. It's composed of heavy strips of black felt hanging from pegs set at various heights on the wall. After sharing from his essay titled "Anti Form," we talked about his desire to investigate the properties of nonrigid material. I then asked participants to find a nonrigid material near them. With items including a scarf, a piece of paper, a tissue, and a window curtain, we together explored our materials through action words, beginning with reading Morris's words "random piling, loose stacking, hanging, give passing form to the material,"[13] I then asked participants to call out action words they discovered while exploring their material—*Twist, braid, fold, swir*—as time passed, possibilities expanded to *tear, wet, burn*. As the program ended, participants asked for a copy of Morris's essay so they could explore the "Anti Form" concepts further. An activity like this can engage participants in concepts surrounding materiality and minimalism from the comfort of their own homes.

In the programs we facilitate, there are real emotional benefits of bringing people together. To foster a comfortable environment for sharing, I have taken an important note from bell hooks in that it's "often productive if professors take the first risk, linking confessional narratives to academic discussions so as to show how experience can illuminate and enhance our understanding of academic material" and that I "must practice being vulnerable in the classroom, being wholly present in mind, body, and spirit."[14] Information and context we offer should connect with lived experience, perception, and memory. One of our recent programs featured Luis Camnitzer's work *Art History Lesson*,[15] in which ten slide projectors perch on various objects like chairs, buckets, and filing cabinets. Each projector is on, faced toward a portion of the wall, as it hums and clicks, but there are no slides in the projectors' magazines. It's a looping cycle of white rectangles projecting onto the gallery walls.

Participants began sharing their perspectives on the work, questioning the format and linearity of art history lessons, as well as who determines which slides are present. Some discussed what and who have historically been left out of art history. They debated whether the work is comedic, tragic, or an expression of possibility by wiping the slate of art history clean.

As we discussed, one participant shared a long-forgotten memory as a young person with macular degeneration. When he was in college in the fall of 1969, the Americans with Disabilities Act had not yet reached fruition. He couldn't take an art history class because, as he was told, "It's all on screen and we can't get you close enough to see the images." His vivid recollection of others determining that art history was not "relevant" for someone like him was poignant and moving for all of us. Following the session, he wrote, "After working for more than 40 years in the fields of vocational rehabilitation and civil rights for people with disabilities, it's quite surprising to me that slide projectors with blank slides can bring up an event that happened in 1969, where someone decided that a legally blind college student didn't have to learn or appreciate art."[16]

Questions and comments from this audience always compel me to look more closely, select my words with greater care, and attune my perception. Often, participants clarify elements of the work that I wasn't fully aware of. "You described the colors as cool, but the scene seems like a summer day. Are the color choices eerie? Or do they evoke a time of day, like early morning light?" I am always learning through participants' astute observations as well as through analogies they draw from nonvisual experience.

While this chapter specifically addresses programming for blind and low vision participants, it's important to acknowledge the intersectionality of identities and experiences that participants may bring to the table. By planning programs with an inclusive design framework,[17] I aim to include participants with disabilities from the beginning. As Leah Lakshmi Piepzna-Samarasinha writes, "When we reach for each other and make the most access possible, it is a radical act of love. When access is centralized at the beginning dream of every action or event, that is radical love."[18] Designing programs, content, and visitor experiences for inclusion aims to welcome people of all abilities and experiences to take part. The Mind's Eye program methodology of unfolding visual information through description, conversation, and sensory experience provides an opportunity to ignite curiosity, cultivate imagination, and deepen understanding for anyone engaging with visual culture. Regarding the intent for this kind of programming, Georgina Kleege certainly says it best:

> So the ultimate goal is not merely to explain visual art to blind people in the hope that this cultural access will compensate for the loss of sight. Rather, the hope is that blind people can bring a perspective that has not been articulated before.

If we can abandon the notion that blindness can only diminish, damage or destroy identity, and adopt instead the idea that the experience of blindness, in all its varieties, can in fact shape and inform other facets of personality and personal history, we will move toward a more genuinely inclusive society. The integration of blind perceptions and experiences will change the foundational assumptions of the culture; change how the human condition is defined.[19]

To foster a space Kleege describes, I have found that my aim as educator and facilitator cannot be a transactional delivery of information. Instead, my role is to provide equal visual access, to frame the conversation through intentional questions, and to connect observations in order to gain collective insight and understanding. It's about valuing perception and lived experience and honoring who brings this expertise to the table—and that's everyone.

NOTES

1. "Mind's Eye Programs," Guggenheim Museum,www.guggenheim.org/mindseye.
2. "Verbal Descriptions," Guggenheim Museum, https://www.guggenheim.org /audio/tag/verbal-descriptions.
3. ABS's *Guidelines for Verbal Description*, http://www.artbeyondsight.org/handbook /acs-guidelines.shtml.
4. Maren Hassinger on *Untitled* (1972/2020), February 10, 2021, Solomon R. Guggenheim Museum, New York, https://www.guggenheim.org/video/maren-hassinger-on-untitled-1972-2020.
5. Perle Fine, *Polyphonic*, 1945. Oil on canvas, 38 x 44 inches. Solomon R. Guggenheim Museum, New York, Estate of Karl Nierendorf, By purchase 48.1172.216, https:// www.guggenheim.org/artwork/1260.
6. Scratch-foam board is distributed by various supply companies. Search for Scratch-Art® Scratch-Foam® board or printing plates.
7. Or find a material that is approved for use in the galleries. Model Magic® is a nontoxic modeling material that dries within two days without kiln firing and has been approved by Guggenheim conservation for use in the galleries. It is manufactured and distributed by Crayola®, https://shop.crayola.com/modeling-compounds /model-magic.
8. *Marking Time: Process in Minimal Abstraction* was on view December 18, 2019–March 15, 2021, https://www.guggenheim.org/exhibition/marking-time-process-in-minimal-abstraction.
9. David Hammons, *Close Your Eyes and See Black,* 1969. Pigment on gold-coated paperboards, 35 7/8 x 24 ¾ inches (91.1 x 62.9 cm). Solomon R. Guggenheim Museum, New York. Purchased through prior gifts of Daimler-Benz in honor of Thomas M. Messer, the National Endowment for the Arts in Washington, D.C., William C. Edwards, Jr., in memory of Sibyl H. Edwards, the Estate of Karl Nierendorf, Mr. and Mrs. Morton L. Ostow, and Dr. Solomon W. Schaefer, 2018.56.
10. Cooper Hewitt's *Guidelines for Image Description*, https://www.cooperhewitt.org /cooper-hewitt-guidelines-for-image-description/.
11. Vasily Kandinsky, *Several Circles,* 1926. Oil on canvas, 55 3/8 x 55 1/4 inches (140.7 x 140.3 cm). Solomon R. Guggenheim Museum, New York, Solomon R. Guggenheim Founding Collection, by gift, https://www.guggenheim.org/artwork/1992.

12. Robert Morris, *Untitled (Black Felt)*, ca. 1969. Felt, six strips, each approximately 670.5 cm long: overall 108 inches high. Solomon R. Guggenheim Museum, New York, Panza Collection 91.3803.
13. Robert Morris, "Anti Form,"*Artforum*, April 1968, 35.
14. bell hooks, *Teaching to Transgress: Education as the Practice of Freedom* (New York: Routledge, 1994), 21.
15. Luis Camnitzer, *Art History Lesson,* 2000. Slide projectors, empty slide mounts, variable stands, and plastic sheets; overall dimensions variable. Solomon R. Guggenheim Museum, New York. Guggenheim UBS MAP Purchase Fund 2014.12, https://www.guggenheim.org/artwork/33084.
16. Anonymous personal communication, March 13, 2022.
17. Institute for Human Centered Design Resources, https://www.humancentereddesign.org/inclusive-design/resources.
18. Leah Lakshmi Piepzna-Samarasinha, *Care Work: Dreaming Disability Justice* (Vancouver: Arsenal Pulp Press, 2018), 76.
19. Georgina Kleege, *More Than Meets the Eye: What Blindness Brings to Art* (New York: Oxford University Press, 2018), 13.

21

Adapting the Tour Planning Template for Adults with Alzheimer's Disease and Other Dementias

Francesca Rosenberg

The Museum of Modern Art's (MoMA) lobby was abuzz with visitors checking in to *Meet Me at MoMA*, our program for people with Alzheimer's disease and other dementias and their care partners.[1] Participants were placed in groups and assigned to an educator charged with leading them on a guided tour through the museum. Attendees exchanged greetings, hugs, and stories.

On this particular day I was leading a tour through MoMA's collection framed around the theme of artist processes and materials. My plan was to take my group of twelve people (six with dementia and six care partners)[2] to look at contemporary works. Rather than lecture, we would engage in a conversation that I would facilitate. My goal was to have them look closely, share their interpretations, and feel connected to the person they came with, the art, the museum, and me. I wanted each of them to feel valued, seen, and heard.

As is my practice, I made the rounds introducing myself to each pair and checking in with them. This gave me a chance to learn a bit about each person, get a sense of their cognitive and verbal functioning, and have a sense of their familiarity with art and MoMA. I was having a jolly chat with Ira, an eighty-four-year-old man who had been diagnosed with Alzheimer's disease. He and his wife had a lovely rapport and the three of us spoke about traveling to the museum and the weather. Despite the challenge of taking a public bus and navigating through Midtown Manhattan in the rain, Ira was in good spirits. He spoke slowly and softly, and with purpose. Since we still had some more time before the tour began, I asked Ira, "What did you do?" With this open-ended question, I wanted to know what he had done in his life, thinking that he might tell me about his profession or provide me with more general information. I was looking backward. I was, despite my twenty-plus years as an educator, looking at Ira through a lens of ageism and bias. I was basically saying to him, "Now that you are older, what was good in your life before?" not considering that there could be more to it now that he was entering his mid-eighties. He said, looking me straight in the eye, "I'm still learning."

There is a misperception that people with dementia do not have the capacity to learn anything new. Art programs can help people with this disease, along with their care partners, to see that they still have many strengths present and the desire and the ability to learn, to be creative, and to connect. Our job as educators is to encourage these opportunities and to validate and honor them.

Dementia is fast becoming a global epidemic. According to the World Health Organization, around fifty-five million people have dementia worldwide, and there are almost ten million new cases each year. More than six million Americans are living with Alzheimer's disease. By 2050, this number is projected to rise to nearly thirteen million. More than eleven million Americans provide unpaid care for people with Alzheimer's or other dementias. In 2021, these care partners provided more than sixteen billion hours of care.[3] A program like Meet Me at MoMA not only provides opportunities for individuals with dementia to engage with art, but it creates a forum for those individuals and their care partners to reconnect with each other through a shared interest and a pleasurable experience. During programming at MoMA, we do not talk about the disease. As Mary Sano, PhD, Mount Sinai School of Medicine, said, "Some of the advantages to such programs is that they de-medicalize individuals with a disease and allow them to go back to being the person they once were."[4] These programs can also provide moments of respite for the care partner. So often, care partners are spouses or family members who suddenly enter into this new, highly medicalized relationship with a family member. Connecting over art gives people a different way of engaging outside of the care partner/care receiver dynamic (see figure 21.1).

MoMA began piloting programming for people with Alzheimer's disease in 2003. At that time, there were very few opportunities for this population and their care partners to remain involved in the community and to participate in meaningful experiences that could be both educational and enjoyable. In 2006, MoMA launched *Meet Me at MoMA*, a program through which the museum regularly offered interactive tours of the collection and special exhibitions for individuals with Alzheimer's disease or other forms of dementia and their care partners. In 2007, MoMA was able to expand and deepen its commitment to working with individuals with dementia and their care partners by scaling this program.[5]

Figure 21.1. At the Museum of Modern Art, a group of older adults stand close to a large painting of water lilies by the artist Claude Monet leaning in to observe the blue and green brushstrokes. *Photographer: Jason Brownrigg*

This disease impacts cognitive functioning and, in particular, memory. We have found that visual art is a perfect tool to use because it does not require memory. It is leveling to have the work of art hanging in the gallery giving everyone the opportunity to connect and respond to open-ended questions about it. At MoMA, each person is encouraged to freely share ideas and interpretations about the work without worrying about right or wrong answers. Sometimes the discussions lead to memories being tapped, but this is not the primary goal.

Engaging with art can have other significant benefits for people with Alzheimer's disease or other dementias. After speaking with thousands of people with this disease as well as care partners, what became clear was that they wanted opportunities for personal growth and self-expression, to be able to connect with others who are going through a similar experience, and to maintain meaning and dignity in their lives. The practice of looking at art together does not focus on improving memory, instead, the goal of the program is to concentrate on quality-of-life outcomes such as increased socialization, self-expression, self-esteem, and decreased feelings of depression and isolation. In his book, Richard Taylor, PhD, author of *Alzheimer's from the Inside Out* wrote, "This isn't a 'go look at the art'; this is a 'go look at yourself,' and the art is just a stimulus for that."[6] So how do we design and lead gallery tours for people with dementia and their care partners? This chapter focuses on the nuts and bolts of an art-looking program.

TOUR THEMES

Select a theme that will be your organizing principle. There are an endless number of themes that you can come up with. Choose a theme that is broad enough to take in various directions that can include varied works of art. The theme should be accessible for everyone and capture the interest and imagination of an adult audience. Some popular themes have been *Landscape*, *Portraiture*, *Art and Music*, and *Animals in Art*. You could focus on highlights from your museum's collection, focus on a single artist (such as Carrie Mae Weems or Martin Wong), an art movement (like impressionism or cubism), art from a geographical region (South America or Japan, for instance), an artistic medium (photography, printmaking, sculpture, etc.), or art from a certain time period. A good idea is to choose a theme that would be of interest to you, your mother, or your neighbor.

SELECTING THE WORKS OF ART AND SEQUENCING

Once you have selected a theme, choose five to seven relevant works for a ninety-minute tour. It is possible that you will not visit all the works within the allotted time, but it is better to be prepared with too many works than not enough. It is always a good idea to have backup works that you feel comfortable using in case something unexpected happens. These unforeseen factors may include another guided group tour happens to be in front of a work you have chosen, a work is unexpectedly deinstalled for conservation or on loan to another museum or crowding in a gallery that might make having an engaging conversation difficult. Learn to be flexible and nimble! You can create positive and purposeful experiences with most works of art, but a rule of thumb is to choose works that you as the leader feel comfortable with and knowledgeable about. Not all works have to be pretty or upbeat. We've found that some of the best works to use with any group are those that are enigmatic and ambiguous. A discussion of Andrew Wyeth's (1948) painting *Christina's World*,[7] for example, can generate many comments because we cannot see the figure's face. This leads to all sorts of interpretations based solely on her gesture, surroundings, and the mood created by the colors and painting style. Typically, we do not include video, performance, or other time-based media when teaching this program. Small works may be difficult for a group to see. Works installed close to others or in a salon-style hanging may be difficult to focus on. Given the more limited mobility of some individuals in the group, works should be chosen that are hanging in relative proximity to one another. It's best to choose works that can be reached relatively quickly to keep the conversation going and to limit fatigue. Also consider the comfort level of the galleries you will visit (lighting, seating, acoustics, and temperature) and be aware of other events that might be taking place and could potentially distract participants.

The sequence of the works should help to connect them with one another under the theme. The order will also depend on the questions you plan to ask.

As a rule of thumb, it is better to begin with works that are simpler in composition and move to those that are more complex or to move from more figurative works to those that are more abstract. Alternatively, you may begin with works that fit your theme in a literal fashion and move toward those that relate more metaphorically or conceptually.

While selecting the works and determining the sequence, ask yourself:

- How will I introduce the theme?
- How do the works relate to the theme and each other and in what order is this best expressed?
- How will I make a seamless transition from one work to the next?
- What are some questions I will ask about each of the works?
- What art-historical or contextual information will I share?
- How will I relate the works to my theme in my summary and conclusion?

FACILITATING PRODUCTIVE DISCUSSIONS: OBSERVATION, DESCRIPTION, INTERPRETATION, CONNECTION

Plan three to five discussion questions that invite exploration of each work. Invite participants to take a close look at the work of art before they take their seats. We provide each guest with a sturdy stool that is lightweight and can be carried from gallery to gallery and set them up in a semicircle in front of the work of art. The seating arrangement should allow for every person to have an unobstructed view of the work. Begin with simple observation questions such as, "What do you see in this painting?" or "What colors in the work stand out for you?" Repeat and summarize all the observations to validate what was said and to create a full visual inventory of the work. As the group gets more comfortable, you can move on to more interpretive questions. Ask questions that prompt participants to reflect on what is not clearly visible in the work but perhaps merely suggested, such as, "What do you think the relationship is between the figures in this painting?" or "What do you imagine might happen next?" Ask for evidence of what they are inferring by looking back at the painting together. Encourage breadth and variety of interpretation. Follow your inquiries with deepening questions, such as, "Could you say a little bit more about that?" or "What do you see that makes you say that?"

It can be most interesting to ask questions that lead participants to make personal connections to a work of art. For instance, having them look at a work such as Madoka Takagi's photograph *Coney Island, Brooklyn*,[8] which features the famous Ferris wheel, we ask participants whether they have ever ridden it or how they feel about amusement parks. This usually leads to conversation about the various things in life that might bring joy (including cotton candy and candy apples!). These conversations enable the group to gain new insights about the work and each other. Tips to keep in mind:

- Ask concrete questions and be specific. Ask, "What do you see in this painting?" instead of "What is going on here?"
- Alternate between open-ended questions and questions with definite answers and be ready to mix in or switch to either/or or yes/no questions to keep the discussion moving. For example, you might ask, "Does this work seem to suggest a specific season?" If no one answers, you could name the seasons, or ask, "Do the colors in the painting make you think of summer or spring?" Or further, you could invite yes/no answers to simpler questions, such as "Does this painting make you think of springtime?"
- Be aware that some participants may not speak. This does not mean that they are not engaged. They are likely benefiting from the experience in multiple ways. Eye and/or body movements may indicate concentration and engagement.
- Be conscious of making comparisons to works you have already discussed if they are no longer visible. The participants may not easily recall them. You should only compare works that are easily visible at the same time.

THE ROLE OF INFORMATION

Balance your questions by sharing art-historical information relevant to the responses you receive from the group to validate individual interpretations, to make connections, and to encourage further discussion. You can find information about each work of art by looking online, in exhibition catalogs, books, museum labels, and museum audio guides. Look for interesting quotes from artists, critics, and curators. Of all this information, select a few main ideas that are relevant to the work and your theme and are conducive to conversation. Settle on a limited number of points for each work (three to four); this will help you to avoid lecturing. Choosing to share points that further the conversation rather than ending it will encourage a wider range of participation.

Art-historical information should be used throughout the discussion to strengthen participants' understanding and appreciation of the work and help place the work in the context of developments in art and world history. When discussing a work always share the name of the artist, date of the work, and materials used. This can be done at the beginning, end, or at a relevant moment during the discussion. The title of a work can even be used to encourage further discussion.

ACTIVITIES

Some people with Alzheimer's disease will be very interested in artmaking and we've had success with these types of programs at MoMA. However, it is important to note that not all adults (with or without dementia) enjoy making art.

People with dementia may also be highly sensitive to feeling infantilized. If they have not made art since they were in high school, they may consider it a childish activity and decline to participate. Any art-making program should be made up of a group of self-selecting individuals that are expecting and looking forward to making art. The art materials should be high quality and sophisticated in keeping with the audience.

There are many other types of low-lift activities that educators can rely on to lead to further close looking and engagement. For instance, a *turn and talk* encourages conversation in smaller groups so that individuals have a chance to connect more directly and personally with others. This activity also gives participants who are more reticent to participate in the larger group a chance to engage on a more intimate level. At some point in the tour, have each pair of participants (the person with dementia and their care partner) join one other pair (for a total of four people in each smaller group). Make sure to go through the observation, description, and interpretation of the work before initiating the turn and talk. Ask the groups to discuss a particular idea or theme that relates to the work of art. Your prompt should be straightforward and appropriate to the participants' cognitive abilities. The discussion should last no longer than ten minutes. At the end of the period bring everyone back together and encourage participants to share their conversation with the whole group.

VIRTUAL PROGRAMS

In 2020 during the COVID-19 pandemic, MoMA piloted its regular programs, including *Meet Me at MoMA*, online. This was a particularly difficult time for people with dementia who were more likely to be immunocompromised and already struggling with isolation, depression, and anxiety, not to mention their care partners. While many of MoMA's other programs could be easily adapted for virtual teaching, this program and audience posed a number of challenges. Many people with dementia have difficulty with computer screens and tracking images on them. At-home devices, that range from smartphones to iPads to laptop computers, generally have screens that are small. In programming on-site at MoMA, we choose larger works of art and make sure that everyone has a clear, unobstructed view of the work that we are discussing. Dyads sit side by side and form a semicircle with other members of the group to encourage conversation. In the virtual realm we were not able to manage the space in the same way. For many, it must have felt like a disembodied voice was coming out of the hardware, which can be very disorienting—not relatable or engaging! Educators are trained to connect with participants by tracking their eyes to see where they are looking and by watching their body language. All of this was very difficult to do virtually. Our goal was to design an online program that would be as engaging as our onsite offering by bypassing some of these barriers.

The onsite programs at MoMA are individual stand-alone programs with a changing set of participants, however, in formulating virtual programs we decided to create a series for the same cohort of individuals, with the goal of building a deeper rapport over time. We would get to know the individuals and become familiar with their language cues and abilities, building trust and opportunities for engagement. This requires both work and time. After several pilot programs, to experiment with various modes of interacting, we finally landed on a successful model through a partnership with NYU Langone's Alzheimer's Disease and Related Dementias Family Support Program. We found through trial and error that twelve dyads could meet weekly online for ninety minutes for five consecutive weeks. The first session, which proved to be a key to success, was an orientation for care partners only. This meeting covered various topics including the goals of the program, how to set up the physical space (sit side by side facing the screen), and the importance of having the care partner present during the whole program. The subsequent four sessions were for the dyads to join together. The content was designed around art cards, which are color reproductions of works in MoMA's collection printed on large postcards. All the images that were shown as part of the slides on the computer were also sent to the attendees in large postcard format in advance of the series so that they had the option of looking at the image on the screen or at the art card, which they could hold in their hands. On the back of each art card, we added a prompt or an open-ended question to be discussed together in pairs at home just as we would in a turn and talk in the museum's galleries. In one session that was built around the theme of New York City and included work by Romare Bearden, Helen Levitt, and Edward Hopper, the question on the back of Hopper's *New York Movie* [9] was, "What's the best thing about going to the movies?" One care partner participant said, "I enjoyed that my partner was so game for it and totally involved the whole time. I loved hearing others' takes on the work as well as the background/story of the artists. It was very engaging and informative and a truly multisensory experience with the microwaveable popcorn that you sent and encouraged us to eat during the program." This comment and the responses from other participants convinced us that we had indeed found a way to translate the *Meet me at MoMA* program for a virtual audience.

In nearly twenty years of working with this audience MoMA has welcomed thousands of participants. One participant put it this way, "I realize that when you have Alzheimer's, you don't know if your memory is correct. The program gave me the confidence to know that I had been able to retain my appreciation of art and that was important. That really was important. And to verbalize it . . . because first you're talking about a perception of it, and recalling it, but then you verbalize that perception, and you are able to verbalize what that means. And boy, is that important!"

NOTES

1. Some content for this chapter is adapted from *Meet Me: Making Art Accessible to People with Dementia*, a book published in 2009 as part of the MoMA Alzheimer's Proj-

ect. Thanks to my coauthors Amir Parsa, Laurel Humble, and Carrie McGee for their extraordinary work. Lara Schweller, associate educator, Access Programs and Initiatives, currently develops innovative virtual programming for this population as well as Social Rx offerings for a broad audience of individuals sixty-five and up. For more information, including research findings and more in-depth guides for creating art programs (also in Spanish), please visit https://www.moma.org/visit/accessibility/meetme/.

2. In the United States the term "caregiver" is preferred, however, there is a fine delineation between being a caregiver versus a care partner. I have used the term care partner because a caregiver gives care, while a care partner, partners in care. It can create a powerful shift in mindset of the role, resulting in a much-improved relationship between the person with dementia and the person who is the partner in care. For more on this term see *3 Strategies for Protecting Your Relationship and Finding Meaningful Moments in Dementia Care*, Valerie Feurich, https://teepasnow.com/blog/3-strategies-for-creating-meaningful-moments-in-dementia-care/.

3. World Health Organization, https://www.who.int/news-room/factsheets/detail/dementia.

4. Francesca Rosenberg, Amir Parsa, Laurel Humble, and Carrie McGee, *Meet Me: Making Art Accessible to People with Dementia*, 2009, Museum of Modern Art, New York, 59.

5. This initiative was funded by a major grant from the MetLife Foundation.

6. Rosenberg, *Meet Me*, 67.

7. Andrew Wyeth, *Christina's World*, 1948, tempera on panel, 32 ¼ x 47 ¾ inches, Museum of Modern Art, https://www.moma.org/collection/works/7845.

8. Madoka Takagi, *Coney Island, Brooklyn*, 1990, platinum palladium print, 7 ½ x 9 ½ inches, Museum of Modern Art, https://www.moma.org/collection/works/98294.

9. Edward Hopper, *New York Movie*, 1939, Oil on canvas, 32 ¼ x 40 1/8 inches, Museum of Modern Art, https://www.moma.org/collection/works/79616.

Appendix 1

This is the email that was sent to my network of museum educators:

An invitation to share your thoughts on gallery and virtual teaching.
Dear Museum Education Colleagues,

A few months ago, the editor of my first book on gallery activities contacted me to ask if I had another book in me. During the process of writing the book on gallery activities, I kept going to thoughts about the rest of the thematic tour planning and facilitating process. And so, I put together a proposal, and I am delighted to report, it has been approved and will be available through Rowman & Littlefield Publishing Group, Inc.

In this new book I plan to detail the process of planning and facilitating thematic tours and also include ways that they can be customized for varied audiences. Unlike my previous book that I wrote, nearly solo, I want this book to reflect many voices and collaborators.

We each come to museum teaching, whether it be in-person or virtual, with our own style and lessons that have been learned through years of honing our craft. I envision that your responses will be woven through the text, offering tips, insights and lessons learned from many of the educators that I so admire.

I have attached a questionnaire where, if you are so inclined, you can share your thoughts on gallery and virtual teaching. You can write as much or as little as you want. My imaginary audiences are other museum educators, classroom teachers and museum education graduate students. Of course, I will credit all contributions. My hope is to provide a wide assortment of strategies and practices that will inform and support more empathetic and effective teaching.

I hope you see this invitation as an opportunity to call attention to the great work you are doing and to share your practice with the field of Museum Education.

I feel so fortunate to have observed so many (although not all) of you teach. I hope to use this platform to make your stellar work more widely known and utilized. However, I don't know every excellent gallery/virtual educator, so feel free to pass this invitation along to others.

Thank you in advance for considering contributing to this project. If you have questions, feel free to be in touch. I would love to hear from you! If you choose to participate, please email the completed questionnaire to me by January 30, 2022.

With admiration and appreciation,
Sharon
Sharon.vatsky@gmail.com

QUESTIONNAIRE ON GALLERY AND VIRTUAL MUSEUM TEACHING

Dear Educator,

Thanks so much for taking the time to respond to this questionnaire. Below are a few questions. Feel free to write as much or little as you would like. Although it would be great if you respond to all the questions, it is also fine to only respond to one, or some of them.

In the book I will acknowledge everyone who returns a questionnaire. If your response(s) are included in the book, they will have your attribution.

Please return this form to me before January 30, 2022.

With deep appreciation for the work that you do!

Sharon

sharon.vatsky@gmail.com

YOUR NAME:

YOUR EMAIL:

TITLE AND/OR POSITION:

AFFILIATION (OPTIONAL):

- What do you think makes an excellent gallery/virtual educator?
- What advice would you give to other gallery/virtual educators who are looking to strengthen their practice?
- What do you want participants to "take away" with them from a gallery/virtual experience that you have facilitated?

- **Planning:**
  How do you go about preparing for a gallery or virtual experience?

- **Facilitation:**
  How do you help participants to feel comfortable enough to participate during a gallery or virtual experience?
  What "lessons" would you want to impart to educators about successful facilitation strategies?

- **Reflection:**
  Following a gallery or virtual tour how do you reflect and learn from the experience?

- What else? Please add any additional comments.

Appendix 2

TEACHING THEME/ESSENTIAL QUESTION

___ A universal lens that is relevant to students' lives and classroom content
___ Either immediately, or through exploration, is visually evident in the work of art
___ Is a concept that can be explored in depth and on many levels
___ Provides a common point of connection through which to frame the objects

OBJECT SELECTION

___ Objects clearly relate to the theme
___ Are sequenced to allow for a greater understanding of the theme throughout the lesson
___ Address the theme in a variety of ways
___ Are developmentally appropriate

QUESTIONS

___Questions are open-ended and invite multiple responses
___Are sequenced from observation to interpretation
___Encourage close looking
___Support the theme and lesson goals

ROLE OF INFORMATION

___ Information is integrated into the discussion and relevant to the conversation
___ Information supports exploration of the theme
___ Information aligns with the lesson goals
___ Information can take many forms

ACTIVITIES (MULTIMODAL APPROACHES)

___One or more approaches (beyond dialogue) is incorporated in the lesson
___The activity relates to the work of art
___The activity instructions are clear
___The activity is aligned to the theme and lesson goals
___The activity supports divergent outcomes

Appendix 3

EDUCATOR: _____

GROUP: _____

THEME: _____

GOALS: _____

ADVANCE ORGANIZER: _____

Object (artwork) Selections: Add a small image (thumbnail) of each work *in the sequence/order* it will be introduced. Depending on the allotted time and group between 3 and 5 tour stops may be included.

Tour Stop 1: Artist, Title, Date, Materials, Dimensions

Transition

Tour Stop 2: Artist, Title, Date, Materials, Dimensions

Transition

Tour Stop 3: Artist, Title, Date, Materials, Dimensions

Reflection/Wrap-up/Conclusion

Open-ended Questions: For *each* artwork write open-ended questions in the sequence/order they will be presented.

-
-
-

Information: Important information about *this* artwork that is related to the tour theme.

-
-
-

Multimodal Activity:

Reflection

Bibliography

About Universal Design for Learning, https://www.cast.org/impact/universal-design-for-learning-udl.

ABS's Guidelines for Verbal Description. http://www.artbeyondsight.org/handbook/acs-guidelines.shtml.

Anderson, Gail, ed. *Reinventing the Museum: The Evolving Conversation on the Paradigm Shift*. Second Edition. Lanham, MD: AltaMira Press, 2012.

Bungard, Brigitta and Jocelyn Meinhardt, December 7, 2011, *"I went to MoMA and...": It's Back!* https://www.moma.org/explore/inside_out/2011/12/07/i-went-to-moma-and-it-s-back/.

Burnham, Rika. *If You Don't Stop, You Don't See Anything*, Teachers College Record Volume 95 Number 4, 1994. https://www.tcrecord.org/content.asp?contentid=88.

Burnham, Rika and Elliot Kai-Kee. *Teaching in the Art Museum: Interpretation as Experience*. Los Angeles CA: J. Paul Getty Museum 2011.

Cai Guo-Qiang Creates New Gunpowder Paintings. Dec 13, 2019.

https://www.youtube.com/watch?v=6al_eiTc67M.

Campbell-Dollaghan, Kelsey. *Frank Gehry At 83: Still Obsessed with Fish*, Fast Company, January 14, 2013, https://www.fastcompany.com/1671622/frank-gehry-at-83-still-obsessed-with-fish.

Carlisle Kletchka, Dana and Stephen B. Carpenter, II. *Professional Development in Art Museums: Strategies of Engagement Through Contemporary Art*. Alexandria, VA: National Art Education Association, 2018.

Cool Culture, https://www.coolculture.org/

Cooper Hewitt's Guidelines for Image Description. https://www.cooperhewitt.org/cooper-hewitt-guidelines-for-image-description/.

Culture Track. https://culturetrack.com/.

Cutler, Nancy. *Planting Curiosity and Harvesting Interest: Capitalizing on Curiosity*, The Docent Educator, Autumn 2001. https://www.museum-ed.org/planting-curiosity-and-harvesting-interest-capitalizing-on-curiosity/.

Davis, Galen and Marie Norman. *Principles of Multimedia Learning*, July 19, 2016. https://ctl.wiley.com/principles-of-multimedia-learning/.

Delamatre, Jackie. *Questioning the Questioning of Questions*, Art Museum Teaching: A Forum for Reflecting on Practice, January 23, 2015. https://artmuseumteaching.com/2015/01/23/questioning-the-questioning-of-questions/.

The Docent Handbook – Revised Edition, Berkeley, CA, National Docent Symposium Council, 2017.

Downey, Stephanie and Amanda Krantz, *Thinking About Art: The Role of Single-Visit Art Museum Field Trip Programs.* Visual Arts Education, Art Education, 2021. https://www-tandfonline-com.tc.idm.oclc.org/doi/full/10.1080/00043125.2021.1876466.

Education Corner. https://www.educationcorner.com/the-learning-pyramid.html.

Elderfield, John, Peter Reed, Mary Chan, Maria del Carmen González. *Modern Starts: People, Places, Things,* New York, Museum of Modern Art, 1999.

Elkins, James. *The Object Stares Back: On the Nature of Seeing.* New York, NY: Simon and Schuster, 1996.

———. *How Long Does It Take to Look at a Painting?* Huffington Post, The Blog, Dec 6, 2017. https://www.huffpost.com/entry/how-long-does-it-take-to-_b_779946.

Falk, John H., and Lynn D. Dierking. *Learning from Museums: Visitor Experiences and the Making of Meaning.* Walnut Creek CA: AltaMira Press, 2011.

Falk, John H., Lynn D. Dierking. *The Museum Experience Revisited.* Walnut Creek, CA: Left Coast Press, 2013.

Fenker, Daniela and Harmut Schütze. *Learning by Surprise: Novelty Enhances Memory*. Scientific American, December 17, 2008. https://www.scientificamerican.com/article/learning-by-surprise.

French, Kathy. *Transitions...The Workhorse of a Tour*, The Docent Educator, Autumn, 1995. Minneapolis Museum of Art, https://artsmia.github.io/tour-toolkit/tour-preparation/transitions/.

Greene, Jay P., Brian Kisida and Daniel H. Bowen, *The Educational Value of Field Trips: Taking Students to an Art Museum Improves Critical Thinking Skills, and More*, (Education Next, 2014). https://www.educationnext.org/the-educational-value-of-field-trips/

Greenhill, Eilean Hooper. "Learning in Art Museums: Strategies of Interpretation" in *The Educational Role of the Museum: Second Edition*. New York: Routledge, 2001.

Halbrooks, Glenn. *Why Tease Writing Is Critical to a Successful TV Newscast*, April 27, 2018. https://www.thebalancecareers.com/why-tease-writing-is-critical-to-a-successful-tv-newscast-2315473.

Hammond, Zaretta. *Culturally Responsive Teaching & the Brain: Promoting Authentic engagement and Rigor Among Culturally and Linguistically Diverse Students*. Thousand Oaks, CA: Corwin, 2015.

Hedeman, Margaret and Matt Kristoffersen. *Art History Department to Scrap Survey Course*, Yale Daily News, January 24, 2020. https://yaledailynews.com/blog/2020/01/24/art-history-department-to-scrap-survey-course/

Hein, George. *Learning in the Museum*. New York: Routledge,1998.

Henry, Barbara and Kathleen McLean, eds. 2010. *How Visitors Changed Our Museum: Transforming the Gallery of California Art at the Oakland Museum of California*, 2010.

Hirsch, Joanne S., and Lois H. Silverman, eds. *Transforming Practice: Selections from the Journal of Museum Education 1992-1999*. Washington D. C., Museum Education Roundtable, 2000.

hooks, bell. *Teaching to Transgress: Education as the Practice of Freedom*. New York: Routledge, 1994.

Hubard, Olga. *What Counts as a Theme in Art Museum Education?* The Journal of Museum Education, Vol. 38, No. 1, City Museums and Urban Learning, Taylor & Francis, Ltd. March 2013. https://www.jstor.org/stable/43305774.

Hubard, Olga. *Art Museum Education: Facilitating Gallery Experiences*, 1st ed. Edition New York, NY: Palgrave Macmillan, 2015.

Impact Study: The Effects of Facilitated Single-Visit Art Museum Programs on Students Grades 4-6, National Art Education Association & Association of Art Museum Directors, 2018. https://www.arteducators.org/research /articles/377-naea-aamd-research-study-impact-of-art-museum -programs-on-k-12-students.

Heumann Gurian, Elaine. *Threshold Fear, Reshaping Museum Space*, Milton Park, England, UK, Routledge, 2005. https://www.egurian.com/omni-um-gatherum/museum-issues/community/accessibility/threshold-fear.

Institute for Human Centered Design Resources. https://www.humancentered-design.org/inclusive-design/resources.

Johnson, Anna, Kimberly A. Huber, Nancy Cutler, Melissa Bingmann and Tim Grove, eds., *The Museum Educator's Manual: Educators Share Successful Techniques,* Second Edition. Lanham, MD: Rowman & Littlefield, 2017.

Kaplan, Issac. *How Long Do People Really Spend Looking at Art in Museums?* Artsy, Nov 7, 2017, https://www.artsy.net/article/artsy-editorial-long-people-spend-art-museums.

Kaupelis, Robert. *Experimental Drawing.* New York, Watson-Guptill Publication, 1980.

King, Brad, and Barry Lord, eds., *The Manual of Museum Learning*. Second Edition. Lanham, MD: Rowman & Littlefield, 2016.

Kennedy, Randy. *Lawrence Weiner, Artist Whose Medium Was Language, Dies at 79*, The New York Times, December 7, 2021.

Kinsella, Eileen, An Estimated 85 Percent of Artists Represented in US Museum Collections Are White, a New Study Claims, Artnet News, February 19, 2019. https://news.artnet.com/market/new-study-shows-us-art-museums-grap-pling-with-diversity-1467256.

Kleege, Georgina. *More Than Meets the Eye: What Blindness Brings to Art.* New York: Oxford University Press, 2018.

Korn, Randi. *Intentional Practice for Museums: A Guide for Maximizing Impact*, Lanham MD, Rowman and Littlefield, 2018.

La Placa Cohen. Culture Track. https://culturetrack.com.

https://www.informalscience.org/sites/default/files/VSA-a0a0x9-a_5730.pdf

Lindsay, Kenneth C., and Peter Vergo. *Kandinsky, Complete Writings on Art*, Cambridge, MA: Da Cap Press, 1994.

Look at Art, Get Paid. Rhode Island School of Design Museum. 2016. http://www.lookatartgetpaid.org/home

Maslow, Abraham H. *A Theory of Human Motivation.* Psychological Review Vol. 50. No. 4.

July 1943. https://docs.google.com/file/d/0B-5-JeCa2Z7hNjZlNDNhOTEtM-WNkYi00YmFhLWI3YjUtMDEyMDJkZDExNWRm/edit.

Morris, Robert. *Anti Form.* Artforum. April 1968.

Oleniczak Brown, Jen. *Improv[e] using Improv to Find Your ...Voice, Style, Self*, Balboa Press, Bloomington, IN, 2018.

Oleniczak Brown, Jen. *Think on Your Feet: Tips and Tricks to Improve your Impromptu Communication Skills on the Job.* New York, McGraw-Hill, 2020.

Piepzna-Samarasinha, Leah Lakshmi. *Care Work: Dreaming Disability Justice.* Vancouver: Arsenal Pulp Press, 2018.

Project Zero, Harvard Graduate School of Education. http://www.pz.harvard.edu/.

Rand, Judy. *The 227-Mile Museum, or Why We Need a Visitors' Bill of Rights.* Curator: The Museum Journal, 44, no. 1, 2001.

Richards, Regina G. *Making It Stick: Memorable Strategies to Enhance Learning. Reading* https://www.readingrockets.org/article/making-it-stick-memorable-strategies-enhance-learning.

Rosenberg, Francesca, Amir Parsa, Laurel Humble, and Carrie McGee. *Meet Me: Making Art Accessible to People with Dementia.* New York, NY: Museum of Modern Art, 2009.

Rowe, Mary Budd. *Wait Time: Slowing Down May Be a Way of Speeding Up!* Journal of Teacher Education 37, no. 1, January 1986.

Schmidt, Laurel. *Classroom Confidential: The 12 Secrets of Great Teachers.* Portsmouth, NH: Heinemann, 2004.

Shulman Herz, Rebecca. *Looking at Art in the Classroom: Art Investigations from the Guggenheim Museum.* New York: Teachers College Press, 2010.

Simon, Nina. *The Participatory Museum.* Santa Cruz, CA: Museum 2.0., 2010.

———. *Come on In and Make Yourself Uncomfortable,* Museum 2.0 February 8, 2012. http://museumtwo.blogspot.com/2012/02/come-on-in-and-make -yourself.html

———. *The Art of Relevance.* Santa Cruz, CA: Museum 2.0., 2016.

Smith, Clint. *How the Work is Passed: A Reckoning with the History of Slavery Across America,* Boston, MA: Little Brown and Co., 2021.

Street, Ben. *How to Enjoy Art: A Guide for Everyone.* New Haven, CT: Yale University Press, 2021.

Tishman, Shari. *Slow Looking: The Art and Practice of Learning Through Observation.* New York, NY: Routledge, 2017.

Tokar, Steve. *Take a Seat.* Museum Magazine, Washington, DC, American Alliance of Museums, September 1, 2008.   https://www.aam-us .org/2008/09/01/take-a-seat/.

Topaz, CM, B. Klingenberg, D. Turek D, B. Heggeseth, PE Harris, JC Blackwood, et al. *Diversity of Artists in Major U.S. Museums.* 2019. https://journals.plos. org/plosone/article/file?id=10.1371/journal.pone.0212852&type=printable.

UDL Guidelines, https://udlguidelines.cast.org/.

Vatsky, Sharon. *Museum Gallery Activities: A Handbook.* Lanham, MD: Rowman & Littlefield, 2018.

Velie, Elaine. *Suffering from Anxiety? Try Visiting a Museum.* Hyperallergic 2022. https://hyperallergic.com/741124/suffering-from-anxiety-try-visiting-a-museum/.

What is the CASEL Framework? https://casel.org/fundamentals-of-sel/what-is-the-casel-framework/.

Young, Tara, ed. *Creating Meaningful Museum Experiences for K-12 Audiences: How to Connect with Teachers and Engage Students.* Lanham, MD: Rowman & Littlefield, 2021.

Index

AAMD. *See* Association of Art Museum Directors

abstract artworks, 37, 65, 127, 168–70, 179

accessibility, 86, 122, 144, 167, 170, 172–73; barriers to, xvi, 118, 129; of multimodal activities, 66–67; of resources, 3–4, 118, 163; of themes, 143, 177; of virtual tours, 162–63

active: learning, 61; listening, 94–96

activities, gallery. *See* multimodal activities

admissions fees, 5, 162

Adsit, Melanie, 116–17

adults, 109–10; with Alzheimer's Disease/Dementia, 175–82, *177*, 183n2; with blindness/low vision , 58n15, 165–73, *166*, *169*; virtual tours for, 155–63, 170, 181–82

advance organizers, 19–20, 69–71, 91, 104, 106, 124

Africa, 34–35

African American artists, 126

age groups, 35, 45, 94, 123, 125. *See also specific age groups*

ageism, 175–76

Akunyili Crosby, Njideka, 124, *125*

Algeria, 34–35

Almerisa, Asylum Center, Leiden, The Netherlands, March 14, 1994 (Dijkstra), 139, *140*

Alzheimer's Disease, tours for adults with, 116, 175–82, *177*, 183n2

Alzheimer's Disease and Related Dementia Family Support Program (NYU Langone), 182

Alzheimer's from the Inside Out (Taylor), 177

American Museum of Natural History, 3

Americans with Disabilities Act, U.S., 172

"Anti Form" (Morris), 171

anxiety, 8, 76, 78, 81–82, 94, 109, 133, 181

appropriateness: developmental, 37–38, 134, 144; in object selection, 37–38, 143–44, 150–51

architecture, 34–35, *35*, 55, 131; of Guggenheim Museum, 104–5, 110, 117–18, 156–57

Art21 (PBS series), 29

art history, 33–34, 51, 172, 180

Art History Lesson (Camnitzer), 172

"Artist as . . ." framework (Whitney), 123–26

artists, xvi, 29; biographical information about, 55–56; of color, xvi, 33–34, 126; materials used by, 34–35, 65–66, 126, *166*, 175; processes of, 57–58, 66, 152, 175; well-known, 33, 35, 37, 61; women, xxiii, 33–34, 38n3. *See also specific artists*

artist's process (activity), 66

art-making activities, 121, 151–53, 180–81

artworks: abstract, 37, 65, 127, 168–70, 179; colors in, 26–28, 36, 65–66, 143, 165, 169; descriptions of, 96, 167–69, 171, 179–81; landscapes and, xix, 28, 41, 57, 127, 178; paintings as, xvii–xix, *xviii*, *xx*, 33, 56, 65, 159, 177; portraits as, 28, 37, 124, 144, 153, 170, 178; reproductions of, 6, 25, 27, 157–58, 182; scale of, 178, 181; as sculptures, 34–35, *36*, 126, *166*; subjects of, xvii–xix, *xviii*, *xx*, 139–40, 144; well-known, 33, 35, 37, 61. *See also* object selection; observations; *specific artworks*

assistive listening devices, 86

Association of Art Museum Directors (AAMD), 4

assumptions, 34, 134, 169, 173, 175–76

attention, 36, 50-52, 71, 93, 132
Attia, Kader, 34-36, *35*
audience. *See* participants/audience/
  museum visitors
audio, 127, 170-71, 180
audiovisuals, 170-71
autistic spectrum, students on the,
  116-17, 129, *135*; facilitation of tours
  for, 132-33; multimodal activities for,
  131, 135-36; participation by, 133-35;
  planning tours for, 130-32
autobiographies, museum-centric, 5, 82

barriers to accessibility, xvi, 118, 129
Begum Lipi, Tayeba, 43, *43*, *44*
behaviors, 7-8, 94, 98, 132, 141; behavioral
  needs, 83, 130
belonging, 83, 139
Bergman, Karen, 118
best practices, 105-7
biases, 118, 168-69, 175-76
biographical information, 55-56
BIPOC (Black, Indigenous, People of
  Color) artists, xvi, 33-34, 126
Black Lives Matter (movement), xvi,
  33-34
blindness, adults with, 58n15, 165-73, *166*,
  169
blue, 27, 177
body language, 92, 94-95, 160, 181; facial
  expressions as, 124, 146
brainstorming, 51, 63, 96-97, 107, 133;
  themes, *25*, 25-28, *26*
breakout rooms, Zoom, 63, 161
breathing/breathing exercises, 77, 85,
  93-94, 123, 132-33, 145
Brooklyn Museum, 27
Bruner, Jerome S., 61, 67n4
Budd Rowe, Mary, 94
budgets, xvi, xxiii
Bureau of Economic Analysis, U.S., xxiii
Burnham, Rika, 36, 47, 85

Cai, Guo Qiang, 57
Calder, Alexander, 122
callouts/thought bubbles (activity),
  62-63, 144-45

cameras in virtual tours, 84, 127, 146,
  160-61, 163
Camnitzer, Luis, 172
Canada, 55
canon, historical, 33-34
caregivers, 85, 116, 130, 151, 161. *See also*
  parents
care partners for people with Alzheimer's
  disease/dementia, 116, 175-77, 181-82,
  183n2
CASEL. *See* Collaborative for Academic,
  Social, and Emotional Learning
  framework
Center for Contemplative Science and
  Compassion-Based Ethics, Emory
  University, 139-40
Cézanne, Paul, 57
Chagall, Marc, *64*, 64-65
challenges, 34, 66, 122; accessibility,
  162, 175; with conclusions, 72; for
  participants, 36, 83, 123, 152; with
  tours for students on the autism
  spectrum, 130-31; with virtual tours,
  127, 181
chat feature in virtual tours, 63, 102, 146,
  159-60
checklists, 42-43, 48n2, 105-7
childbirth analogy, 17
children, 3-4, 47-48, 82, 153-54;
  caregivers for, 85, 116, 130, 151, 161,
  183n2; evaluations from, 110, *111*;
  as subjects, 139, *140*, 144. *See also*
  students
Christina's World (Wyeth), 178
civil rights, 172
closed-ended questions, 134
Close Your Eyes and See Black (Hammons),
  168
cognitive abilities, 134, 175, 177, 181
collaborations, xv, 11-14, 63, 119, *135*,
  167-68
Collaborative for Academic, Social,
  and Emotional Learning (CASEL)
  framework, 124, 141-42
collaborative poetry (activity), 63
collages, 124, *125*, *135*, 153
collections, museum, xvii-xviii, xxiii, 11-12,
  176, 182

colonialism, 35
colors, 26-28, 36, 65-66, 143, 165, 169
comfort/comfortability, 77, 82-83, 171;
    in family tours, 151; participation and,
    84, 91-92; in tours for student on the
    autism spectrum, 129-31
communication, 95-97, 119; for field
    trips, 122-23; in introductions, 86-87,
    123, 133; power of, 94; in tours with
    students on the autism spectrum,
    130-36
conclusions, 72-73, 106-7, 136-37; in Tour
    Planning Template, 19-20
Coney Island, Brooklyn (Takagi), 179
conferences, 139-40
confidence, xxii, 37, 83, 140, 182
Connecticut, xxii, 3
Connecting Collections (institute), 11-14,
    18, 54, 159; on inquiry based learning,
    41, 49; on theme selection, 24-25,
    28-29; on use of information, 52
context/contextual information, 57, 105-6,
    127, 157-58, 170-71
conversations. *See* discussions
Cool Culture (organization), 5
Cornell, Joseph, 71
costs, xvi-xvii, 5, 162
Cotter, Katherine N., 8
couscous, 34-35, *35*
COVID-19 pandemic, xv-xvi, 8, 140-41,
    171; Guggenheim programming
    during, 155-159, 161, 170; isolation
    experienced during, 153, 156, 171, 181;
    MoMA programming during, 181-82;
    virtual tours/programming during,
    126-28, 153-54, 155-63, 170, 181-82;
    Whitney Museum programming
    during, 126-27
Crystal Bridges Museum of American
    Art, 4
cultural activities, xxii
cultural institutions, xv-xvi, 3-5, 8, 11-12,
    33-34, 156, 162. *See also specific
    institutions*
Culture Track (research organization),
    xxii, 7-8, 162
curatorial tours, xvi-xvii, 41-42

curricula, school, 11, 18, 104-6, 109, 117,
    122-23, 143

daily tours, xvi-xvii, *115*
"dead end" questions, 46-47
DEAI (Diversity, Equity, Access, and
    Inclusion) goals, xvi, 34
debriefing in reflections, 103
decision-making (CASEL competency),
    141-42
Delamatre, Jackie, 45
dementia/s, tours for adults with, 116,
    175-82, *177*, 183n2
Le Demoiselles d'Avignon (Picasso), 33
Demuth, Charles, 123-24
Department of Cultural Affairs, New York
    City, xvi
descriptions of artworks/objects, 96,
    167-69, 171, 179-81
deskilling activities, 152-53
developmental appropriateness, 37-38,
    134, 144
Dewey, John, 60, 67n3
Dierking, Lynn, 115-16, 136-37
digital platforms: Google Meet, 126-27;
    Miro, 63, 67n7, 160; Padlet, 63, 67n7,
    160; Padlet (platform), 63, 67n7, 160;
    Zoom, 63, 126-27, 159, 160, 161, 170
Dijkstra, Rineke, 139-40, *140*, 144, *145*
disabilities, 84, 86, 118, 172. *See also
    specific disabilities*
discussions, 6-7, 73, 106, 150, 179-89;
    facilitation of, 41-48; on field trips, 124;
    guided, 133-35; inquiry-based, 12, 45,
    47-49, 52-53, 60, 96, 121; participation
    in, 133-35; around theme, *25*, 25-27,
    26; turn and talk, 97, 99n13, 181; in
    virtual tours, 181-82
distractions, xxii, 51, 56, 92, 152, 158
Diversity, Equity, Access, and Inclusion.
    See DEAI
diversity/diversification, xvi, xxiii, 33-34;
    of artworks, 125; of object selection,
    170; of participants, 118
drawing activities, *64*, 64-65, 110; tactile,
    168, *169*, 173n6
dual responsibilities, 123

Ecker, Holly, 110
Édouard, Vuillard, 152
educators, museum, xv–xxii, 3–4, 95–98, 116, *135*; brainstorming activity for, *25*, 25–27, *26*; flexibility, 121–22, 126, 128, 133, 178; inclusivity facilitated by, 83–84; online tours by, 157–59; orientations by, 81–88; power of, 85, 117; previsits by, 130–32; previsit sessions for school tours, 117–18, 122–23, 130–32; professional development, 46, 72, 104; research by, 129, 143–44, 151; responsibilities of, 38, 75, 121, 123, 128, 155–56; self-reflections by, 72, 147, 171; tour conclusions by, 19–20, 72–73, 106–7, 136–37; tour objectives of, 104–5. *See also* facilitation; introductions/greetings; multimodal activities; object selection; preparation/planning; reflections; sequencing; teaching strategies
educators/teachers, 91, 117–18, 122–23, 139–40, 142–43; evaluations from, 109; of students on the autism spectrum, 130–33, 137
Edwards, Melvin, 126
Elkins, James, 6
emails, xv, 52, 109, 111, 117, 122–23, 130
Emory University, 139–40
emotional intelligence, 141
emotions, 4, 17–18, 82, 123, 146
empathy, 8, 85, 124, 132–33, 140–41
engagement, 141–42, 146, 167, 180; comfort and, 92; on family tours, 151; for students on the autism spectrum, 130, 132
Europe, 34, 144
evaluations, 11, 107, *108*; from adult tour participants, 109–10; from children, 110, *110*; from supervisors, 110–11
everyday objects (theme), 29, 71, 143, 162
exclusion, 128, 170
exhibition tours, 23–24
expectations, 84, 88, 91, 132
experiences, 13, 83, 85, 105, 107, 154, 165; in-person, 73, 156–57, 161; of isolation, 153, 156, 171, 181; positive, xxi, 82, 119, 121; sensory, 167–68, 170–71

experimentation, 98, 152
eye contact, 94–95

facial expressions, 124, 146
facilitation, *54*, 83–84, 97–98, 104–5, 155, 171; of discussions, 41–48; of tours adults with Alzheimer's disease/dementia, 175–76, 179–80; of tours of students with autism, 132–33; of virtual tours, 146, 158–63
Falk, John, xix, xxi, 115–16, 136–37
family tours, 149; information in, 151–52; multimodal activities for, 152–53; questions in, 150–52; virtual, 153–54
fears, 81–82, 132
feedback, xv, 171; participant, 129, 147, 156–57, 163–64. *See also* evaluations
fees, 5, 162
field trips/school tours, 3–5, 38, 121, 124–28; curricula and, 11, 18, 104–6, 109, 117, 122–23, 143; previsits for, 117–18, 122–23, 130–32; for students on the autism spectrum, 116–17, 129–37
Fine, Perle, 168
first impressions/listing observations (activity), 63
first-time visitors, 81–82
Fisher, Mayrav, 104
flexibility, 121–22, 126, 128, 133, 178
follow-ups, 52, 117, 136–37; questions as, 42, 122–23, 125, 134, 167
France, 57, *64*, 152
free admissions, 5, 162
free-choice learning, xix, xxi, 109
free tours/programming, 161
French, Kathy, 71
fun, xvii, xxii, 67, 83, 87–88, 145, 163

gallery activities. *See* multimodal activities
gallery stools, 70, 75, 91–92, 119, 132, 179
Gehry, Frank, 55
gender, 25–26, 33, 56, 82, 118, 126, 169
Getting' Religion (Motley), 123–24
Getty Museum, 66
goals, 18–20, 56, 104, 143, 150, 172–73; DEAI, xvi, 34; of virtual tours, 181–82
Golemann, Daniel, 141
Google Meet (platform), 126–27

graduate school/students, xvi–xvii, xxi, 5, 26, 51, 82, 86
grandparents, 92, 153
grounding exercises, 145
grouping icebreaker, 23, 24, 24
group management, 123
Guggenheim for All program (Guggenheim), 116–17, 129, 135
Guggenheim Museum. See Solomon R. Guggenheim Museum
guided tours. See thematic tours/ interactive museum tours
gunpowder, 57

Hammons, David, 168
hands-on activities, 135–36
Harvard Graduate School of Education, 109
Hassinger, Maren, 168
Hayden Planetarium, American Museum of Natural History, 3
Head Start (program), xxii, xxivn7
hearing impaired participants, 86
The Hermitage at Pontoise (Pissarro), xvii–xix, xviii, xx
high school, 125, 139–40
Hill, Ryan, 87
historical canon, 18, 33–34
History of Art (Janson), 33, 38n3
home (theme), 153
hooks, bell, 171–72
Hopper, Edward, 182
Hubard, Olga, 36, 39n12, 52, 95, 97, 98n8, 103; on color, 28; on thematic tours, 30

ice breakers activities, 23, 24, 24, 133, 146
identity/identities, xxi, 115–16, 118, 172; as a theme, 70, 143
imagination, 124, 165, 167
Imperial Hotel (Japan, Wright), 55
improvisational theater, 96–97
inclusion/inclusivity, 33, 104, 118–19, 161, 172–73; DEAI on, xvi, 34; museum educators facilitating, 83–84; of themes, 30
An Incomplete History of Protest (Whitney exhibition), 125–26
in-depth inquiry, 126, 128

inequality, 118
Infinite Blue (Brooklyn Museum exhibit), 27
information, 13, 42, 49, 72–73; art historical, 180; biographical, 55–56; contextual, 57, 105–6, 127, 157–58, 170–71; in family tours, 151–52; in information auctions, 54, 54–55; in information strips activity, 53, 53–54; in object exchange activity, 50–52; about processes of artists, 57–58; in Tour Planning Template, 20–21; in tours of adults with Alzheimer's disease/ dementia, 180; in tours with students on the autism spectrum, 131–32, 134–35
information auction (activity), 54, 54–55
information strips (activity), 53, 53–54
in-person, xv–xvii, 60; experiences, 73, 156–57, 161; previsits, 130–32
inquiry-based teaching/learning, 97, 104, 106, 119–20; discussions in, 12, 45, 47–49, 52–53, 60, 96, 121; open-ended questions in, 41–42
inquiry checklists, 42–43, 48n2
interactive museum tours/thematic tours. See also specific topics
interests (participants), 167; of students on the autism spectrum, 130–32, 134
intergenerational participants, 91, 149, 152–53
internet, 18, 57, 75, 77–78, 159
interpretations, 4, 11, 46, 134, 177, 179–81
intersectionality of identities, 172
intradepartmental communication, 119
introductions/greetings, 70, 81–84, 91, 105; communication style in, 86–87, 123, 133; museum rules in, 87–88; name tags in, 85–86; for tours of adults with Alzheimer's disease/ dementia, 175–76; in tours with students on the autism spectrum, 117, 133; in virtual tours, 84, 159–60
iPads/tablets, 146, 168
Ira (tour participant), 175–76
isolation, 155–56, 171, 177, 181

Jamboard (application), 63, 160

Janson, H. W., 33, 38n3
Japan, 28, 55
Johnson, Sarah Anne, 55

K-12 education/students, 3-5, 13, 121-28, 139-47
Kai-Kee, Elliott, 47
Kandinsky, Vasily, *135*, 169
Kaupelis, Robert, 6
Keogh, Carolyn, 102, 110, 112n5
kinesthetic activities, 136
Kleege, Georgina, 172-73
knowledge, 28, 69, 98, 134; prior, 42, 45-46, 52, 69-70, 106, 134
Ko, Queena, 117
Kruger, Barbara, 72

landscapes, xix, 28, 41, 57, 127, 178
language, xxi-xxii, 84, 93, 134, 142; body, 92, 94-95, 124, 146, 160, 181; of questions, 46-47; in theme selection, *26*, 26-27; tone and, 158
lecture-style tours, 41-42, 47, 49-50, 157, 175
Leigh, Simone, *166*
Lipsett, Missy, *7*, 84
listening, 94-96, 124
listing observations/first impressions (activity), 63
Loophole of Retreat (Leigh), *166*
Love Bed (Begum Lipi), 43, *43*, *44*
low vision, adults with, 58n15, 165-73, *166*, *169*
Luca (participant), 110, *110*

marginalized communities, 5, 33, 128
Marking Time (Guggenheim exhibition), 168
Martin, Agnes, 65
Maslow, Abraham, 83
materials, 57; of artists, 34-35, 65-66, 126, *166*, 175; for multimodal activities, 66-67, 75, 136, 161, 173nn6-7, 180-81; touch/touchable, 65-66, 87-88, 134, *166*, 167-68
Mayer, Richard, 158
Mazzola, Lisa, 117
mediums, 19-20, 28, 30, 35, 127, 161, 178

Meet Me at MoMA (MoMA tour), 116, 175-82, *177*, 182n5
Mehretu, Julie, 65
memory/memories, 5, 26, 35, 49-51, 55, 121, 182; of participants, 150, 172
Messina, Jodi, *135*
Metropolitan Museum of Art (the Met), xv, 11, 159
middle school, 125
mindfulness, 123, 141
Mind's Eye program (Guggenheim), 117, 165-67, *166*, *169*, 171-72
Miro (platform), 63, 67n7, 160
mistakes, xxi, 98, 103, 128
Mitchell, Joan, 65
mobility, 122, 178
Modern Starts (MoMA exhibit), 28
MoMA. *See* Museum of Modern Art
Monet, Claude, *177*
Monkman, Kent, 159
Morris, Robert, 171
Mostow, Sarah, 56, 72, 86, 92-93, 95-96, 98n3, 102; on object selection, 37; on tour preparation, 17
motivations/motivators, xxii, 56, 83, 107, 115-16, 130-31
Motley, Archibald John, Jr., 123-24
Mountains at Saint-Rémy (van Gogh), 56
movement activities, 125
movement wave (activity), 66
multimedia guides, xvi-xvii, xix
multimodal activities, 13, *59*, 59-61, 67n2, 105-6; accessibility of, 66-67; for adults with Alzheimer's disease/dementias, 180-81; art-making, 121, 151-53, 180-81; drawing activities, 64, 64-65, 110, 168, *169*, 173n6; for family tours, 152-53; materials for, 66-67, 75, 136, 161, 173nn6-7, 180-81; multisensory, 65-66; for students on the autistic spectrum, 131, 135-36; time/timing for, 61-62; in Tour Planning Template, 20-21; in virtual tours, *60*, 62-66, 127, 161-63; writing activities, xxi-xxii, 62-63, 93, 144-45. *See also specific activities*
multisensory activities, 65-67
Murphy, Shannon, 37, 82, 103

Museum Gallery Activities (Vatsky), xv, 59

Museum of Modern Art (MoMA), xv, 11, 33, 111, 141–42; *Meet Me at MoMA* tour, 116, 175–82, *177*, 182n5; *Modern Starts* exhibit, 28

museums/museum tours. *See specific topics*

My Egypt (Demuth), 123–24

NAEA. *See* National Art Education Association

names/name tags, 75, 85–86, 91, 133

National Art Education Association (NAEA), 4

needs, 122; behavioral, 83, 130; of participants, 129–30; sensory, 130, 132

nervousness, 76–78, 146

Netherlands, 144

New Mexico, 57

New York, xvi, 3–4, 11–12, 139, 155, 182; World Trade Center attacks, 117–18

New York Movie (Hopper), 182

New York University, 6

Nigeria, 124–25

novelty, 35–36

NYU Langone, 182

Object Exchange (activity), 50–52, 162–63

objectives, 34, 42, 104–5

object selection, 36, 105, 170; appropriateness in, 37–38, 143–44, 150–51; for family tours, 150–51; sequencing and, 145, 178–81; in Tour Planning Template, 19–20; for tours of adults with Alzheimer's/dementias, 178–81

observations, 98, 167; power of, 51, 117; questions and, 150; by students, 123–24, 139, 144; in tours adults with Alzheimer's' disease/dementias, *177*, 179–81; in tours adults with blindness/visual impairments, 172

O'Keeffe, Georgia, 57

O'Leary, Gabriela, 95, 98n7, 103

Oleniczak Brown, Jen, 92

One Work, One Hour (Guggenheim tour), 7, *7*

online. *See* virtual programming/online tours

open-ended questions, 94, 96–97, 105, 122, 124, 129, 133–34, 180; in discussions, 41–48; in Tour Planning Template, 19–20; at tour stops, 61–62; via online chat, 160; in virtual tours, 27, 158, 182

orientation, 81–88. *See also* introductions/greetings

pace/pacing, 92–94, 127, 160

Padlet (platform), 63, 67n7, 160

paintings, xvii–xix, *xviii*, *xx*, 33, 56, 65, 159, 177

pairs/pairing, 53, 58n4, 175, 181–82

paraphrasing, 95–96

parents, 144, 151, 153

Paris through the Window (Chagall), *64*

participants/audience/museum visitors, xvii–xix, *23*, *24*, 97–98, 115–20; active listening, 94–96; comfort and, 84, 91–92; distractions for, xxii, 51, 56, 92, 152, 158; diversification of, 118; evaluations from, 109–10, *110*; fears of, 81–82, 132; feedback from, 129, 147, 156–57, 163–64; first-time, 81–82; interests of, 130, 167; intergenerational, 91, 149, 152–53; memories of, 150, 172; name tags for, 85–86, 91, 133; needs of, 129–30; pairing of, 53, 58n4, 175, 181–82; perspectives of, 172–73, 175; prior knowledge of, 42, 45–46, 52, 69–70, 106, 134; silence and, 92–94. *See also* engagement; experiences; observations; *specific participant groups*

participation, xvi–xvii, 97–98; active listening and, 94–96; comfort and, 84, 91–92; discussions and, 133–35; silence and, 92–94; by students on the autistic spectrum, 133–35; in virtual tours, 160–61

Pawelski, James O., 5, 8

performance art, 178

performativity, 76–77

perspectives, 104; of participants, 126, 172–73, 175

phones, 18, 75–76

photographs/photography, 55–56, *140*, 144, *145*, 179; as contextual information, 57, 158; in previsits, 131
Picasso, Pablo, 33, 55
Piepzna-Samarasinha, Leah Lakshmi, 172
Pissarro, Camille, xvii–xix, *xviii*, 49–51, 57
place (theme), 28, 30, 57, 70, 150
Place Vintimille (Vuillard), 57
planning. *See* preparation/planning
point of view (activity), 63–64
Polyphonic (Fine), 168
Portals (Akunyili Crosby), 124, *125*
portraits, 28, 37, 124, 144, 153, 170, 178
positive experiences, xxi, 82, 119, 121
postvisit activities, 137
power, 5, 13, 27, 56, 139, 156; of communication, 94; museum educators, 85, 117; of observation, 51, 117; themes and, 23, 30
PowerPoint (program), 127, 159
Prabhu, Vas, 101–2, 111n1
preparation/planning, 142, 145–47; advance organizers in, 19–20, 69–71, 91, 104, 106, 124; for family tours, 151–52; research in, 129, 143–44, 151; for students on the autistic spectrum, 130–32; time, 75–77, 168–69; for virtual tours, 75, 78, 157–59
previsit sessions for school tours, 117–18, 122–23, 130–32
prior knowledge, 42, 45–46, 52, 69–70, 106, 134
privacy, 131, 161
processes, artist, 57–58, 66, 152, 175
professional development, 11–12, 46, 72, 104
Project Zero, Harvard Graduate School of Education, 109
public spaces, xvi, 82, 86, 97
Pyramid Up and Down Pyramid (Edwards), 126

quality/qualities, 177, 181; of museum educators, 95; novelty as, 35–36; time, 153
questions, 4, 13, 73, 93–94, 123, 132, 142–43; "dead end," 46–47; in discussions, 134, 179–80; in evaluations, 107,

109–11; in family tours, 150–52; follow up, 42, 122–23, 125, 134, 167; in tours for the blind/visually impaired, 167. *See also* open-ended questions
quotes, artist, 56

race, xvi, xxiii, 118, 124–26; white people and, xvii, 33–34, 82
Raimondo, Joyce, 88, 89n16, 103
Rand, Judy, 83
rates of visitation (museum), xv–xvi, xix, xxi, 3–5
Rauschenberg, Robert, 36
reassessments, 133
red, 27–28
reflections, 73, 101–7, 136–37; self, 72, 147, 171; in Tour Planning Template, 19–21
refugees, 144
remote programming. *See* virtual/online tours
representation, 33–34
reproductions, artwork, 6, 25, 27, 182; in virtual tours, 157–58
research in tour preparation, 129, 143–44, 151
resources, 11, 69, 118, 141–42, 146, 168, 171; accessibility of, 3–4, 118, 163; internet, 57; virtual tours and, 126–27
responsibilities, 33, 124; of museum educators, 38, 75, 121, 123, 128, 155–56
Resurgence of the People (Monkman), 159
retrospective evaluations, *108*
rights, 172
Ringgold, Faith, 55
Rivlin-Nadler, Emily, 54, *54*, 85, 88n9, 116
Rosenberg, Francesca, 116
Rothko, Mark, 65
rules, museum, 87–88, 132
Russia! (Guggenheim exhibition), 27–28

Sano, Mary, 176
scale, of artworks, 178, 181
Schmidt, Laurel, 47–48, 86, 95
school tours/field trips, 3–5, 38, 121, 124–28; curricula and, 11, 18, 104–6, 109, 117, 122–23, 143; previsits for, 117–18, 122–23, 130–32; for students on the autism spectrum, 116–17, 129–37

scratch-foam board, 168, 173n6
sculptures, 34–35, *36*, 126, *166*
SEE (Social, Emotional, and Ethical) Learning (program), 139–40
SEL. *See* Social-Emotional Learning
selection, object, 33–38, 143–44; for tours of adults with Alzheimer's/dementias, 177; for tours of adults with blindness/visual impairments, 170
selection, theme, 12–13, 23–30, 178
self-awareness (CASEL competency), 124, 141–42
Selfhelp (nonprofit), 155
self-management (CASEL competency), 141
self-reflections, 72, 147, 171
sense/sensory, 57, 60, 87, 122; experiences, 167–68, 170–71; needs, 130, 132. *See also specific senses*
sensory-friendly spaces, 132–33
sequencing (artworks/objects), 33–38, 105, 145; for field trips, 123–24, 128; for tours of adults with Alzheimer's/dementias, 178–79
Several Circles (Kandinsky), *135*, 169
sexual content, 38, 43, 150–51
share-back (activity), 126
Shulman, Rebecca, 95, 97, 98n8, 103
silence, 92–94, 139
Singapore, 43
slides/slideshows, 127, 131, 158–59, 172, 182
Slurzberg, Zev, 159
smartphones, 18, 75–76
Social, Emotional, and Ethical Learning program. *See* SEE Learning (program)
social-awareness (CASEL competency), 124, 141
Social-Emotional Learning (SEL), 123, 139–47
social narratives, 131
Socratic method, 42, 48n1
Solomon R. Guggenheim Museum (Guggenheim), xvii–xix, *xviii, xx,* 34–35, *35,* 46, 54, *54, 115,* 119; architecture of, 104–5, 110, 117–18, 156–57; in Connecting Collections institute, xv, 11; during COVID-19 pandemic, 155–159,

161, 170; Guggenheim for All program at, 116–17, 129, *135*; inquiry checklist, 42–43; *Marking Time* exhibition, 168; Mind's Eye program at, 117, 165–67, *166, 169,* 171–72; *One Work, One Hour* tour, 7, *7, 7; Russia!* exhibit, 27–28
Song, Jamie, 86–87, 98, 99n16, 103
soundscape (activity), 65
speaking, 86, 94–95, 146, 158, 160, 180
"speed dating" (training activity), 119, 120n7
Starry Night (van Gogh), 33
stools, gallery, 70, 75, 91–92, 119, 132, 179
storytelling, 29, 86–87, 124
strategies, teaching, 11–12, 58n4, 102, 111, 116, 119, 132; active learning, 61; in "Artist as . . ." framework, 124; COVID-19 based, 140–41, 156; improvisational theater, 96–97; introduction, 84; open-ended questions in, 47–48, 94; prior knowledge in, 69; virtual tour, 156
stress/stressors, xxii, 8, 77–78, 110–11, 131–32, 141
stroller tours, 85, 116
students, *35,* 38, 55, 87–88, 93–98, 141–47; on the autism spectrum, 116–17, 129–37; curricula of, 11, 18, 104–6, 109, 117, 122–23, 143; graduate, xvi–xvii, xxi, 5, 26, 51, 82, 86; Head Start, xxii, xxivn7; high school, 139–40; K–12, 3–5, 13, 121–28, 139–47; museum field trips for, 121–28. *See also* school tours/field trips
subjectivity, 33, 169
subjects of artworks, xvii–xix, *xviii, xx,* 139–40, 144
supervisors, museum, 110–11
surveys, xv, 108, 111
SVSC. *See* Virtual Senior Center, Selfhelp

tablets/iPads, 168
tactile drawing activities, 168, *169,* 173n6
tactile objects, 57, *166,* 167–68
Takagi, Madoka, 179
take a pose (activity), 66
Tar Beach (Ringgold), 55
Taylor, Richard, 177

teachers. *See* educators/teachers

Teaching in the Art Museum (Burnham, Kai-Kee), 46

teaching strategies, 11–12, 58n4, 102, 111, 116, 132; active learning, 61; in "Artist as . . ." framework, 124; COVID-19 based, 140–41, 156; improvisational theater, 96–97; introduction, 84; open-ended questions in, 47–48, 94; prior knowledge in, 69; virtual tour, 156

teasers (in media), 71

technical difficulties, 127, 159

texts, 93, 127, 131, 135, 158

thematic tours/interactive museum tours, 11–12. *See also specific topics*

themes, 42, 69, 91, 104–5; accessibility of, 143, 177; brainstorming, *25*, 25–28, *26*; for family tours, 150; for field trips, 123; power and, 23, 30; selection, 12–13, 23–30, 150, 178; in Tour Planning Template, 19–20; in virtual tours, 30, 157. *See also specific themes*

thought bubbles/callouts (activity), 62–63, 144–45

threshold fear, 81–82

thumbnail images, 19–20, 37

time/timing, 42, 87, 133, 136, 153; for multimodal activities, 61–62; preparation, 75–77, 168–169; silence and, 92–93; "wait time," 94

tone/voice, 86–88, 95–96, 104, 158, 170–71

touch/touchable materials, 65–66, 87–88, 134, *166*, 167–68

Tour Planning Template, xv, xxiii, 4, 11, 13, 17–21, 61, 119–20, 127–28; for adults on virtual tours, 155–64; for adults with Alzheimer's disease/dementias, 175–82; for adults with blindness/visual impairments, 165, 167–73; for family tours, 149–54; SEL in, 139–47; for students on the autistic spectrum, 129–37

tours. *See specific topics*

tour stops, 34–35, *35*, 45, 91, 121; open-ended questions at, 61–62; in Tour Planning Template, 19–20; transitions,
19–21, 71–72, 106, 132. *See also* sequencing (artworks/objects)

transitions, tour stop, 71–72, 106, 132; in Tour Planning Template, 19–21

Tree Planting (Johnson), 55

turn and talk discussions, 97, 99n13, 181

TV news programming, 71

UDL. *See* Universal Design for Learning Guidelines

United States (U.S.), xxii, 125–26, 183n2, xxivn7; Americans with Disabilities Act, 172; Black Lives Matter movement, xvi, 33–34; cultural institutions, xv–xvi, 3–5, 8, 11–12, 33–34, 156, 162. *See also specific states*

Universal Design for Learning Guidelines (UDL), 118

University of Arkansas, 4

University of Pennsylvania, 5

Untitled (1972/2020, Hassinger), 169

Untitled (Black Felt) (Morris), 171

Untitled (Ghardaïa) (Attia), 34–35, *35*

U.S. *See* United States

van Gogh, Vincent, 33, 56

Vatsky, Sharon, xv, *23*, 59

verbal descriptions, 167–69, 171

videos, 37, 57, 127–28, 158, 178; in virtual tours, 170–71

viewfinders (activity), 65

virtual programming/online tours, xvi, 30, 130–32; for adults, 155–63, 170, 181–82; cameras in, 84, 127, 146, 160–61, 163; chat features in, 63, 102, 146, 159–60; during COVID-19 pandemic, 126–28, 153–54, 155–63, 170, 181–82; discussions in, 181–82; facilitation of, 146, 158–63; for families, 153–54; introductions in, 84, 159–60; multimodal activities in, *60*, 62–66, 161–63; participation in, 160–61; preparation for, 75, 78, 146, 157–59; reflections on, 102; for students, 126–28

Virtual Senior Center (VSC), Selfhelp, 155

visitation, museum, xv–xvi, xix, xxi, 3–5

visitors. *See* participants/audience/
museum visitors
"Visitors' Bill of Rights" (Rand), 83
visual biases, 168–69
visual schedules, 133
Vo, Dahn, 153
voice/tone, 86–88, 95–96, 104, 158; in
virtual tours, 170–71

Wadsworth Atheneum, 3
"wait time," 94
Weiner, Lawrence, 46
Welcoming the Newcomers (Monkman),
159
well-being, xxi, 141–42
well-known artist/artworks, 33, 35, 37, 61
"What else?" (prompt), 96–97
white (color), 28, 36
Whiteboard, Zoom (platform), 63, 160
White Painting (Rauschenberg), 36

white people, xvii, 33–34, 82
Whitney Museum of American Art, xv,
123–27
Woman Ironing (Picasso), 55
women, *xviii, xx,* xxiii–xix, 33–34, 38n3
World Health Organization, 176
World Trade Center attacks (2001),
117–18
Wright, Frank Lloyd, 55, 110, 117–18
writing activities, xxi–xxii, 62–63, 93,
144–45
Wyeth, Andrew, 178

Yale University, 33
"Yes, and . . ." (prompt), 96–97

Zoom (platform), 126–27, 159, 170;
breakout rooms on, 63, 161;
Whiteboard, 63, 160

About the Author

Sharon Vatsky is a lifelong art educator. Her career in museum education includes a decade as curator of education at the Queens Museum and more than twenty years at the Solomon R. Guggenheim Museum, most recently as director of visitor engagement.

She has conducted workshops for teachers and museum educators at universities and art museums in the United States and internationally and has taught graduate level courses in museum education at the City University of New York; Teachers College, Columbia University; and New York University's graduate program in museum studies as well as undergraduate courses in drawing, painting, design, art history, and arts education. Her first book, *Museum Gallery Activities: A Handbook* was published in 2018 by Rowman & Littlefield.

About the Contributors

Melanie Adsit is a museum educator and arts accessibility and education consultant. She has worked in cultural institutions for over twenty years, including the Whitney Museum of American Art, the 92nd Street Y, the Museum of Modern Art, the Queens Museum of Art, and most recently served as senior manager of youth, family, and inclusion initiatives at the Solomon R. Guggenheim Museum. In this role, she developed and managed *Guggenheim for All*, an initiative to create welcoming and accessible museum experiences for visitors with autism and sensory sensitivities. Melanie has also trained staff and helped developed accessible arts programming at the Queens Botanic Garden, the Noguchi Museum, the Lower East Side Tenement Museum, the New York City Department of Education, and contributed to the Special Education section of the NYCDoE Blueprint for Teaching and Learning in the Arts. Melanie is an adjunct professor in the Department of Art Education at Queens College, CUNY. Her education includes a BA from Boston University (art and psychology); an MA from the Teacher's College, Columbia University (art and art education); and an EdD (ABD) from the Teachers College, Columbia University (art and art education).

Karen Bergman is the assistant director of interpretation and access at the Solomon R. Guggenheim Museum, where her work centers on inclusive design and interpretation in the galleries and facilitating dynamic educational programs for visitors of all abilities and experiences. A trained painter, her love for site-specific education grew during the years she worked for a studio art program in Orvieto, Italy. She has previously worked in education and visitor experience roles at the Whitney Museum of American Art, the Philip Johnson Glass House, and the U.S. Pavilion at the Venice Biennale.

Jackie Delamatre has been a museum educator for nearly twenty years. She currently teaches writing to Rhode Island School of Design (RISD) graduate students and adult programs at the RISD Museum. Jackie taught school programs at the Guggenheim Museum, Museum of Modern Art, and Whitney Museum for nearly fifteen years. She has written teacher curricula for museums across the country and founded museum programs for different audiences—from babies to teens to university faculty. She designed and taught a graduate course on informal learning for Brown University's Center for Public

Humanities. She holds an MFA in writing from New York University and a BA in education history and policy from Brown University. Jackie lives in Providence, Rhode Island with her husband and two daughters.

Queena Ko is a museum educator and director of education at The Noguchi Museum. She has held roles as manager, academic engagement at the Solomon R. Guggenheim Museum, and taught gallery tours and workshops for wide-ranging audiences at the Whitney Museum of American Art, the Museum of Modern Art, Cooper Hewitt Smithsonian Design Museum, the Getty Center, and Hammer Museum. Queena is passionate about developing arts programming that empowers students to share diversity of thought and self-expression. She is an advocate for education initiatives that bring under-represented artists and artworks to the forefront and has worked on collaborative projects including *Student Conversations on Art*, a student-created bilingual audio series, and *Teaching Modern and Contemporary Asian Art*, a free digital resource for K–12 teachers. Queena has her BA in art and architectural studies from the University of California-Los Angeles.

Lisa Mazzola has been working in the field of museum education for over twenty-five years. In her current role as the director of young learners in the Department of Learning and Engagement at the Museum of Modern Art, she develops programs and resources to help K–12 teachers, students, teens, and lifelong learners make connections to the art and ideas in MoMA's collection. Prior to her work at MoMA, Lisa coordinated gallery education and special projects at the Cooper-Hewitt National Design Museum, Smithsonian Institution, and helped facilitate school programs at the U.S. Holocaust Memorial Museum in Washington, DC. Her professional and personal journey are inspired by a background in wellness. Lisa has extensive training in Western and Eastern healing techniques and has a wellness counseling certificate from Cornell University. An avid cyclist and cycling coach, she is continually striving to provide health and wellness resources to the communities she serves. Lisa received a BA from the State University of New York, College at Oswego, where she majored in art history and minored in museum studies and an MA in liberal studies with a concentration in urban education from the CUNY Graduate Center in New York City.

Emily Rivlin-Nadler is manager of family programs at the Solomon R. Guggenheim Museum. For the past twelve years she has been designing and overseeing all family programming including exhibition specific family guides and activity packs, drop-in programs, tours and long-term community partnerships. Emily has been involved in art museum education since she participated in the Whitney Museum's *Youth Insights* program as a high school student. She holds a master of science in museum education from Bank Street College of Education.

She has discovered digital programming to be an exciting way to connect with people all over the world and a chance to rethink what a museum visit can be.

Francesca Rosenberg is the director of community, access, and school programs at the Museum of Modern Art (MoMA). In her twenty-seven years with MoMA, Francesca and her team have won national and international respect for MoMA's focus on disability equality and inclusion. Most recently, MoMA received awards from the Alzheimer's Association; American Association of Museums; Museums and the Web; Ashoka's Zero Project for social impact and scalability; and the Hearing Loss Association of America. Francesca is a founding member of the Museum, Arts and Culture Access Consortium and currently serves on its emeritus steering committee. She is a former board member of Studio in a School and DOROT. Francesca is the coauthor of *Meet Me: Making Art Accessible to People with Dementia* and *Making Art Accessible to Blind and Visually Impaired Individuals*. In 2020, she coproduced disability equality training videos with advocates from the disability community.